OUT OF CONTROL

OUT OF CONTROL

How My Addiction Almost Killed Me and My Road to Redemption

Cathal McCarron

with Christy O'Connor

Author of the award-winning
The Club

**SIMON &
SCHUSTER**

London · New York · Sydney · Toronto · New Delhi

A CBS COMPANY

First published in Great Britain by Simon & Schuster UK Ltd, 2016
A CBS COMPANY

1 3 5 7 9 10 8 6 4 2

Simon & Schuster UK Ltd
1st Floor
222 Gray's Inn Road
London WC1X 8HB

www.simonandschuster.co.uk
www.simonandschuster.com.au
www.simonandschuster.co.in

Simon & Schuster Australia, Sydney
Simon & Schuster India, New Delhi

A CIP catalogue record for this book
is available from the British Library

Trade paperback ISBN: 978-1-4711-5784-4
eBook ISBN: 978-1-4711-5785-1

Typeset in the UK by M Rules
Printed and bound by CPI Group (UK) Ltd, Croydon, CR0 4YY

MIX
Paper from
responsible sources
FSC   FSC® C020471

Simon & Schuster UK Ltd are committed to sourcing paper that is made
from wood grown in sustainable forests and support the Forest Stewardship
Council, the leading international forest certification organisation. Our
books displaying the FSC logo are printed on FSC certified paper.

CONTENTS

ACKNOWLEDGEMENTS

I would like to express my sincerest thanks to everybody who has helped me throughout my life, especially during the most difficult and troubled part of that journey. In my darkest moments, I often thought that I was on my own, that I was completely alone. I never was.

To Mummy and Daddy. I know we had some difficult times. I am sorry for putting my parents through such turmoil and hardship but I want to thank them so much for always supporting me, and for their unwavering love and affection. Daddy was never a big football man but it has been brilliant to watch him become such a loyal Dromore and Tyrone supporter. Meeting Mummy after the 2016 Ulster final in Clones was a special, special moment, one that I will never forget.

My brother Barry has always been my big brother, the guy I always looked up to. In my most troubled hour, Barry was there for me, just like he always had been. We don't see each other now as much as we would like but we will always have that special connection, that unique brotherly bond, which we've had since we were kids growing up in Tummery.

My sister Eimheár has always been a really special person in my life. There may have been plenty of times when I didn't show her that affection, when I didn't let her know how viii | OUT OF CONTROL

much she meant to me, but she always has. It means so much to me too that she gets on so well with my girlfriend, Niamh.

Niamh is my rock. She has been for a long time now. When so many people had made up their minds on me, Niamh was brave enough to make her own decision. When I let her down, she still stuck by me. She always has. I am so thrilled to be starting a family with her. I love Niamh so, so much. I am really excited about our future together.

The Cuan Mhuire charitable organization has done so much for people in Ireland. It continues to do so every day. I was blessed and fortunate to go through that system, which helped me deal with my addiction, and become a better person.

So many people in the organization had a massive impact in turning my life around; Sister Consilio; Liam McLoughlin; Derek, Barry and Ciaran, who worked alongside me in Athy; Nicola Kelly. I would also like to thank Joe Kelly and the Kelly family, great footballing people, great people, from Athy.

I would like to extend my deepest gratitude to Mickey Harte, not only for always having faith and trust in me as a footballer, but for giving me the chance to wear a Tyrone jersey when I never thought I would get that chance again. I hope I have repaid that faith and trust. Thank you, Mickey.

To my Tyrone team-mates, not just the current lads, but all the Tyrone players I played with throughout my career. We have all been extremely lucky to wear that sacred jersey, and I have always felt so privileged to have been given that opportunity. Tyrone people are some of the most passionate football supporters in the country. In the coming years, hopefully we can reward that passion and loyalty with another All-Ireland title.

The Dromore St Dympna's club, and the Dromore people, have always been very close to my heart. I let those people down so often at stages of my life, but the Dromore community always was, and will be, part of my DNA. My greatest moment as a footballer was the day we won our first county title in 2007. It was what we had always dreamed about. I have great, great friends in the club. There are too many to mention, but they all know who they are.

I also want to thank the wider GAA community for welcoming me back into their family when I returned home from London. They never made me feel uncomfortable or out of place. I always felt at home on a football field. The GPA deserve a special mention, too, for all the support they have given me over the years.

I would also like to pay a special tribute to the Athy senior football team, who I trained with during the latter half of 2014. At that time, I thought football might be behind me, but those boys rekindled my passion and love for the game through their generosity and kindness. They took me on nights out to help me assimilate myself back into the public domain. I will never forget those lads for that support. It meant more to me than they will probably ever know.

I am so grateful for having been given that second chance, for having been given the opportunity to show my potential beyond a football pitch. Geraldine Doherty, my boss at Temple Recruitment in Dublin, has always been very supportive of me. I want to thank Geraldine so much for showing such deep faith in me, and in my potential as an employee.

I will also never forget Martin Sludden for his kindness. When I moved home to Tyrone in 2015, I had no work.

Martin was the one person who stood up and took me on. I didn't stay too long in that position, but I will never forget Martin for his loyalty at such a difficult time in my life, when I was desperately trying to put the pieces back together.

Paul Coggins, the former London manager, was another man who came into my life at a very difficult time and had a hugely positive impact at such a difficult hour. So many people had that effect on me, mostly without even knowing it. The time I worked in the drug rehab centre in Cuan Mhuire in Athy was one of the most rewarding of my life. I was helping those people but they helped me in ways that they will never know.

To Christy O'Connor, I want to thank him so much for writing my story. I couldn't have got a better man to guide and direct me through this project. We got on so well, but Christy's empathy and understanding was hugely important in helping me to articulate my thoughts. It was a real pleasure to work with such a talented writer, and somebody I have massive respect for. Thank you also to Iain MacGregor, Jo Whitford and the team at Simon & Schuster.

The reason I wanted to write this book was to tell my own story as honestly and graphically as I possibly could, to let everyone know how much addiction can impact on – and destroy – your life, to describe the destruction it caused me. It's not an excuse for some of my actions but addiction, especially gambling addiction, has become such a huge blight on modern society that addressing these issues is a huge challenge for that society, a challenge that cannot be ignored or undervalued. And I hope that telling my story can assist in that massive battle.

Cathal McCarron, September 2016

HELL

P ing. It was after 11pm when a tweet landed in my phone. I was lying in bed in a small apartment in south London. Ping. Ping. Any phone alerts dropping that late normally just melted into the background noise outside as I drifted off to sleep, but this time the regularity pricked my senses. Ping. Ping. Ping. I sat up in the bed. Ping. Ping. Ping. Ping. Ping. The Twitter feed was relentless, like a jammed doorbell that wouldn't stop ringing.

What the hell was going on? Had something happened at home? I glanced at the phone in trepidation. The first three or four tweets went over my head until I spotted one from Owen Mulligan.

'Holy fuck, what am I seeing here, lad?' said Mugsy. 'What have you gone and done now?'

That was the trigger point. I dropped the phone. I didn't want to read any more. I knew my secret was out.

A fear enveloped me like a wave of cold water washing over my whole body, the dampness seeping into my bones. In my own mind, my life was over. I couldn't see a way out of this.

Everything I had done as a footballer was almost irrelevant. I'd crossed such a line that nobody would have any respect for me again. Who would ever take me seriously now? There was no way back from this.

My mind started scrambling for options. They were so limited, I distilled it down to two: go on the run to Mexico or someplace nobody would know me; or else kill myself.

What was the easiest way of taking away the anguish and distress, of shedding the shame and the guilt? What could be the most painless way?

I wanted to do it there and then. All that stopped me was thoughts of my family. I knew my brother and my father would be calling as soon as they found out what everyone else on social media seemed to know.

As I waited for that call, my mind was ransacked with terror. Sweat flooded out through my pores. The anxiousness coursing through my body was almost paralysing. It was the worst night of my life. It felt like hell on earth.

I hadn't closed an eye when my brother Barry rang at 6am. I didn't answer. He rang back thirty times, but I couldn't bring myself to talk to him out of shame for what I had done. His texts started dropping relentlessly. 'Are you okay? Call me. Please call me.'

I couldn't. I texted him. 'I'm okay, but I don't know how much longer I'll be okay. I'm in a bad way. I'm just fucked from gambling.'

The disease was so overpowering and self-destructive that it had taken a complete grip on my thought process, on my ability to rationalize between right and wrong. There was no right and wrong. I just needed money and I didn't care how I got it.

There was a SPAR store near where I lived in London which was run by a Pakistani boy. Every day when I walked past it, with nothing in my pocket, and less in my belly, I thought about robbing the place. I often went in, bought nothing and tried to formulate in my head how I might pull it off as I walked around. If I caught him unawares and hit him a smack, I'd have been able to clean out the till in no time.

I never had any problem stealing money to feed my gambling addiction. Before I was twenty-one, I had blown around £200,000, most of which I had stolen, the vast majority from my own father. I took so much money from my mother that she was forced to call in the fraud squad. I stole from my employers. When I was sacked, I took even more money off my next employers. When that wasn't enough, I began breaking into houses to steal from neighbours and friends. When I was caught in one friend's house by relatives, the story made the front page of a Sunday newspaper. The headline screamed: 'Red Hand Star Caught Red-Handed'.

I had gone too far. I'd crossed too many lines. I was forced to leave Tyrone. I was told that unless I got out of the country I'd be shot.

I had moved to London with good intentions. To stay away from gambling, to begin a new life. I tried. I couldn't. Gambling just wouldn't allow me to.

I didn't have any money. I wasn't working. People wouldn't trust me any more. Any collateral or good faith I had built up with people I knew had long been exhausted. I didn't have the same easy access to cash that I had at home, so I was always on the lookout for some way or means of generating money to feed my gambling addiction.

I was on the train one day when I spotted an advertisement in the *Metro* newspaper looking for male models. I sent off a picture of myself in my boxer shorts. I thought nothing more of it, until an email landed in my inbox six weeks later requesting me to come in for an interview.

The company was based in a fancy office block in north London and looked like a legit model agency. It didn't take me long to discover it was something more. After a brief introductory chat, a girl asked me if I would be able to urinate in front of a camera. I was about to get up and leave until she said it was worth £200. I was unzipping my jeans before the words had barely left her mouth.

I hadn't a penny in my pocket. My bank account was empty. On the way to the interview, I jumped the barrier of a Tube station to get the train to this place. I didn't even have £1.50 to pay the fare. I could have been arrested for that stunt, but risk and dare had been hardwired into my system. I was a gambling addict. That's what I did, it was all I knew. I gambled.

A week later, they called me back. They were straight up. They weren't a modelling agency. They were a porn company. They enquired if I'd be interested in some work.

The money was an obvious appeal, but the risk was still too great. They sold it to me on the basis that they only dealt with US hotels, where the porn was exclusive to the hotels' pay-per-view channels. Anyone in their right mind knows that uploaded material can appear anywhere, but I wasn't in my right mind. I accepted the offer of some work.

When I came back to my first shoot the following week, I assumed it would be with a woman, or women. I love women. I nearly fell off my chair with excitement when they said the shoot was worth £3,000. 'Great,' I said, 'let's get started.'

They said that one of their actors had let them down. They wanted me to have sex with a man.

'Boys, not a chance,' I said.

They asked me again. 'No way, I can't do that.'

The boy I was dealing with said that if I signed the disclosure form after doing the scene, I would be paid in cash. I remember physically shaking in the chair. I couldn't do this. I didn't want to do it. But there was £3,000 on the table. Could I really reconcile this in my heart?

My head started to compute the pain to come further down the road if I debased myself in this manner. 'Ah no, I can't do this.'

Still, £3,000 was an attractive way of easing that pain. My mind went into overdrive in those few seconds.

'Sure, this will only be seen in the US,' I thought to myself. 'Jeez, I might get away with it. I'll just block it all out and get it over and done with. Yeah, I will get away with it. Nobody will ever see this stuff.'

My decision was made in that instant.

'Fuck it,' I said. 'I'll do it.'

I'm not homophobic but the very thought of gay sex always felt unnatural to me. In some clichéd concocted storyline, I played a character called Fergus, a footballer from the country who grew up in a rural area where gay sexual adventures were limited. Now that Fergus was living in the big city, he wanted to try it out.

In real terms, the first part of the story is true. The second was in a different stratosphere from my reality, but the only reality guiding me at the time was the desperation to feed my gambling habit.

If someone had told me in the past that I'd sink that low, that I'd end up in a gay porn film, I'd have thought I must have been close to death's door. I was still fit and healthy, but the disease is so destructive that a gambler repeatedly gambles with death. Your mind is so skewed, so warped from reality, that you descend into another dysfunctional world. It's a place where you could end up killing someone, somebody might kill you, or else you'll just do it yourself.

I never got to the stage where I could have killed somebody, but if I'd kept on the same course I was headed, I could have taken somebody's life. It might even have been that poor wee Pakistani boy who was slaving all the hours in the day to make a living. That is the perverse and deformed existence of a serious gambler.

Staying alive, finding that next pound to make that next bet will only briefly sate your craving, but it's all that sustains you.

The guy I had sex with was straight like me. He was getting married a few months later. His fiancée would allow him to have sex with men but not women. What did that do to his mind? That's how sordid and dehumanizing the porn world can be.

A country boy from Tyrone like me had never met a porn actor before, never mind sharing a bed with one. He told me to treat the experience like a job, to shut out whatever emotions I was feeling.

He could sense my unease and anxiety. I was trembling. 'I don't know you,' he said. 'I'm never going to see you again. This is work. Just get on with it.'

As we had sexual intercourse, I did everything to suppress my real emotions, to dislocate myself from the moment. All I was thinking about was the money I was going to receive afterwards. The end would justify the distorted means.

By that stage, I'd reached the point of no return. If the director had told me that I had to lie down and let the other boy beat me to a pulp with a baseball bat, I'd have ground my teeth and sucked up the pain.

When the filming was over, I felt physically sick, disgusted that I had allowed myself to sink into such an abyss of degradation and humiliation. As soon as I was handed a brown envelope with £3,000, that feeling began to dissipate. I walked across the road into a betting office and gambled away half of my earnings.

While I was there, all my troubles left me. I was happy again. I still knew the feeling would be fleeting. It always is. Those few moments are only a brief respite from the endless vortex of pain and suffering and chasing that comes with the habit. The collateral damage is an insufferable reality that you just learn to suppress.

The money was soon gone. I had nothing again. The

pressure to get more money was overbearing. Placing that next bet is only a minor release valve from the torment, but in your own head you're treating the disease. In truth, you're just spreading a virus that will eventually collapse your system and possibly kill you.

Your mind is not really your own. When the fear came over me that a recording of me in a gay porn film might get out, I reassured myself that it wouldn't. The more you try and rationalize the risk in your own head, the more you justify the reasons for doing it.

When I eventually got caught, my first impulse was to keep running. I looked up flights to Panama at 3am. Since I didn't have the money to go that far, running in front of a train seemed like the only viable alternative.

I was there when a boy had done it two weeks earlier in a Tube station. Everyone was standing on the platform waiting for the train to arrive. As soon as it did, people started roaring and screaming. There was this wild commotion at the top of the platform. Blood was everywhere. The poor fella had been snapped in half.

That memory came back to me. 'There's a quick death anyway,' I thought.

I believed that was how I was going to kill myself. I was sick and tired of running, of hiding this disease. I couldn't take it any more. I wanted it to be over. Life would go on without me.

I left my apartment at 6.30am and walked to Wimbledon Park Tube station. I stood for forty-five minutes on the platform. I never moved. I never looked at a single person. Every time a train whizzed past, the warm gust of air would press against my face, blow back my hair. I waited and waited. I wanted it to be over. I was trying to convince myself to jump. I was trying to stoke up the courage to make that fatal leap.

I just couldn't.

It wasn't that I didn't have the balls to do it. It was more that my survival instincts wouldn't allow me to. As human beings, we want to survive. Even though I so desperately wanted all the pain and anguish to go away, something inside me wanted to stay alive, to keep going.

I was still lost. My mind was vacant. I wasn't thinking about anyone or anything. I was crying, but I was still emotionless. I probably looked to be in a disturbed state, but nobody came near me. I was just a dot in the blur and madness of a city wiping the sleep from its eyes.

Eventually, I snapped out of the daze and made my way towards the exit. It was close to 8am by that stage. It already felt like the longest day of my life.

Hell was only warming up.

CHAPTER 1

ADDICTED

I used to hang around Dromore with a boy called Billy T. There was a small bookie shop in the town and the two of us went in there one Saturday. My first bet was a £1.50 double on some nag. The horse won. I got back £6. The buzz was deadly and I was hooked immediately. I was sixteen.

I was bricklaying at the time so I had the money to spend, the collateral to risk. My wages were £250 a week, so I started betting with tenners. Some days were profitable, others weren't.

My first big bet was £50. It was even money on a hot favourite, which I thought was a certainty. The horse didn't win. The loss hurt so much that I became obsessed with winning the money back. I risked the rest of my wages on horses I knew nothing about. The adrenaline was pumping through my body like a narcotic. I was shaking with anxiety but I got lucky. I left the bookies with £800. I thought I was God.

I went out that night and spent £200, just blew it. I woke up the next morning and my first thought was, 'I gotta get that £200 back.' I was only seventeen but gambling had already taken a firm hold of me.

On the good days, when I won big, I'd showcase my wallet to my friends, the leather bulging with notes. On the bad days, when the wallet was as thin as a piece of paper, I'd leave it rooted deep in my pocket.

The money always only lasted hours, long gone by the following morning. I'd go into Omagh late on a Saturday evening and splurge on new clothes, mostly designer stuff. The night was a haze of beer and good vibes, with rounds of drink for everyone. Everybody wanted to get the taxi home with me, because I'd always pay for it.

At seventeen, you can get trapped in the fog of alcohol exploration, but gambling always dictated the journey I was undertaking. I always wanted to be the big man. We had a business at home, McCarron Fuels. We were well off. I wanted to maintain that front, to embellish that image even more.

Daddy worked hard and was successful. As kids, we were spoiled rotten. Anything I ever wanted, Daddy gave it to me. If I didn't have it, my father became the easiest resource for me to get it, to feed the habit after I had blown every penny.

When that well ran dry, as it invariably does, I began to steal. I'd poke around the house for money. Unless it was nailed down, it was mine. Gradually, I became more resourceful. Customers would come to the house to pay bills. I'd take the money, write them out the receipt and pocket the cash.

Daddy had to get a couple of safes put into the house, but that wasn't enough of a deterrent for me. I'd wait until he was asleep, until I could hear him snoring. Then I'd crawl up the stairs like a cat burglar, sneak into the room, take the keys from his pocket and rifle money from the safes.

Thousands of pounds would be stacked in the iron boxes, but I played it cute. I'd only lift £50 or £100, but all those small thefts gradually added up. Daddy knew what was going on. Money was clearly missing. People told him I was living in the bookies. He knew I was heading down a very dangerous road, but Daddy was still always there for me.

Unknowingly, he was doing me untold damage. He might make me suffer for a while, but the purgatory never lasted long. If I wanted £50 or £100, and I couldn't get hold of it, Daddy would still always hand it over. I was his son and he loved me. I never doubted that love for a second, but I often wondered too if he was trying to compensate for what he could never really pay back.

I don't know where my father and mother met. We just never asked. My mum, Margaret Catterson, was from Castlederg in Tyrone. My father, Seamus McCarron, grew up in Irvinestown in Fermanagh. Daddy was a joiner. He did a lot of travelling in the USA and Germany before returning home to start a business on the road with one fuel tanker.

We lived in Irvinestown until I was ten. An uncle of my father left him a house in Tummery, just outside Dromore, off the main Omagh to Enniskillen road. It was farmland at the end of a lane, but my father reconstructed the house and built a yard for oil tanks to expand his business.

My brother Barry is two years older than me. I have a younger sister, Eimheár. On the outside, we had it good. We were financially well off. We had everything we wanted. On the inside though, we were a family in turmoil.

My parents got married young and they just gradually fell out of love. They stayed together for our sakes, until we were older, but it was a sham arrangement that fooled nobody.

I was ten or eleven when I first began to notice how much damage their relationship was doing to us all. My parents would fight the whole time. Barry and I shared a room. We would sit up most nights, waiting for the arguments to start. Invariably, they always did.

Daddy was fond of a drink but he was never a social drinker. He drank at home. My mother liked a few glasses of wine. It was their way of unwinding after we had gone to bed, but alcohol was like loose petrol around a smouldering fire. One spilled drop would ignite into a blaze.

My parents just didn't get on. They struggled to be in one another's company, and some of their arguments were fierce. There was never any physical violence, but anything would be said. Some of it was personal stuff we shouldn't have heard as kids.

They were arguing so badly one evening that I dialed 999 and just hung up. I was terrified. The police arrived at the house to investigate the matter. I was dragged out of bed and admonished for making bogus phone calls.

As children, we did our best to try and make our lives

easier. At the weekends, Barry and I would often pour bottles of vodka down the sink and fill them with water. It would make Daddy even angrier, but it was our only way of trying to stop something which we were ultimately powerless to do.

Mummy and Daddy were great parents in so many ways. They loved us so much. They did their best, but there was so much anger in our house. We were young and it affected all of us. There should have been a release with the counselling. There was some form of escape for me with football. But not enough.

As a wee child trying to stop constant rows between your parents, you are completely limited in that capacity. You always felt that helplessness at home, of being unable to stop what you knew was inevitable.

There were some scary times. After a desperate row one evening, Daddy left the house in an awful temper. A few miles down the road he wrote off his jeep, turning it over on its roof. The police rang shortly afterwards. A neighbour called in a panic. I remember fear overpowering my young body. I thought my father was dead. I was only eight at the time.

We had some great moments as a family, some happy days, but it's only natural for a child's mind to store the emotional and psychological trauma that shatters your sense of security.

I was fifteen when my parents eventually separated. Mummy was always threatening to leave. The threat was issued so often that it eventually sounded hollow. We never thought she would walk, but we came home one day and she was gone.

Over the following few days, the trail was noticeable: clothes, a clock, some cutlery, had all been removed from the house. For some reason, I remember the hoover was missing.

Daddy wasn't happy with Mummy's actions but that was part of the baggage that comes with a family break-up. Daddy had given Mummy money as a form of settlement. She rented a place fifteen minutes away in Enniskillen. Our mother, who had always been there for us, was suddenly no longer around.

It was a huge shock to our system. We had been spoiled. Mummy cooked dinner every night. She did our washing. She ironed our clothes. It was tough at fifteen to have to learn to fend for yourself, especially when you never had to before.

We were all in a bad way. I was all over the place for a long time afterwards. I was close to my mother. If something was bothering me, I could approach Mummy easier than Daddy. Now, that outlet was effectively gone.

Initially, I was in complete denial. I didn't believe Mummy was really gone. I thought it was just a bad row and that it was only a matter of time before she would be back. It took me about a year before I realized that Mummy wasn't coming home.

In the meantime, I kept the front up. I didn't tell my close friends that my parents had split up. I was still projecting this image of us as the perfect family, where we had everything and wanted for nothing. Emotionally, I was bankrupt.

Deep down, I knew the separation was final when I went

to visit my mother in her new house. It was a tough experience but it also made me realize that it was for the better. My parents' fighting and rowing the whole time was only tearing them further apart. It was only causing more damage to us as kids.

Mummy asked me how I was doing. I said I was great, but I wasn't. I was full of hurt and sorrow, but I just put up the front again. I needed an escape. And gambling provided the perfect release for me.

By seventeen, I was gambling so heavily that I was already disconnecting myself from reality. I was viewing my parents' separation, which had such a detrimental effect on me, as an opportunity. My mother wasn't living at home any more, but she still had an address there. So I applied for three credit cards in her name.

Mummy had a good credit history, so getting approval was easy. Each card had a £5,000 limit, which handed me the licence to cut loose. The scam was easier to conceal, and prolong, when my mother wasn't around home any more, and had less reason to suspect the scam. It gave me even more control.

In my own mind, I was just risk taking, using the money as a leverage to make more, before putting back what I was taking out. The mind of a compulsive gambler doesn't think rationally. Collateral damage is irrelevant; the wreckage you leave behind is always hidden, stored away for a reason. All you see are potential outcomes: what you could win, what you might win. Ultimately, you just keep losing. And when you're losing, you're always chasing.

The letters from the lending institutions started arriving as soon as the cards were cleaned out. I knew what those letters contained, so I just dumped them. When I feared my father might get suspicious, I started intercepting the post. I knew the postman's routine, so I'd meet him at the top of the lane.

I'd tear up the documents as soon as they were in my possession, but that strategy certainly wasn't fireproof. I needed a back-up plan so I concocted a new, and false, address for my mother and got the correspondence rerouted there.

It was complete disregard for Mummy, but I never had any difficulty justifying my actions to myself, of reconciling their wider ramifications. I wanted money. I needed money. And I didn't care how I got it.

Mummy rang Daddy one day and said she was calling in the fraud squad to investigate the credit card scam in her name. The fraudster was her own son, but I never said a word. When Daddy mentioned it, I didn't even bat an eyelid.

I was living in a dream world. I was still making good money working as a bricklayer. I had just turned eighteen when I marched into Gormley's Vauxhall garage in Omagh and bought a new Vauxhall Astra Sport. The car was just on the market, £14,000 brand new. I was playing with the Tyrone minors, thinking I was untouchable.

I paid the first three months of the car loan, but the repayments stopped as soon as the money ran out. I was lying in bed one morning when I heard a truck passing by the window. I looked out and saw two boys getting ready to repossess the car. I lost the head with them.

I was disputing their rights, and arguing mine, but it was

all futile anger. The repossession was more of an assault on my ego than anything else.

I wasn't fooling anybody, but I still made a good attempt. I told friends that the car was damaged when I bought it and that I made the company take it back. Everyone knew the real story, but they were too embarrassed for me, too uncomfortable with my warped sense of denial to challenge me on it.

That moment was the beginning of the first real sense of shame, the first real heavy awareness of guilt. It was an awakening of sorts, but a compulsive gambler's acknowledgement of his problems has a certain cut-off point. The consciousness and acceptance of the chronic disease tearing you apart only extends as far as the next bet, as far as the craving to find more money and sate that burning desire to gamble. It's all a big lie, but you don't give the big lie a second thought.

Nothing changed. Daddy got me an old banger of a car so I could get to work and training. I used it to go to Irvinestown and Omagh to lay my bets, away from the glare of Dromore.

Everyone knew I had a serious problem. My boss at the time, Adrian O'Neill, a good Dromore football man, tried to talk some sense into me one day. He may as well have been talking to the wall. I wouldn't listen. It was the same attitude I had to the credit card fraud. 'It will be alright, it will just go away.'

I was an arrogant bastard, but I didn't see myself in that light because I wasn't living in the real world to be able to make the distinction between arrogance and reality. People were working all the hours God sent them, struggling to bring up their children, finding it hard to make ends meet. I was working too, but I didn't want to pay for anything. I didn't.

My reputation around Dromore was gradually coming apart. People were losing respect for me. I was a cautionary tale in everyday life, but being a Tyrone minor insulated me from the hard truth I needed to hear.

Nobody would say it to my face. Gradually, I was getting worse. I was becoming more devious, more daring with my dishonesty. I stole a chequebook from Daddy and wrote out a batch of cheques for £100. I cashed a couple of them in the local chipper. The owner knew what I was up to, but he underwrote the risk by ringing my father and telling him the story. He knew Daddy was good for the money. He always was.

Daddy thought gambling was just a craze I would grow out of. So did people around Dromore. Many were turning a blind eye to my actions, like my father, which only fed the monster more.

I continued to steal off my father. I used to justify it on the basis that, given it was Daddy's money, I had an entitlement to some of it. It made life at home very uncomfortable. We were arguing the whole time. Some of the words exchanged were mean and nasty. I had heard some of those words before when I was a child. The cycle was just repeating itself all over again.

Daddy would repeatedly tell me to cop myself on. I couldn't, but neither of us knew at the time that this was an addiction, a disease. It wasn't something that I was just going to 'grow out of'. The disease needed to be treated.

Even though I couldn't hold onto money for any longer than a day, and that I was out of work at the time, I decided to move out of home. I was struggling financially, but I was masquerading as somebody flush with cash.

I needed to be able to pay for the place I was now renting, a classy apartment in the park in Dromore. I bought a big flat-screen TV and had all the lads around in the evenings when I wasn't training. It was almost an effort to convince them of my false security as much as myself.

It didn't take long for the walls to crash in. I came home one evening and all the doors of the apartment were open. I rushed through the front door. Five undercover police officers were standing in the kitchen. The fraud squad had traced the credit card scam back to me.

I was arrested. My rights were read out. I was handcuffed and led through the park to the awaiting unmarked police car. I was charged with serious fraud at the police station in Omagh.

The police officer who interviewed me quickly identified that I had a serious gambling problem. I didn't have any money stored away. I wasn't hoarding cash. The money I'd stolen wasn't tied up in stocks or shares, spent on flashy cars or a big house. It made no difference. I was going to court.

During that night in the cell, my concerns lay elsewhere. Shame and fear were my dominant thoughts. 'Did anybody in Dromore see me being led away to the cop car?' Although the front was coming down, I was still trying to maintain it for as long as I could.

It was all around the town that I'd been lifted by the cops. That was bound to happen in a small place like Dromore, but I still tried to cover up the mess. I belittled the experience, concocting a story that there was a mix-up over one of my mother's credit cards.

When I ended up in court, Mickey Harte came to my assistance. He gave me a reference which helped my case. I received a suspended sentence. I was in the clear.

For now.

CHAPTER 2

ANARCHY

Dr McKenna Cup final, Athletic Grounds, Armagh
23 January 2016

There were five minutes remaining when Gareth McKinless wrote off Ronan McNamee with a sliding tackle. McNamee got up and banged into McKinless' upper chest with two closed fists. There was force behind McNamee's reaction, but the Derry boy hit the ground like he'd been smashed with a sledgehammer.

Niall Morgan charged from his goal in frustration at McKinless' actions and started pulling him up off the ground. As soon as I arrived on the scene, I put my left hand out as a loose cordon to prevent other players, including our own, igniting a potential melee. That peace-making approach lasted about a second. Out of the corner of my eye, I spotted the Derry manager Damian Barton coming across, plumes of smoke billowing from his ears.

I made a go for him. I don't know how I connected with Barton but I did. Whatever it was – a dunt, a half-box, a slap – I nailed him. As soon as Barton hit the deck, a full-scale brawl kicked off.

I did some clipping in the scrap, but it was more wrestling than anything else. I don't know if it was for boxing Derry fellas or for nailing Barton but the referee showed me a straight red card.

I was bulling because I thought that was me gone for the following weekend's opening league game against Cavan. I found out afterwards that the suspension only kicked in for the following year's McKenna Cup. If I'd known that at the time, I'd have hit Barton a lot harder.

I already had recent history with Derry going into the game. When we met in the competition a couple of weeks earlier, I didn't start. I was on the bench, but I spent all my time watching Emmett McGuckin and our full-back Paudie Hampsey going at it for the whole first half.

I came on for Paudie at half-time to do a marking job on McGuckin. I had marked Emmett a few times and there had never been any friction or trouble between us. He hit me a shoulder into the back. We exchanged a few words.

'When did you grow a set of balls?' I asked him.

There was an incident later in the game. A ball came in between the two of us and I read it first. I had a yard on McGuckin but he put his arms around me and we ended up wrestling on the ground.

I got him in a headlock and held him in it for a few moments. When he got up, he started shouting to the referee that I tried to choke him out.

I was defending myself. I wasn't thinking, 'I'm going to choke this boy and leave him unconscious.'

I do some mixed martial arts (MMA) training. I know all those moves, but I would never go out to knock somebody out. It's a dangerous game and it's irresponsible. You go so far, but you don't go to that extreme.

It was more to restrict his movement and keep him penned down, but McGuckin didn't see it that way. He was even more furious when a second yellow card for the altercation with the headlock got him his marching orders. He approached me after the game and unleashed his frustration.

'You're a dirty bastard McCarron, you knew exactly what you were at.'

'Emmett, if you're going to start something, don't bother unless you're going to finish it.'

The flames from that bonfire of bad blood were still visible two days after that game on the back page of the *Irish News*. A headline, directly quoting McGuckin, screamed: 'McCarron Was Sent On To Get Me Sent Off'.

Barton was of the same mindset. 'A forward is surely trying to get space,' he said.

What planet were they both on? They were only deluding themselves. Believe me, McGuckin is not Peter Canavan. Mickey Harte wasn't devising a plan to stop McGuckin in our dressing room at half-time. His ego was running away with himself.

I could have run to the newspapers as well with my own story, to tell of the sledging I had to put up with. I was pushing McGuckin away at one stage and he turned around and let me have it.

'Get your filthy hands off me McCarron, I don't know where they have been.'

I just laughed. I'd heard all that stuff before. Was that not McGuckin trying to rile me? When we met again, Derry were probably expecting a reaction from me, which they got. With the teams due to meet in the league and the championship, maybe Derry were already thinking: 'McCarron can be targeted now. We can get him agitated and sent off.'

It was my first time getting a red card for Tyrone in my career. I wasn't riled. I didn't feel I overreacted. When I saw Barton coming, I just felt as a manager he had no right to be there. He can say he was defending his player, but his players should be big enough to fight their own battles. We have been in plenty of scrapes over the years and you never saw Harte stuck in the middle of any of them.

The most important thing for us was how we reacted after the melee. I was gone. McNamee walked on a second yellow. We were down to thirteen men and trailing by three points with only five minutes remaining.

The game looked over, but our boys dug in. Conor Meyler replied with two points before Darren McCurry levelled the match in the sixth minute of injury time. We had all the momentum. Six successive points in the first half of extra-time reflected the control we had on the match, before McCurry sealed the outcome with a late penalty.

Job done.

In that *Irish News* piece, McGuckin claimed that my actions 'didn't belong on a football field'.

Did they? I can't say that I intentionally went out to hurt

Emmett, but it scared me afterwards when I looked back on what I had actually done. If I'm being honest, I probably lost the head for those few seconds.

It wasn't a move I had learned from MMA; it was more a form of protection, an impulse reaction after finding myself grappling with McGuckin on the deck. I didn't want to be walked all over, but the difference was I was on a pitch, not in a cage.

I have always been well able to handle myself. I did karate when I was younger before moving into Muay Thai as I got older. As I got stronger, MMA appealed to me. I liked the challenge but I also saw the benefits it could add to my football, purely from a strength point of view.

A couple of years ago, I started going to Victor Hugo da Silva's Underground Fitness gym in Dublin. I took classes, started doing rolling matches with Da Silva and some of his top fighters in the cage.

I was down there one morning before work recently. It's an animal workout, but it is more tactical and technical than hammering the shite out of one another. You're trying to read the other guy's moves, locking and holding and often ultimately trying to extricate yourself from a web of legs and arms.

The top exponents of the sport like Conor McGregor are thinking four or five moves ahead. You are thinking how to get out of a stranglehold you're in, while he is thinking about how to counteract that move if you make it. It's not just a cage fight; it's a tactical mind game as much as anything else.

Three rounds of rolling, each three minutes long, wipes

you out. When you're running, you rarely use your hands, but MMA is brilliant for tackling because your hands have to work so fast and so often.

I'd love to leave football in good enough shape that I could give MMA a rattle for a year or two, to see how far I could push it. I feel I could turn my hand to it, definitely. When I'm in that cage, that environment, I turn into another person. Unlike football, I'm not depending on my wing-back or midfielder or corner-forward, it is just me. There is nobody else to blame, only yourself. I like that control.

If a fella wants to wrestle with me or take me on, he's going to meet his match. I know what I can do and I'd be confident enough of looking after myself if someone squared up to me.

I always loved combat. Even when I was in primary school, I always seemed to be stuck in rows. When I excavate deep now into that layer of my past, it was probably a form of escapism from the trouble going on at home. It was my way of unleashing that anger and frustration already building in me as a child. There was a lot of resentment inside me that I didn't have the happy family life that all my friends appeared to have.

Even though Daddy was never physically violent, he often came across as verbally agressive or angry. I probably picked up those traits. When I was a child, Mummy would often come into our room at night crying. There were two sides to the story, but she made it look like Daddy was always the bad guy.

When Daddy was drinking, the atmosphere in the house was always horrible, but when I was confronted with conflict involving people my own age anywhere else, I felt strong enough to be able to deal with it. And when that anger from deep within my gut was stirred, it was a dangerous cocktail.

In school, I was totally disobedient, disrespectful. I never did what I was told. I was forever being thrown out of class. I had Mrs Reynolds for English and I spent more time outside the door than in her class. Teachers would pass me in the corridor and expect nothing else.

It was my way of attention seeking before everyone else in the class, because I had a reputation for being a hard man around school. It was more a sense of comfort for me, having that power and strength over someone else. It was nothing to do with wanting to win, it was a sense of exercising that power. 'You either listen to me or fight me. And if you do, I'll take you.'

The slightest spark would ignite me into a fireball. We might be having a harmless slagging match at school and a loose comment would provide me with the ammunition to hammer someone. I often used it as an opportunity to initiate a fight. Me, or my friends, were always in rows. The schoolyard was often a constant battleground.

At one stage, it was the ring for an ongoing feud between Dromore and Fintona students. Those scraps weren't just a few slaps. We used to think up ways of how we were going to get these boys. We'd often pair lads off together, a Dromore fella against a Fintona boy, like an arranged prize-fight without the money. Honour was far more powerful. We killed one another.

I don't know where all that violence stemmed from, but it was a dangerous fusion of testosterone and hormones and local pride. Most of those Fintona lads were sound fellas, but perspective has no place in a just war. I was coming out of last class one day – it was actually Religion – when I heard this barrage of thuds, that unmistakable but sickening sound of bone and flesh pounding against bone and flesh. A Fintona boy was lying in the corridor in a pool of blood. The Dromore fella who had left him in that state was just casually walking out the door to get the bus home. Job done.

Nights out became an extension of that battleground. I was in a nightclub in Omagh one night when I got hit with an awful skite on the blindside, right into my eye. The fella who landed the haymaker was five or six years older than me. He had a mean and nasty reputation, but I was so full of temper and fury that I was tempted to get a hurley from the boot of my car and beat him to a pulp with thirty-six inches of ash.

My attitude always was if you're going to fight, use your fists, but I felt I needed a weapon to take this boy down. The more my eye swelled, the more I thought about doing it. Thankfully, I never followed through. If I had, God only knows what damage I'd have inflicted. I'd definitely have been locked up.

At sixteen, I thought this was normal, that it was just part of growing up. We were full of badness, thinking we would grow out of it. We did but that environment I lived and operated in skewed my perspective of normality. And the gambling completely exacerbated a dysfunctional existence.

I often found it difficult to reconcile that madness with my personality. I knew I had a good heart. I wanted to help people, to look out for them, and I did. I trained under-age teams in the club. I did good turns for my friends, but then the addiction would make a mockery of that personality.

The kind-hearted fella remained hidden behind the mask. All anyone else could really see was a young man full of anger and resentment and violence.

It got worse when I was gambling. If I lost money on a Saturday and I was drinking that night, I was liable to do anything. I could easily get it into my head to destroy somebody.

When I was eighteen, a group of us were out in Enniskillen one Christmas. We came out of a nightclub and got into a car one of the lads owned. The window was down and I wolf-whistled at a girl who we passed. When the car stopped a few yards away, the girl's boyfriend squeezed his frame in through the window and planted me with a headbutt.

I was dazed but I couldn't get the door open quickly enough to exact retribution. One of my friends got out with me and we beat the shite out of the boy the whole way up the street. I think we broke his jaw.

As soon as his pals realized what was happening, all hell broke loose. A mad brawl broke out, and within five minutes five cars had pulled up as reinforcements. They were druggies and drug pushers from the town who meant business. One of the cars was a swanky sports model and I noticed the boot flying open. The occupants of the other cars quickly gathered around and started pulling out baseball bats and other dangerous weapons.

These boys had no interest in playing baseball or golf on the streets of Enniskillen. My friend and I knew if we got back into the car that it would have been wrecked, and we'd have been beaten to a pulp. We ran up through the town and headed for Dromore, which was fifteen miles away.

All I had on me was a pair of jeans and a pair of shoes. I was bare-chested because the T-shirt I'd been wearing had been ripped from my back. My friend's clothes were torn up like a scarecrow's. We looked like two degenerates high on drugs.

It was impossible to negotiate a safe passage through the town. Five cars were trying to hunt us down. No matter where we turned, what lane or alleyway we took, this particular car seemed to be reading our movements. At one stage, my friend and I debated jumping on the bonnet of the car, luring the driver out from behind the wheel and beating the hell out of him.

We shelved that plan and just kept going. Our phone batteries were dead so we couldn't call anyone to come and lift us. Eventually we knocked on someone's door and asked for the loan of a phone. We made some calls, but we were calling from an unknown number at 3am so nobody answered.

We laid low for a while. When we thought the circus might have rolled out of town, we made our way towards the big roundabout that leads to all routes out of Enniskillen. When it loomed into view, about ten cars were parked around it. Our pursuers had called for more backup. They had turned into the local law enforcers, stopping and searching cars to try and find us. It looked like half the Russian mafia was on our trail.

We had our heads down but one of them spotted us. They all got into their cars and started chasing. We were outside the Donnelly Brothers garage. Directly behind the premises was a river cordoned off by a huge barbed wire fence, with three coils of wire wrapped around the top. The adrenaline was firing so hard within us that my friend and I scaled the fence. We had to. If we didn't, we'd have been killed stone dead.

The wire ripped flesh clean off my back and torso. We were hiding in the field in the dark, but the gang still hadn't given up on hunting us down. In the pitch dark, all we could hear were these repeated thudding noises around us.

Thunk. Thunk. Thunk.

They were trying to identify our position by throwing these huge, heavy bricks in our direction, and, if they could, take us out in the process. Those boys meant business. They wanted to do us serious harm.

We kept our heads down. We didn't want to blow our cover by running so that they might cut us off in another direction. They waited for another twenty minutes before walking back to their cars. They were so full of hatred and poison, so hell-bent on damaging us, that we couldn't be fully sure they had given up the chase.

We still had to get home, to try and navigate a pathway through fields and ditches in the pitch dark. We had walked for miles before Irvinestown came into view. Once we got our bearings, we used a back road as our chief navigating route to get into the town. Anytime a car approached, we jumped into the ditch in case it was our pursuers.

It is ten miles from Enniskillen to Irvinestown and we walked every inch. As the adrenaline wore off, hypothermia began to set in. At least it was numbing the pain from the wounds on my body, but it was a freezing night and my system was beginning to shut down. When we arrived in the town, we couldn't go any further. We knocked on a door and pleaded for the use of a phone. I rang my neighbour,

Marie Fitzpatrick, who had been like a second mother to me. When Marie brought us home, I collapsed into bed and fell into a near coma.

Nothing more came from the incident. A few days later, the news around Enniskillen was that a few Dromore boys had been fighting drug lords. We realized then how lucky we had been. You often hear these stories of boys being rounded up and killed. If we had been caught that night, we were dead men. We'd have been found in a dark alley, scraped off the ground and scooped into body bags.

We weren't always that lucky. After a league game against Galbally in April 2010, I ended up in a nightclub with the same set of pals. Our reputation for fighting was well known to many people by then and clubs everywhere had our cards marked.

One of my close friends is always full of energy. He was hopping around the place, high on a cocktail of fun and good vibes, when security threatened to throw him out if he didn't tone it down. He warned him again shortly afterwards. It was purely personal by then. When the guy came over the third time, he pinned said friend against the wall. I tried to intervene. I asked the boy what he had done. The security guy just grabbed him and pulled him out the door and into the alleyway.

As I was following the two of them out, the door began closing in front of me. Just before it did, I could see the two of them grappling outside, but I couldn't get near them. When I eventually did, my friend was in a heap. The boy had choked him out. He fell and hit his head on the ground. He was unconscious.

We got him into a taxi and brought him to the urgent

care and treatment centre at the local hospital. From there he was taken by ambulance to the Erne Hospital in Enniskillen. He eventually came around in the ambulance. He was discharged the following morning but had to return later that day. He was all over the place. His brain had started to swell. After being transferred to the Royal Victoria Hospital in Belfast, he was put into an induced coma. The following Wednesday, he underwent a four-hour operation.

By the time he eventually left hospital, he had lost three stone. He had to learn how to walk and talk again from scratch. He had been a key player for Dromore, but he never played football again.

It could have been worse. At least he was still alive.

In 2009, I got sent off against Moy in a club game. A huge brawl kicked off in our forward line and I ran the length of the field, not to get involved, but to try and diffuse the situation. I was pulling boys out of the melee, but I lost the head with the referee in the process. He was letting everything go during the game and a powder keg of a match was only craving a fuse for it to explode. The row was an inevitability.

'This is all your fucking fault,' I roared at him. 'You started this. If you were doing your job properly, this would never have happened.'

I had my arm out and I pushed the referee with the back of my hand. However, the match officials did not agree with me. It was a headless act and a straight red card. Nobody knew what I had been sent off for because they hadn't seen me do anything, but I was suspended for three months for minor interference with an official.

Tyrone won the Ulster title that year and reached an All-Ireland semi-final, but my year was a write-off. On the day Tyrone beat Armagh in the Ulster quarter-final at the end of May, a group of us had spent the afternoon drinking in Dromore. At midnight, Seán O'Neill, Shane McMahon and I were in the chipper, Salt & Pepper in the town. Another group were in the corner. They thought we had skipped them in the queue and heated words were exchanged. We went outside to sort it out.

It escalated into a nasty battle. There were three lads and one girl in the other group and she tried to break a bottle over Seán's head. It got mean and dirty. One of them came at me swinging and I just clocked him with a box on the temple. I knew immediately that I had done damage to the boy. The legs went from under him, and he collapsed in a heap. He hit his head on the ground when he fell.

The mayhem stopped when everyone realized what had happened. The boy was in bad shape. The other group were gathered around their friend, who was unconscious. The three of us were so scared that we all ran up the fields and hid.

You could run from debt but there was no escaping or hiding from an incident as serious as this. We were loitering around in the dark, cramped behind a ditch, out of our minds with worry when my phone rang shortly afterwards. It was Daddy. He wanted me home straight away. The police were already in the house, looking to interview me.

I was arrested as soon as I walked through the door. The case went to court a few months later. One of the witnesses was that girl who had been in the middle of the fight. She claimed that I tried to stamp on her friend's head as soon as he hit the ground. I would never descend that low. I recoiled from the boy the second I saw him lying unconscious. The sight frightened the life out of me. That's why we ran. I thought he was dying.

I was on trial for grievous bodily harm. Our case was constructed on pure self-defence, which is exactly what it was. Their case was built on witness evidence from the night, but the judge accepted my account of events. I ended up with a warning and a fine of £250.

It wasn't my first time in court. I had my hood pulled up. I was hiding in the court house, but it was more out of concern of being spotted by somebody I knew, or who knew me through Tyrone football, than being up for GBH. I still wasn't dealing in negatives. It was me suffering again from positivity, which basically means I didn't deal in consequences. They meant nothing.

The outside perception of me at that stage was not good. I was behaving like a headcase, a loose cannon liable to explode at any minute. This was my second court appearance for a serious offence inside a couple of years but, in my own head, everything was fine. I was still insulated inside my own little bubble.

When I wasn't sentenced, a residue of bad blood flowed through the town. I knew the boy's sister fairly well. We grew up together, in the same class at school. The incident naturally polluted the atmosphere between me and their family, and the people in the town connected to that group.

In a place as small as Dromore, the fallout was hateful; dirty looks and a cloud of discomfort, little twigs and branches of rumour and innuendo gradually forming into a ball of spiteful tumbleweed.

When the GAA season finished, I used to play soccer for the local club Tummery Athletic. After that incident, I couldn't play for the first team any longer, because the boy I had hit was an ingrained member of the club.

The bad blood and its scent lingered in the air for a long time. You'd see and sense it off their friends, especially in the pubs around Dromore. A mouthing match ignited one night. They were trying to antagonize me into a response, but I was bound to the peace for six months. If I had hit anyone, I'd have been locked up.

A lot of the anger within me at that time stemmed from gambling. I was drinking the day before the incident, but I don't think I'd have found myself in that position if my head hadn't been as distracted from gambling.

I have done a lot of work in managing my anger, but there are still traces of it in my system. Not long after I started dating my current girlfriend Niamh Delahunt, this fella made comments about me on Twitter. I had no idea who he was but he knew Niamh and he was offering her some friendly advice. 'What are you going out with that fella for? Sure, he's gay.'

I was fit to do damage to him, but I let it go at the time. Then at the end of 2015, Niamh and I were out one night in a café in Athy in Kildare. There was a group of six fellas seated nearby and Niamh pointed out the tweeting keyboard warrior.

It wasn't the time or the place for a confrontation but I had drink in me and couldn't contain my anger. I approached and asked him to explain his actions. The hurt of what he had written was still vivid in my mind's eye. I flipped. I didn't care who was around or what backup he had. I decked him. Twice.

The keyboard warrior went to the Gardaí and reported me for physical assault. He just forgot to disclose the information which had sparked my outburst. The Gardaí said that he was within his rights to take action but that I was also entitled to pursue a case for defamation of character. He dropped the case immediately.

It worried me, because even though I had done so much work on myself, I was still out of control when I had drink in me.

I realize now that I need to keep going, to keep trying to make myself a better person. I try not to get involved in rows these days. If something kicks off, of course I'll defend myself. But I prefer to talk my way out of a fight now than cut and smash my way out of it like a threshing machine.

There was a time when I was mad for starting rows. It allowed me to vent the pent-up anger and hurt raging inside me like a volcano, and to hurt people in the process. It was my way of releasing the ball of bitterness and fury rolling around inside my mind and body, but all that angst denied me the clarity of thought to be able to recognize why I was so angry in the first place.

This battle doesn't get any easier. I just need to keep working on myself. Day after day, after day, after day. I understand now that it often takes a bigger man to calm a row down, or just walk away, than it does to hit someone. Then again, maybe I should have thought like that when I saw Damian Barton coming towards me.

CHAPTER 3

FRUSTRATION

National League Round 2
Tyrone 1–11
Galway 1–9
Pearse Stadium, Salthill, 7 February 2016

We stayed in Mullingar the night preceding the game, before travelling on to Galway on the Sunday morning. When the bus returned to Mullingar on the Sunday evening, I headed straight for my car, barely pausing to speak with anyone. As soon as I sat behind the wheel, I vented my complete frustration, roaring at the top of my voice to nobody but myself.

'YOU STUPID FUCKING BASTARD.'

I was substituted at half-time because I'd picked up a ridiculous yellow card a minute before the break. I didn't even concede a free. It was just a case of myself and my marker, Adrian Varley, being thick.

There had been an edge between us throughout the half. It's usually the forward who gets the benefit of the doubt in any altercation, but Varley had been pulling me and I told the umpire to keep an eye out for him.

'What would I be pulling you for?' Varley asked.

I shot back immediately. 'Sure, why wouldn't you? I've won the last four balls. You have to try something to win a ball off me.'

He drove his shoulder into me. I drove mine back into him. The referee arrived and doled out two yellow cards.

I didn't know if Mickey Harte would keep me on or not, but I knew my odds weren't good. Fresh jerseys were handed out in the dressing room at the break, because the ones we were wearing were saturated from the driving rain. I grabbed the garment and quickly pulled it on in a show of false hope. Then Mickey spoke. 'Cathal, you know the yellow-card rule here. I have to pull you.'

Harte might have had a different approach in a bigger game but I still should have known better, especially at this stage of my career. I had to keep my aggression under more of a lid, because it had bubbled over the top too often in the past month. I didn't know what the hell had been wrong with me over the last few games. I'd seemed angry again. Why? I didn't know.

Watching the second half from the stand was torture. It had been a long time since I'd been among the substitutes for a league game. The frustration was compounded by the stupidity of what put me there. I was in foul humour the whole way up the road to Dublin. There was serious competition for places everywhere in our team, especially in the full-back line. It didn't matter who you were, Harte wouldn't pick you if you had not been playing well or were fucking about like I had been lately.

I needed to cop myself on.

On my day, I know I can mark the best forwards in Ireland. I love a shit-hot forward in a good vein of form coming in my direction. Nobody likes man-marking jobs, but I do. Most defenders hate having huge tracts of space in front of them, but that is right up my street. My game is all about looking my man in the eye and saying to him, 'Right, let's go here. Just you and me, let the best man win.'

The first half was very open against Galway. I saw plenty of ball, which I preferred than having sweepers or cover in front of me cutting possession out. Bernard Brogan, Cillian O'Connor or James O'Donoghue would normally cut loose in those situations, but they are the boys you wanted to test yourself against. If I had all that extra space to contend with as well, better again. Bring it on.

I always had pace. Some people might say I'm arrogant, but all county footballers have that belief which is more an extension of confidence than arrogance. There is a difference, because confidence hardens and strengthens that belief you already have in your own ability. If you doubt yourself, especially against top forwards, you have no chance of surviving.

You are always aware of the great defenders who went before you. I learned from some of the best of them in Tyrone. Ryan 'Riccy' McMenamin was a legend. Despite the perception many had of him, and the reputation he carried, Ricey was a brilliant defender. So was Conor Gormley. No bells and whistles, Gormley always got the job done efficiently.

I had always looked up to those boys. My family didn't have a footballing background or tradition. Dromore never had a strong history of producing footballers for Tyrone, but then Ricey came along and changed everything for all of us in the club.

When Tyrone won the All-Ireland for the second time in 2005, I watched the game from Hill 16. We all jumped the barriers afterwards. As we celebrated on the pitch, I wanted it even more. 'I'm going to be on this pitch, with these boys some day, after winning an All-Ireland.'

Three years later, I was. That hunger and desire drove me on, because I was so desperate to make it happen. In 2005, I was in the Tyrone Under-16 development squad, but I couldn't make the starting team. I felt I was good enough, but I had to suck it up.

I had to keep sucking it up. Tyrone won the All-Ireland minor title in 2004, but I couldn't even make the squad. Liam Donnelly of Trillick – father of Mattie and Richie – was manager. Liam was well within his rights not to select me when I hadn't shown up on his radar the previous year at Under-16s, but I was a different animal by 2004. I was playing senior club football by then; Shane McMahon and Seán O'Neill, who were on the Tyrone minor panel that season, weren't. I actually made my senior debut against Trillick before I turned seventeen. I played well. Liam was at the match, but it made no difference.

I felt my history of having left Trillick was a factor in Liam not selecting me. He was fully justified by winning the All-Ireland, but I was really bitter about it. Then I just let it go. I wanted to prove him and everyone else wrong. I did.

Liam selected me in 2005. He was a good manager who was always fair to me afterwards. We had an excellent minor team that season, but our campaign was derailed in the first round against Down in Omagh. We were two points ahead in the fifth minute of injury time when Down got a thirteen-metre free. They went for goal. The ball was blocked. It pinged back to James Colgan who pulled the trigger. Colm Cavanagh got his fingertips to the ball, but it spun into the net and we were gone. Down went on and won the All-Ireland.

It was one of the hardest defeats I ever experienced, but at least I was on the right track. I had played well. All the lads who had been ahead of me when I was fifteen, sixteen and seventeen had drifted away. I was beginning to hit my stride.

In my last year in the Under-21 team in 2008, I made the Tyrone senior panel. I had a good Dr McKenna Cup. I damaged ligaments in my shoulder in the final against Down, but I still knew Harte was going to give me a chance at full-back during the league.

I missed a couple of weeks' training, plus our opening league game against Kildare, before we played Kerry in Tralee in Round 2. I could barely lift my arm at the time, but I was named on the panel for the trip. Conor Gormley had started at full-back against Kildare and was due to wear the number 3 jersey against Kerry, but Harte pulled me aside when I boarded the bus in Omagh. 'Are you fit?' he asked. 'Are you ready to mark Donaghy?'

I was almost shaking with the thought of the challenge, but it was a healthy mix of nerves and excitement. I was still only about 60 per cent fit, but Harte was never going to get the full medical update. I struggled to raise my arm above my head. The injury had left me extremely vulnerable and exposed, but there was no way I was turning down such a good opportunity.

When the first few balls dropped in between myself and Kieran Donaghy, I could feel myself minding my shoulder. Donaghy grabbed one out of the sky and nearly planted it in the net. His shot just shaved the crossbar, but it was the only score he got. I couldn't hold back any longer. I attacked the next ball like a crazed wolf and absolutely wrecked my shoulder.

I knew there was an opening at number 3. Tyrone had started four different full-backs in the 2007 championship – Gormley, Cormac McGinley, Ciaran Gourley and Joe McMahon – and had settled on none of them. I was confident of making the jersey my own, because I didn't see too many alternatives.

That day I left the field in Tralee, Justin McMahon took over on the edge of the square. I didn't see Justy as a threat. I certainly didn't see him staying there for too long. Justy had played midfield and centre-back for the Under-21s. I don't think he had played much at full-back, but he settled into the position and made it his own. He won an All-Star at number 3 that year.

We stayed in Limerick on the night of the Kerry game and ended up in a pub. We were all drinking, then a row broke out. One of our team was throwing boxes. Another lad got involved. Then I got stuck in. Even though my arm was in a sling, I started swinging.

When I woke up the following morning, my shoulder and arm were in bits. I was hung over from drink. My head was a mess. Reality hit because I knew I'd be out for at least a month. A glorious opportunity to nail down a place had passed. I was actually out for six weeks and never made up that ground I lost. The injury cost me whatever chance I had of starting or playing in that 2008 season.

I believed I was good enough to play, but I wasn't. I didn't have that security in myself to make that step up. Tyrone played Galway in the league in 2008, and Pádraic Joyce and Michael Meehan cut loose. I was almost in awe of watching these boys do their stuff. Mentally, as much as physically, I wasn't ready to handle forwards of that skill and class.

Harte knew it too. When I got back to full fitness that season, I was too aggressive in my play. I was too tight to boys. I was fouling too much. I needed more experience to wipe that naiveté from my hard drive. It was the only way I was really going to learn the nuances of defending at the top level.

I still wanted it to happen quicker than I was able to make it happen. Harte always asked for the best and I was frustrated when I couldn't consistently deliver that standard. If my man won a ball, I'd be thinking, 'He can't win the next one now.' Defending is often about marrying that desire with timing and technique, but in my case manic desire was overruling everything else.

You can't fast-track experience. It's difficult to achieve a complete performance every time you play, but it has never stopped me from trying to reach that goal. As a defender, there are set ways of measuring that level of elite performance: keeping your man scoreless; making him as ineffective as you possibly can; covering space and blocking channels; communicating with and supporting your teammates on the ball; getting forward when you can; making something happen when you have possession; not conceding any frees.

As a defender now, I try not to make a mistake. I want there to be a positive aspect to everything I do, but I also appreciate that meeting those standards is not always a realistic demand. Some of these top forwards are so good now that you couldn't keep them scoreless if you tied them up and chained them to the railings on Hill 16. They'd still find a way around the traps you set.

You just learn to accept that reality, but when you're a young player in a hurry, everything is a blur because you want it all to happen straight away. My game became a contradiction. I'd clean out some of these top Tyrone forwards in training, but I couldn't carry that form into league games. I was going out with the intent of attacking and winning every ball, but I was holding back as soon as the ball was kicked or passed in. I was playing with fear, especially when I was marking a top-class forward.

The contradiction was even harder to reconcile in my mind, because it went against everything that got me on the Tyrone panel in the first place. I loved the challenge of marking all the best forwards in club games. It excited me even more when I played for the county, but not always being able to meet that challenge exacerbated my frustration. Fouling and conceding too many frees was an unavoidable by-product.

I was young and inexperienced, but it was harder for me to process all that information because I had no space in my brain for introspection. I needed to set more realistic targets; to understand that I couldn't win every ball. I couldn't always keep my man scoreless; holding my man up for a few seconds until the rest of the defensive pack arrived was just as important as trying to win the ball back.

Most of that only comes with hard experience, but I still wasn't mentally ready to establish myself during my first two years on the Tyrone panel. You need to give it everything. I did, but only when I was training and playing.

All my other waking hours were focused on gambling.

I was suspended for the summer of 2009 and didn't make my championship debut until 2010, against Antrim. It was a vivid championship Sunday in Casement Park. The stand and terrace creaked, the grass was baking beneath a relentless sun. I only came on with two minutes remaining, but Tyrone won and all was great with the world.

I didn't see a minute's game time in the semi-final win against Down, but I'd got my foot in the door and was hell-bent on kicking it in. I was marking Stevie O'Neill most evenings in training that summer. It was the best induction and education I could have hoped for.

Stevie was one of the best forwards of the last twenty years, a two-footed assassin who could land a score from anywhere. He moved around the pitch like an eel, but I knew that if I could mark Stevie I could live with any forward in the country.

Mickey Harte knew it too. Dermot Carlin had started the two previous games at corner-back, but Harte felt my form was better than Dermy's and he went with his rookie for the Ulster final against Monaghan.

Throwing me on Tommy Freeman increased the challenge on my first start, but I was primed as a greyhound after chasing Stevie around like a hare for the previous month. Tommy only got one point from play. I was shortlisted for *The Sunday Game* man of the match. Tyrone won by ten points.

It was my first Ulster title, but the overriding emotion afterwards was of pure emptiness. There was hardly anybody on the field when Brian Dooher lifted the cup. The Anglo–Celt trophy was sitting on the table in the dressing room afterwards and nobody even went near the big, glistening canister. It was Tyrone's third Ulster title in four years and our post-match mood reflected that familiarity.

It was a strange feeling, but when I began to recognize the sensation for what it really was, I realized it was just the standard of expectation Tyrone had set for themselves at that time. Ulster titles weren't a priority. All-Irelands were all that mattered.

When Dublin squared up to us in the All-Ireland quarter-final, they were undergoing a major identity change. After Meath buried them with five goals in the Leinster semi-final, Pat Gilroy established a new defensive template designed to make them harder to beat. They allowed us to go short with all of our kick-outs and a complete war of attrition ensued.

Dublin won, but my day was over after twenty-five minutes. I knew I was gone the second I picked up a stupid yellow card for a foul on Bernard Brogan. I pleaded with the referee. 'You might as well send me off,' I said to him, 'because I'll be going off now anyway.' Two minutes later, my number went up on the board and Dermy Carlin was back in.

Ricey or Gormley might have got away with that offence, but that was Harte's rule, especially in the full-back line. Mickey has far more trust and faith in me now, but I didn't have that luxury at the time.

It was still a good debut year for me, but looking back now, I don't know how the hell I did it. I could stand in a bookies for the whole day, from ten to six, then go to training, with maybe just a sandwich in my belly for nutrition. I wasn't drinking nearly enough water to be sufficiently hydrated to train properly. It was a mystery how I even had the energy to train most of the time.

A gambler's day is like a constant spin on a rollercoaster: highs and lows, dips and peaks. You're jacked up on adrenaline and emotion. The amount of energy I used up was ridiculous. In my own mind, I'd been through three sessions already that day without having even run a yard. It was a manual for how not to be an inter-county footballer.

I could lose thousands of pounds in a bookies and torment myself with stress and anxiety, but once I had football training to go to afterwards, I could leave everything at the door. It was just a pure release.

I thought that was enough to get me by, but it wasn't. I was wasting away my career, and Harte could see it without having any knowledge of how bad my addiction was. I started the 2011 Ulster championship quarter-final against Monaghan at full-back, but Harte hauled me off again on sixteen minutes after another silly yellow card.

He wasn't going to keep putting up with that petulance. Harte couldn't fully trust me and he wasn't prepared to take any more chances. Tyrone played four more games in that 2011 championship and my game time was limited to just a handful of minutes in garbage time against Longford.

I was going nowhere.

Fast.

CHAPTER 4

LOVE

'I see John's [not his real name] young fella was found dead on the streets of Belfast on Saturday. It's a nightmare what addiction does to you.'

That text from Donal (not his real name) dropped in my phone late on a wet Monday evening in February 2016. John was a lovely man. When I was in recovery in Cuan Mhuire in Newry in 2014, he was two weeks ahead of me. His son would come to visit him at the weekend. John would tell you himself that he only came to look for money. He was a drug addict. It was always obvious that he was strung out on heroin or whatever other evil concoction had taken control of his mind and body.

John knew he wasn't really helping his son, but he loved him and he always gave him whatever money he could. There was no other way around it. The son didn't want help. He spent five days once in recovery and got up and walked out the door on the sixth day. He couldn't handle rehab. It was too hard. Drugs eventually claimed his life on a Belfast street.

Addiction stalks you in so many ways. If your mind shows any weakness, addiction will attack it. Seán (not his real name) was one of eight in my recovery group in Newry. He was a lovely young fella, talented in so many ways. He was a brilliant guitar player, a great musician. He used to sing at Mass, with a voice as sweet as honey.

Seán had a good support network. His mother and family used to come and visit him the whole time. He was doing well, but you could still always see the strain in Seán. He was fighting a constant battle with depression. We would all stray and drift along our path, but Seán oscillated more wildly than anyone else. Shortly after he left Cuan Mhuire, an overdose claimed his life.

Recovery will only take you as far as you allow it. Of those eight in my recovery group, Donal (not his real name) and I are the only ones still sober. The other five have strayed off course. All of them have been back in the house in Cuan Mhuire. Turmoil is still part of their daily lives. Most of them have lost their wives and families. The pain is insufferable.

Addiction never leaves you. When I was in Cuan Mhuire in Athy working in the recovery section of the drugs unit, I used to help out in group therapy. I would offer my advice on my addiction, but I could see how some people's minds were working, how they were taking in the recovery process. They go in on a five-month programme and think they are cured when that time is up.

You are never fully cured. I will always think of putting on a bet. That urge will never leave me, ever. It's the same with a recovered heroin addict; they will always have that desire to drive the needle into their veins, to feel that crazy rush the narcotic provides. Cuan Mhuire doesn't remove those thoughts. It just gives you the tools to suppress them, to channel the urge in other ways.

It does scare me that I will relapse sometime. I would regularly attend Gamblers Anonymous once I had come out of recovery. When I missed a meeting, I could feel my mind was just not as strong as it needs to be. Now I never go longer than a week without going to a GA meeting.

The longer you last without breaking, the easier it gets. You have to be in the world of recovery to say you have recovered. If you go outside the loop or drift away, you're a goner. There is no way back.

The fear of relapse will never stop you gambling. What I went through with my whole experience, what I suffered mentally, that will never keep me away from a bet. A gambler doesn't live by consequences.

You can't do much more damage to yourself than to your reputation. I took a wrecking ball to my name. And then went back for a tonne of dynamite. What I did is heavily frowned upon. It disgusts a lot of people, many of whom, no matter how hard they try, will always perceive me in that way.

Others look at me differently. They see the journey I have undertaken. They think, 'Look at what that man has been through. Look at how well he is doing now. He will never gamble again.'

That means nothing. That is not reality. Reality is that if I don't keep going to my meetings, I will do worse than I already have. I could even end up killing somebody.

Fear motivates me to go to GA meetings, but fear alone will not be enough for me to survive. I don't know any addict in recovery who doesn't go to his meetings, who doesn't stay around counselling and who doesn't try to help other addicts in some way.

The boys who were in recovery but who you don't hear about any more, they are the fellas back gambling again. I was at a GA meeting in Athy recently. Someone said that this guy had not been going to meetings. He had been attending them sporadically, but you could see it in his eyes that he was back gambling. His mind was racing. He couldn't settle.

I knew he hadn't stopped gambling. When you stop, your mind slows down, like a car moving back down through the gears before the brakes are applied.

Sister Susan, who is based in Athy, is one of the few people in Ireland qualified to specialize in gambling addiction. She had never gambled in her life but had studied the subject extensively in the USA and was an expert on it. She once neatly described to me the difference between a gambler and an alcoholic. An alcoholic's mind is like a washing machine. You throw in your clothes and turn it on. If you look inside, you can pick out your red jumper, or spot one of your yellow socks. A gambler's mind is like a spin drier. You look in and can see nothing.

They are completely different addictions. The rate of recovery is about 60 per cent higher for gambling, but you never know when anyone is really recovered. The change in an alcoholic's appearance is stark during that recovery process. They start putting on weight again. They look far healthier, but nobody knows what state their mind is in.

The closest thing to gambling addiction is heroin. The opioid going into my body was money, endless streams of cash providing me with the same euphoric effects that heroin gives to junkies.

You can spot a heroin addict a mile off: the gaunt face, the skeletal physique, greasy hair, shabby appearance, with the sole concern of the next hit, irrespective of how they get it. You'll often only see junkies gathered in groups, convening beside a methadone dispensary in the most beat-up part of town.

You could walk down O'Connell Street in Dublin in the morning and see guys dressed in the best suits, looking like a million dollars. At least one of those fellas is up shit creek from gambling, but he is still too proud to look anything other than unbreakable.

Appearance is only a smokescreen to hide the real torment and chaos in your head. An alcoholic can spend just a handful of euros on a bottle of vodka or whisky, but the deep burn it provides at the back of his throat is enough to sate his desire for the time being. A gambling addict could blow thousands of euros and still not be able to stave off the terror about to ransack his mind over the impending hours and days.

There are numerous strands to any addiction. I didn't always need money to satisfy my addiction. Unconsciously,

I got a buzz from that constant search for money. The high from the chase was just as good for me.

And I was always, always chasing.

When I first started gambling, I was always in the red more often than the black. If I needed money, I just took it. I began by lifting fivers and tenners out of my mother's purse. My brazen attitude again governed everything. 'Sure, my parents have loads of money, they won't notice another fiver gone.'

All the fivers eventually added up. Mummy knew something was up. We were driving one day when she stopped the car on the side of the road. 'Cathal, did you take money from my purse? Own up now, tell the truth.'

I was sixteen at the time and I let fly with a volley of denials. She knew I had taken the cash, but she couldn't prove it. Mummy certainly wasn't going to get an admission of guilt, because I'd say black was white.

Before long, fivers and tenners were no good to me any more. I needed hundreds. With Daddy having a cash business on my doorstep, it wasn't that difficult to get access to that kind of cash as a sixteen- and seventeen-year-old.

Anytime Daddy left the house, I'd set myself up as the secretary of his fuel business. People would come down the lane to pay for fuel. The average payment would be around £500. Usually, I'd blow every penny of it at the bookies. Then the chase would start again. The chase was the buzz: I need money; I've got to get money; then when I get it, I've got to get more.

Customers eventually copped on to my actions. I was

there too often in my father's absence for them not to. It eventually got to the stage where people wouldn't pay me.

'Is your father around, Cathal?'

'No, he's not,' was my standard reply, even though he could have been upstairs or down the yard. His car could be outside in the driveway, which was another giveaway, but I wouldn't relent for a second.

'He's gone for the day and he won't be back.'

'Well, sure, I'll come back tomorrow then.'

It was their way of telling me that they didn't trust me. You would get the odd fella who wouldn't know me, or who wouldn't be into football, and he would pay me. He didn't know he was a victim, or that he was feeding a frenzy. As soon as the money was handed over, the adrenaline would start flowing inside my body like electric honey. That person wouldn't be out the gate before I'd be on the way to a betting office.

I didn't possess the ability to form rational thoughts, to process what I should do ahead of what I knew I was going to do. I was in the bookies in Irvinestown one day having blown a huge wad of cash. I was down to my last tenner. I knew I needed that tenner for fuel for the car to get me home, because the red light had been flashing for over twenty miles. I just about had enough juice to get me to the local garage before heading for home.

I wasn't thinking in those terms. I was only thinking of what I could win with that tenner. I won £1,000 once starting from a tenner, one of those days when I backed ten favourites and they all won.

This time I staked the tenner on a favourite and lost. I

went back to the car, poked around the glovebox, rummaged deep underneath the seats and cobbled together £4 in loose change. It might have been enough to get me home, but I only entertained that thought for a second. I went back into the bookies, laid a bet, and lost.

As soon as I turned the key in the ignition, the frame of the car started chugging, its belly gasping for a drink of diesel. I managed to get it on the road, put the gearstick into neutral, and was freewheeling into the filling station when it stalled just as I entered the forecourt. I jumped out before anyone saw me and pushed the car up beside the pumps. I put £20 into the tank and told the fella behind the counter that I'd left my wallet at home. I drove the ten miles home, got the £20 off Daddy, and drove back again to pay.

It wasn't the first time I'd run out of fuel. I was on the road one day with £500 in my pocket and zero diesel in the tank. I drove past a filling station because I wanted to gamble every penny of that £500. Before long, I only had £20 left. I wanted to gamble that too, but I knew I'd be stranded if I did. When the car gave up on the side of the road, I had to walk a mile to the filling station. It killed me to pay a fiver for a little oil drum before pouring £5 of diesel into the plastic container.

I had my hood pulled up as I carried the oil drum back to the car, but I was fooling nobody. Most of the people who passed knew it was me and the likely reasons for finding myself in that predicament. As soon as I got the car started again, I drove to another betting office and lost the remaining tenner.

As my gambling addiction became more corrosive, so did my worth as a person. I had no respect for anyone. I was a conniving, sneaky bastard. I stood for the complete opposite of the majority of principles we espoused as a footballing team in Tyrone: loyalty, honesty, trustworthiness. Off the field, I stood for none of those traits.

My moral compass extended so far it was bipolar. On the field, I'd die for the guy beside me. Once we both stepped outside those four white lines, I'd have sold him out for a few pounds that I could gamble with.

I was always setting people up. I stole a chequebook from my mother once and cleaned out every last penny of the £1,500 in the account. I gambled most of it, but I also used some of the funds as a Machiavellian tactic to build up the perception of my own personal stock, to generate more revenue.

Gary Walker had a classy menswear store in Irvinestown. I loved going shopping there, but I was often thinking about more than just the next Lacoste top or Boss shirt. I was a regular customer, but part of my regularity was to create a false trust. I bought a pair of jeans and two T-shirts one afternoon which amounted to £80. As payment, I asked Gary to cash a cheque for £500, which he did. The cheque bounced.

I paid him back and swore that it was a harmless mistake. I still had the cheek to pull that same stroke many times again. As a small businessman, Gary was willing to take a chance on a loyal customer. It was in his best business interests to keep me coming into the shop. He knew I was good for the money, but he also probably reasoned that the mark-up on the clothes I was buying provided enough of a buffer against the risk my custom provided.

I never actually stole money from Gary. The bounced cheques were always paid back, because I'd give him the cash weeks later when I had it. In my mind, I looked on Gary like a loan shark, without the interest or the muscle.

The shop is closed down now due to the recession which hit small businesses hard, but looking back on those cowboy tactics, of the discomfort and worry all that scheming may have had on Gary, causes me a lot of unease now. It's humiliating baggage to have to carry. I can feel it on my shoulders now, but I was completely blind to the damage and hurt I was causing at the time, to the trail of destruction I was leaving beside my name.

I had no concept of the destruction and vulgarity of cheque fraud, of how soul-destroying and demoralizing it is for an honest, hard-working person to be screwed around by someone they thought they could trust.

I was bouncing cheques all over the place and I didn't care. It was a criminal offence, but that meant nothing to me. I was never embarrassed or concerned about what the victims, some of whom were local people, thought of me. Once I had that cash in my hand, all I felt was euphoria. I was going gambling.

If I won money, I would pay back what I owed, but not everyone got paid. I took one man for £1,500. I was working for a company and we used to cash cheques in his business. It presented the ideal opportunity for me to lob in my own cheques, written from an old McCarron Fuels chequebook years out of date, the account long closed.

I was in such desperate straits at the time that I just ran away from the problem. I made no attempts to pay him back. He is a big GAA man and he never came after me. I told him that I would pay him back when I got my life back on track, but he gave me a fool's pardon. I only heard afterwards that he was recovering himself from a gambling addiction.

An addiction is like someone who wants to remain hidden. A wee devil, who sits on your shoulder so he can roar and shout into your ear: 'Defend me here, don't let me down.'

The wee devil gradually grew into me, was subsumed into my whole body, and took complete hold of my existence.

I was a thief. I was stealing thousands and thousands of pounds from my father. And I didn't care.

Every time my father and I had a row, Daddy would attack me over taking money. I would hit back with the lowest form of counter-attack I could summon.

'You're taking too much drink.'

'You're a fucking alcoholic.'

'You're the one with the problem, not me.'

'You're addicted to drink, go and sort that one out, don't be hammering me about my problems.'

Daddy was always fond of a drink, but he didn't have a problem. It just made it easier to justify my addiction by suggesting that he did.

There were times when Daddy did drink too much, but he never once missed a day at work. He always paid his bills. He was regarded as an honest and decent hard-working man in the community, somebody who would never see someone out of pocket if a bounced cheque was connected to the McCarron name.

Even when business people around our area knew I was a lying and dishonest bastard, they still cashed the cheques because I was a footballer, or because they knew my father would cover the cost if I couldn't.

I was squandering and stealing the money Daddy worked so hard to earn, but I still had the bare-faced cheek to tell my father that he was the one who needed help, not me.

It was a form of cruelty from me. I never thought how hard it must have been for Daddy to listen to my constant lies and abuse, to have to put up with the incessant anxiety my gambling problems caused him. If he did drink too much at times, it was probably his way of dealing with the frustration my actions were creating.

We squared up to each other plenty of times. It was just pushing and shoving, never any swinging fists. Daddy did make a go for me once when he was drunk, but I pushed him and he fell over.

I still regret that moment. To see the pain and torment in his face as he struggled to get up off the ground is a hurtful memory. He didn't deserve that humiliation, that lack of respect.

Only for my father I'd be in jail or dead, but he always bailed me out or did his best to protect me. I had no appreciation of that love he always showed me. Behind everything, I still loved my father. At that time though, the only things I showed any love for were money, gambling and football.

The addiction was turning me into a terrible person. It was Daddy's house, but I was the boss. If I wanted something, both he and I knew I was eventually going to get it, one way or another. As I got older and stronger, and my gambling began to spiral out of control, Daddy became more afraid of me, and what I was capable of.

I would feel guilty about that treatment of my father, but the pain was always only fleeting. It never stayed long enough in my system for me to consider not causing any more pain. A county final defeat was a hundred times worse than the torment I caused my father. It should have been the other way round, but that was how my mind functioned.

I knew how to prey on Daddy's emotions, how to exploit his weaknesses. Daddy carried a lot of guilt from how his relationship with my mother broke down. He shouldn't have had to carry that burden, but my behaviour was a constant reminder of the impact it had on me, and on us as a family.

God only knows what the man was thinking at times. Daddy is like any hard-working country Irish man who grew up in the 1960s and 1970s. Living in Northern Ireland at that time probably increased those insecurities. He was a closed book. He never expressed his emotions, but he must have been under serious pressure trying to deal with all my shit. He had nobody to talk to about it.

I never had a close relationship with my father. I never spoke to him about personal issues or football or trying to make my way in the world, because the thought never even entered my mind. It was something you didn't do.

It wasn't that we weren't loved. Daddy spoiled us. He showed us huge love and affection, but it was still restricted access, never extending beyond a certain threshold. It was just probably a male emotional response, where Daddy would only allow himself to go so far, to only express himself so much.

I just drifted. I think we all did as a family. Our home situation wasn't ideal, but we all just managed as best we could. As a child, you have a very innocent family outlook. You think everything is going to be like the movies, that everyone will be happy. You never think that your mother and father will break up. That heightens the shock when you turn around one day and Mummy is suddenly no longer there.

I don't hold it against Mummy in any way for leaving, because she and Daddy were both so unhappy. They are happy in their own lives now. That is all you ever want for your parents, but as a child, you don't know how to process the oscillating emotions of a failed and ultimately doomed marriage.

As a family, we never dealt properly with that whole experience of their separation. At the time, parents didn't split up, especially where we were from. It was a shame on our family, so we covered the whole thing up for over a year. That wasn't easy to hide in a country place where everyone knows your business. You tried to avoid talk about your family everywhere: school, work, football. It felt like a black cloud constantly hanging over us.

You just learned to cope because we always had. The fighting and arguing were going on since I was five or six. It was a way of life for us. The routine was almost like clockwork. When Daddy and Mummy had taken a drink, we knew what was coming. We were often so afraid of something terrible happening that we would come up from our bedroom late at night to intervene, hoping our presence would somehow diffuse a clearly volatile situation. Mummy and Daddy would just hunt us back to bed. Our actions only postponed the inevitable. As soon as our heads would press gently against our pillows, the din would start again. Nothing could close out that noise. Sleep never came easy, the turmoil still ransacking our young minds.

The wheel kept turning. When I was older and was arguing with my father, I often vindictively returned him to the soundtrack of my youth.

'You're arguing with me now because Mummy isn't here and you've nobody else to argue with. Are you fucking happy now she's gone? Do you want me gone too? Do you want all of us gone?'

It was another form of nasty manipulation. When I think back on it now, I was so horrible to my own father. Daddy was arguing with me for a good reason. I was stealing thousands of pounds of his money. I was on a road to self-destruction. He was more than entitled to question my erratic and dishonest behaviour.

As I got older, I began to see Daddy's true feelings come out when he was drunk. His anger towards me and my actions was festering and bubbling inside him. When he had drink in him, it would all come out. He would go mad. He would threaten to beat the shite out of me.

I was stronger by that stage, a Tyrone minor footballer who believed he was untouchable. Being the arrogant gambler as well, I'd just invite Daddy to take his chances. I fancied the odds. 'Come on ahead so, show me what you've got.'

I feel so sorry now for what I put the man through. If I could turn back the hands of time, I would love to take all that hurt back. I'd do anything to remove the stain it has left on me.

It wasn't on Mummy's doorstep, so she didn't have to deal with it. Daddy did.

We all suffered, especially my sister. After Eimheár moved in with Mummy, she returned to live with us for a while in Tummery, alternating between both homes until she was old enough to find her own place.

As a young girl growing up and dealing with my parents' break-up while trying to find her own path in life, Eimheár knew her needs and priorities were often subjugated for my actions. There were times when she needed Daddy, when he could have done more for her, but he was preoccupied with cleaning up the trail of destruction I'd left behind me.

Daddy spent thousands and thousands of pounds on getting me out of trouble. At the time Eimheár resented both Daddy and me for it. He was doing so much for me, expending so much needless energy, that Eimheár thought Daddy loved me more than her.

I could do anything and get away with it. Daddy still gave her everything he could but, even as a young child, Eimheár was fully aware of the extravagant amounts of money Daddy was wasting on me. In her mind, she knew some of that money could, and should, have been for her.

It caused a lot of friction between the two of us. There are six years between Eimheár and me, but the age difference never stopped us fighting, much of it residual anger built up from our home situation which we vented on each other as some form of release. I remember lifting Eimheár clean off the ground one day, putting her outside the door and locking my baby sister out in the cold.

We should have had counselling, especially Eimheár. She was very young and shouldn't have had to deal with that stuff on her own. Barry and I were much older. We had each other. Eimheár didn't have a sister. She was exposed to a lot of domestic unhappiness at a dangerous age. She has grown up now into a wonderful young woman, but when I look at her sometimes, I can still see traces of unhappiness in her demeanour. I don't doubt that everything that went on had an effect on Eimheár.

Girls are different. Barry and I were Daddy's boys. Eimheár was more Mummy's girl. She is big-time Daddy's girl now, but she didn't always see Daddy in that light because of the shade I was continually casting over him.

My gambling impacted on my sister, not just through the money I wasted, but through the instability it created around our family environment. For Eimheár, it wasn't always easy to find her feet among the debris and crumbling wreckage.

Daddy wasn't showing Eimheár any less affection than me, but in protecting me he was still unknowingly hurting my sister. In the broader scheme of events, Daddy was hurting me too, rather than helping me, but that was more through love than any acknowledgement of my illness. Throwing more money at me wasn't treating my problem; it was only making it worse.

Daddy didn't know that. He was just trying to do his best for me. Like John (not his real name), he just loved his son.

CHAPTER 5

DROMORE

We live in the Trillick parish. A river runs through a field at the bottom of our lane which acts as the boundary between Trillick and Dromore. Ronan McNabb lives just across that field, close enough from our front door that I could kick a football onto his roof but into a different parish.

When we were kids, Barry and I played for Trillick. It was our parish, so it was where we were expected to kick a football. We did for a couple of years until Barry fell out with the club. He wasn't getting on with a couple of under-age managers and wasn't getting a game. Barry was only a child but his read on his demotion was that unless you were from a big footballing family in Trillick, or had deep historical connections to the club, you wouldn't be picked ahead of those other kids bound to the club by those ties.

Our family had no footballing history or status. We were

effectively blow-ins, having moved from Irvinestown a few years earlier. Our next-door neighbours, the Fitzpatricks, had also played for Trillick before moving to Dromore. There were four lads in that house. We were friendly with them and they asked us to switch clubs to Dromore.

Barry was mad to go and I was always going to follow my older brother's lead. I was ten, Barry was twelve. Neither of us were protégés at the time. We were kids starting out on a footballing path with no idea of where it would lead to, but the move didn't go down well in Trillick.

My parents were never big football people. The game just wasn't part of their lives growing up. They wouldn't have even understood the implications of moving to a rival club, because they had no grasp of how parochial and intense the GAA culture can be.

They just let us go. I don't know where I drew my talent from, because nobody had any interest in even watching football, or following Tyrone, in our house. My father goes to matches now, but it is only to support me.

Barry was a good player until he damaged his cruciate ligament. He fell head over heels in love with a girl at sixteen and never went back to the game. By that stage, I was trying to drive myself to the next level.

I started off as a goalkeeper before graduating to the full-back line. When we began playing competitive matches at Under-12s, a neighbour up the road, Hughie Quinn, used to lift six of us in a wee Volkswagen van and take us everywhere around Tyrone.

Seán O'Neill, Snowy O'Neill, Shane McMahon, Mark Teague and Emmet O'Neill – our group became very close friends. We still are to this day. Even when we were Under-12s, we realized the importance of the bond we had and how powerful a force it really was.

We were driven bastards on a football field. Even at twelve years of age, I remember the six of us driving training with the tone and temper of adults. Dromore was such a fanatical footballing town that you were nobody unless you played football. I was desperate to be somebody.

When I was at Under-12s, I marked Aidan Cassidy – one of my best friends now – in a game against Clogher and he absolutely destroyed me. I was full of anger afterwards. I swore to myself, 'I'm going to get that fucker the next time I meet him.'

When we met Clogher again two years later at Under-14s, my sole intention was to take Aidan out of the match. Football was irrelevant. I was hitting Aidan, mouthing off, trying to antagonize him. I did alright, but Aidan still scored a few points off me and he ended the game in greater credit than I did.

I couldn't channel my anger in the right way. The emotion was so powerful that it was detracting from my own game rather than enhancing or improving it. So I began focusing on pure football and just being better than my opposite number. When we met Clogher again at Under-16s, Aidan Cassidy never touched the ball.

We were driven to win and to succeed but we never did at under-age level, always coming up short. Our first big breakthrough was reaching the minor final against Carrickmore in 2004. It was a huge occasion, made even bigger by the senior team's progression to the senior final, also against Carrickmore.

The town went crazy. Both county finals were on the same day in Omagh. Carrickmore were our biggest rivals. They were going for their fifth county title in ten years. They were hot favourites, but Dromore were convinced that we would win at least one of the titles, and, at a stretch, two. Disaster. Carrickmore turned us over in both finals.

The town was absolutely devastated. The hurt was never as raw. Dromore had never won a senior championship, but losing the minor final as well to Carrickmore was like shovelling salt into a gaping wound.

The longing went on. When we were growing up, Fabian O'Neill, Seán O'Neill, Shane McMahon and I always did weights training together. We'd pump iron in a gym in Omagh and then sweat out all the toxins in the sauna and steam rooms.

Some of the heaviest and deepest discussions we had about football took place where we could barely see each other's faces from the steam. Many of those talks resembled the scene from the movie *Any Given Sunday*, where the characters 'Steamin' Willie Beamen (Jamie Foxx) and Shark (Lawrence Taylor) speak about the real meaning of football.

We always talked about what winning a county senior title would mean. We dreamed the dream, but we wanted to live it for real. 'What would it be like to win the first senior title for Dromore? What would the town be like? Imagine. Imagine.'

That was our favourite word – imagine.

It was all the town ever aspired towards. One of our greatest supporters, Tommy Hunter, was very sick in the middle of the last decade. He was dying, but he said all he wanted was to see Dromore win a championship so he could leave this world happy.

The legend around Dromore for years was that the club would never win a championship. The club had supposedly been cursed after falling out with a local priest over land in the 1940s, but the young crew had no truck with that rubbish. That drive our group had always shown as young players transported itself to the senior team as soon as we arrived en bloc in 2005. We always believed we would win a senior championship. It was only a matter of time.

I played senior championship for the first time in 2005. By 2006, most of the rest of the young crew had graduated as we stormed to the league title, coming up from 1B to 1A, winning every game, which was unheard of in Tyrone.

Noel McGinn and Seamus Goodwin had carefully nurtured us through from minors to seniors and we were finally ready by 2007. I had gone from corner-back to full-back. The other young boys had matured at a progressive rate. The older and more experienced players knew our time had come, that the chemistry was finally right.

We went into that championship like men possessed. We were desperate to be part of the first Dromore team to win a county senior title. It didn't matter who stood in our way, we were going to blow them out of the road. By the time we met Coalisland in the final, they hadn't a chance. At half-time, we led by seven points. We were ten ahead at the final whistle.

When that whistle finally blew, I collapsed to my knees and thanked God. The sense of relief and satisfaction was nothing like I had ever experienced before or since. I will probably never have that same feeling again.

All of our people basked in the warm afterglow of finally being crowned champions. Tommy Hunter was still alive. It was the greatest day of his life. It was a day of days for everyone associated with Dromore St Dympna's football club.

When I looked into the eyes of my team-mates, I didn't have to imagine any more what this feeling would actually be like. Now, we were all experiencing that elation, drinking it in, inhaling the deep sense of satisfaction.

It felt absolutely magic.

The night of the county final, we were paraded around the town like kings. Over 5,000 people turned up in Dromore to celebrate with the team and its supporters. They came from all over Tyrone, Derry and Fermanagh. It was like a fiesta. The party lasted for a week.

It was no surprise that so many outsiders arrived on our doorstep, because Dromore always had a big reputation as a drinking town. If you were from Tyrone and you wanted fun and craic, you went to Dromore. Even when Dromore were beaten in championship finals and semi-finals, everyone would come to Dromore to drink, instead of going to the team and club that had just beaten us.

That whole atmosphere and outlook didn't sit well with many of the new generation. Why would you celebrate defeat and continual failure? We understood that boys were devastated after losing big games and that drink removed some of the pain associated with those losses, but, to many of us, it reflected something deeper – a lack of real hurt, a lack of real want from some of those players.

We had a different attitude. We had a real chip on our

shoulders over the legacy of failure which we were hell-bent on altering. We weren't going to stand for failure or failing to close out championships, which had happened so often in the past. We knew if we brought our A game, nobody would beat us.

Prior to 2007, Dromore had only contested six county senior finals in their history. Five of those appearances had come over the previous thirty years, but they hadn't done the business in any of them.

We created our own unique history, left our own celebrated legacy. Between 2007 and 2012, we contested six county finals, winning three titles in 2007, 2009 and 2011. We won three leagues in the same timespan. Dromore wasn't known as the place for just craic any more. We changed everything, especially the football club's identity.

Like anything, no matter how delighted your people are for you, there is still bound to be residual resentment for what you have achieved. It's just a deep-seated Irish mentality. The great players who went before us failed. We didn't. Our legacy was secured. Theirs would always be tarnished, especially now when compared with ours.

None of those boys set out to lose finals. It just seemed to be the mentality in Dromore, that they'd get to finals and lose, and then drink for a week as if they had won. We couldn't get our heads around that lack of ambition. With drink taken, we often used it as a stick to beat some of the older generation with.

Stupid words were often exchanged, needless sentiments expressed. 'You were just happy to get to the finals. We went ahead and won them.' It created some bitterness between the groups, and within the town. It wasn't fair for some of those great players to have that accusation rammed down their throats. Some of those guys did as much as anyone else to win some of those games for Dromore. It wasn't their fault that it never happened.

Tyrone have always had this image of having a black soul, perceived as this nasty shower of northern bastards that you didn't fuck around with, a crowd that would cut your throat to win.

Much of that was refracted through the prism of Ryan 'Ricey' McMenamin, and how he played. Ricey got a lot of negative attention when Colm Cooper had bite marks on his arm after marking Ricey in the 2003 All-Ireland semi-final. His bad-boy image went to another level after he sunk his knees into Tony McEntee's chest when he was on the ground late on in the 2005 Ulster final replay. By the time Ricey was suspended for eight weeks after digging Paul Galvin in the balls after a league game against Kerry in Omagh in 2009, he was being portrayed as a mini-Satan.

In Dromore, he was always a god. Ricey didn't grow up as this talented under-age player on the teamsheets of All-Ireland winning teams, minor and Under-21 teams that Tyrone churned out in the 1990s and early 2000s. He was a grafter who would just grind and grind his man until he had worn him down, until he had beaten him into submission.

After Peter Canavan marked Ricey in a club game between Errigal Ciarán and Dromore in 2002, Canavan rang Art McRory, then joint-manager with Tyrone and told him to get this boy onto the panel straight away. The following year, Ricey was the first man to bring the Sam Maguire Cup back to Dromore.

As a crusader from our club, he was the guy everyone looked up to. Everybody wanted to emulate Ricey. Every one of us wanted to be like him. It was natural that a player with that kind of status would influence how we projected ourselves, how we wanted to be perceived. Ricey was a master at the dark arts. He was lethal with the verbals and notorious for sledging. He didn't glorify in how he behaved, but it worked for him and it naturally rubbed off on all of us.

Dromore are probably the most despised club in Tyrone. Everyone hates us. When we cross that line, we will do anything to win. Everybody expresses that sentiment, but we always follow through on it. We are always true to our word. Growing up, you knew you had to do whatever it took to win. If it meant taking a boy out, you just did it.

I knew boys who went down the sledging route because it gave them an edge. It suited them to do it. Others advanced the dark arts onto another level. I preferred to focus on the football, but I saw how some boys got inside the heads of other players and, if it meant winning the game, I had no problem justifying some of those nasty actions.

I marked Benny Coulter when we played Mayobridge in the 2007 Ulster quarter-final. The story goes that after Benny's mouthguard fell to the ground, one boy picked it up, stuck it inside his shorts and underpants, rubbed it around his crotch and genital area before handing it back to Benny.

I didn't see it happening. I have heard Benny speak about it. The boy has never admitted to doing it, but he does laugh at that story anytime it comes up. If he did do it, he was just trying to piss Benny off and get inside the head of one of the best forwards in Ulster football at that time. Benny only scored one point. We won by two.

Nobody likes our attitude, our belligerence, even our strut and stride. We have been successful, but we tend to flaunt our authority. When we score, we always let the other team know about it, like a peacock preening its feathers.

What you see is what you get. If you beat us, you earn it. Teams respect us now, but we had to work hard, and wait a long time, to earn that respect. When we won our first championship, we didn't get the respect we deserved. It was only after our second championship in 2009 that we began to receive the proper acknowledgement for what we had achieved.

Strife and friction, often all-out war, was a direct by-product of our quest for true respect within Tyrone. We were going up against the established clubs, trying to smash their citadels and plant our flag on top of the castle. Before we won our first title in 2007, Errigal Ciarán and Carrickmore had shared twelve of the previous fourteen championships. Neither of them were happy to see us coming like men on a mission intent on smashing that cartel.

We had serious history with Carrickmore. When we met in the 2006 county semi-final, we had them on the ropes. They had used up their five subs and were only hanging on by a thread. They needed something drastic to dig them out of the hole, and it arrived with a highly contentious blood substitution. They managed to scramble an equalizing point deep in injury time. They beat us by a point in extra time.

It left a deep scar on our psyche and that of our supporters. It wasn't even about football any more. We hated them. They hated us more. Anytime we met, you could smell the sulphur and cordite in the air.

There had always been little bushfires of animosity igniting on the pitch anytime we met, before it finally erupted in a blaze during the 2011 county league final in Ballygawley. All hell broke loose on the pitch and it spread into the stand. Supporters were leaning over the barbed-wire fence, whacking players on the head with umbrellas. It was mean and nasty. The brawl spiralled out of control. Young children were terrified by what they saw. One supporter had part of his ear bitten off.

You couldn't condone what went on that day. Both clubs were heavily punished afterwards. We couldn't play each other for three years, and then when we did play, we had to meet on neutral grounds.

People are so passionate about football that it takes them over. When we lost the 2008 county final to Clonoe after extra time, a mass brawl broke out on the pitch. Our manager, Noel McGinn, dropped a boy with a headbutt. One of their players then nailed McGinn with the force of his head. Both incidents were caught on camera and made national TV headlines.

Noel is a primary school teacher and he nearly lost his job over the incident. He ended up publicly apologizing. You couldn't condone his actions for a second, but people get lost in the haze between passion and aggression.

I won't deny that it happens in Tyrone probably more than anywhere else. When I was only seventeen, Dromore played Ardboe in a league game that was abandoned. The two teams literally just beat the fuck out of each other.

It was a free-for-all. Nobody could stop it. It was vicious. I was only a young fella, but I got stuck in and started throwing boxes like everyone else. I got a right skite on the side of the face from a 28-year-old. I had no complaints. If you're fit to throw a box in a senior match, you have to be prepared to take one.

Everyone was getting stuck in. This guy from Ardboe arrived out of nowhere and clocked Eoin McCusker, one of our best forwards, on the side of the head. Eoin was knocked out cold.

When he came around ten minutes later, Eoin was like a demented lunatic. Some of our boys had to hold him down, because he was frothing at the mouth looking for retribution. Your man was lucky Eoin didn't find him – he could have caused him serious damage.

There was bad blood between the clubs for years but, like Carrickmore, it never contaminated the dynamic in a Tyrone dressing room. Anytime we played Carrickmore, Conor Gormley would go through you, walk right over you if he felt it would be of benefit to his club. We never had an issue with that approach, because we had the same attitude towards him and his team-mates – we'd beat the shite out of them on the pitch if we had to. Gormley and I didn't always see eye to eye, but there was always that respect there when we put on a Tyrone jersey.

The tension between Dromore and Ardboe lingered for a long time after that league game, but it still didn't make any difference to our approach, which had helped propel us from the margins into the middle of the conversation. And Ricey continued to drive it.

That internecine stuff at club level can poison an inter-county dressing room but, whatever it is about Tyrone, players put all that stuff to one side because they all just want the same thing. You can beat the fuck out of a boy and then go and drink tea with him afterwards. I have never held a grudge against someone who has done something gruesome on the field to me. I have got hit low blows plenty of times, but you just forget about it.

That is what annoyed me about boys who ran to the media, crying like babies. Many a Tyrone boy ended up in a far worse state and there was nothing said about it.

At times, we're probably our own worst enemies in Tyrone. Players have been targeted and seriously hurt out of pure badness and vindictiveness, often because they are county players viewed as a legitimate target. Joe McMahon got his jaw broken in a club game once and lost so much weight afterwards that he looked like an emaciated greyhound.

Brian McGuigan nearly lost the sight in his eye one night in Aghyaran after a late and dangerous elbow. It took eight stitches alone to close the gash in his eyelid. McGuigan's retina had been detached, and the lens behind his eye had become dislocated because all the ligaments holding it and the iris together had been torn apart. It took four operations to fully restore McGuigan's vision.

That stuff is crazy, but it goes on because Tyrone is often almost like its own police state. The cops are rarely called over incidents and offences, which, if committed on the street, would lead to incarceration. Maybe it's because most of us are Republicans and the police, who have always been viewed with suspicion up here, are often seen as a last resort.

That still doesn't deny that the club culture in Tyrone is rife with hatred, sheer venomous hatred. The Tyrone senior championship is probably the most physical and draining in Ireland. Only one Tyrone club – Errigal Ciarán – has won an Ulster club title, but that's more down to the conditions than the standard. With everyone beating the fuck out of each other, the county champions are often hardly able to walk by the time the provincial championship comes around. Our best chance to win Ulster came in 2007 when we lost to Crossmaglen Rangers by one point.

In Tyrone, football comes ahead of religion, and nearly everything else. The ongoing trouble at club games reflects how the worst of the club rivalries has seeped into the roots of the county. The accumulation of incidents over the years suggests Tyrone has a problem. We don't see it as such. We accept that serious issues need to be addressed, but that most of them are containable.

The rivalry in Tyrone is vicious. We all fight for our own clan, to defend the honour of our own tribe. But when the Tyrone flag is raised on the battlefield, we all go to war together.

CHAPTER 6

FREEFALL

By the time I was eighteen, gambling had infiltrated every part of my being. Apart from football, it was my only focus in life. I could never leave a bookies without putting on a bet. Mostly my limit was £100, but I was lethal for £200 doubles. One day, I did a £200 double on a betting terminal but I made a mistake, pressed the wrong button and backed the wrong team in a different game. It was Olympic handball and I'd just staked £200 on some crowd who were getting the shite beat out of them.

I hadn't a penny left. I was going to wreck the machine. I thought of asking the boy in the bookies for my money back, but that's always a futile exercise in an industry that doesn't deal in compassion. As a form of personal punishment for my mistake, I decided to watch the match, in some false hope that Austria or Turkey or whoever the hell was playing would somehow dig out a result.

The odds on them at this stage had stretched out to 15–1. Gradually though, they started pinging in goals. As they shaved more and more points off the scoreboard, it was like driving nails into my skin. A narrow defeat would have inflated the torment. With less than a minute to go, the game was a draw. Bastards. Even worse again, with twenty seconds remaining, the screen went blank after the feed collapsed. Holy Jesus.

I was broke, despondent, sick and disgusted with myself for throwing away good money through a basic lack of concentration. Then the misplaced bet ended up like a merciless joke.

Before I walked out the door, I pressed the refresh button on the machine, expecting to see a long set of zeroes on my account. Instead, there was the figure of £2,500 staring back at me. Turkey, or whoever the hell I had backed, must have scored the winning goal with their last play. It was like Tyrone had scored a last-second goal to win the All-Ireland. The buzz was electric. I was in the black, alive again.

I cashed in the winnings. Having that much money in my hands, at just eighteen, felt overwhelming. I thought about booking a nice holiday, putting a deposit down on a new car.

I wanted to. But I just couldn't. I wouldn't allow myself.

I returned to the bookies again the following day and started pressing buttons on the terminal, thinking I'd double my earnings: £200, another £200, £200 again, and again. By the time I'd left, I had blown £1,700.

The loss was sickening, but I wouldn't let it defeat my purpose or train of thought. I returned the following day convinced I'd win it all back. By that evening, every penny was gone.

The cycle repeats itself, because whatever money you win is never really your own. You may have it in your hand, but it's in the bookie's name. It's only a matter of time before they have it back in their till.

Anytime the bookie hands over money to a compulsive gambler, it is like a silent, twisted transaction. The concealed smile, the glint in their eye is clearly visible. He or she knows. You know. The money is only changing hands for a short period. I used to wonder, if deep down, the bookie was laughing at me.

You know you're fucked when the person behind the counter knows your first name, not through football or personal interest, but for your custom. I was leaving the bookies in Irvinestown once when one of the girls working there said, 'See you tomorrow, Cathal.'

I had just lost a big wad of cash but the girl's comment, as harmless as it may have been intended, fuelled me with rage and anger. 'That fucking bitch thinks I'll be back here tomorrow to hand over another ball of money to her boss.'

I wanted to prove her wrong but, deep in my gut, I knew she was right. I had no money, which meant the craving would drive me back there. Once I had a tenner again, I'd be straight in the door.

That stuff could drive you demented, but it never did. I always slept well. Even when I owed thousands, when I was involved in scams that could have had me locked up, I never worried. The only time I felt anxiety was knowing the bet I had just laid was going to come up short.

Most of the time, I hadn't a clue about form or who I was betting on. I would just bet on anything: handball, volleyball, women's beach volleyball. What the hell do I know about that sport? I wasn't even studying the women's asses, because all I would watch was the score.

It was the same when I bet on tennis matches. That was complete torture: 15–love, 15–all, 30–15, 40–15, 40–30, Deuce. Jesus, it was like a slow march to madness, until Nadal or Federer or some other fella I knew nothing about won or lost the fucking match.

I was living from day to day. My daily existence didn't rhyme with my footballing life. I could have a thousand pounds in my pocket, but I'd often still be hungry, wanting and feeling the need to reserve every penny I had for gambling. I wouldn't even buy a teabag for the house.

Football was always my collateral. I left school at sixteen. College held no interest for me. I had already started labouring at weekends when I was in third year, and having a steady income supply was a far more appealing prospect than investing in an education that could take years to see a return. By the age of sixteen, my gambling was already an issue. I needed money. I couldn't wait to get it.

School was a waste of time. Teachers didn't even bother with me in class. They let me do my own thing, which is what I always did anyway. I would go to the bookies at lunchtime. I'd often sneak out during class to lay a bet.

Making good money at sixteen fed the addiction even more. Gambling and football was all I focused on. Work was only a means of getting money. During the boom times, when bricklaying work was everywhere and the money was good, friends of mine in the trade did really well for themselves. They were smart with their wages. Mine would often be gone less than an hour after I'd opened the wage packet.

When the recession hit and I was out of work, I had to improvise. I needed money. If I couldn't steal it off my father, I'd somehow have to get it somewhere else.

The only money I had coming in was my weekly dole allowance, but I often abused the system. I lied through my teeth on occasion, looking for emergency payments when I didn't need them. I got a payment of £300 once and gambled every penny of it.

Even though I didn't have as much cash as I used to, I'd become as much addicted to money as gambling. If I was flush from a win and had £200 in my pocket on a night out, I'd still think it was nowhere near enough cash. I'd have a great time, but the night would only be complete if I knew I had enough money to go gambling the following day.

Saturday gambling soon segued into an all-weekend craze. Betting shops don't open in Northern Ireland on a Sunday, so I'd drive for close to an hour over the border and into Bundoran in Donegal.

It sated my habit, but it never halted the fury and wildly oscillating emotions crashing around inside my head. I don't know how I managed to play inter-county football. The energy my gambling required was exhausting: hiding, lying, cheating, stealing, conniving. It stirred a crazy concoction of emotions. I could sleep, but anxiety still coursed through my body when I wasn't gambling.

The only minor strand of anxiety connected to my gambling was caused by embarrassment. I was a senior county footballer by then and afraid of being spotted. I often went into bookies with the same appearance I had when stealing into the dole office: hoodie up, pulled right down over my eyes, like a convict who was about to rob the place.

I was only hiding from myself. Everybody else in Dromore knew my form by then, fully aware of my capabilities, of how low I could sink. When you start fleecing people in a small rural area, it doesn't take long for you to get tagged as trouble.

The only reason I got away with so much cronyism and deception was because I was a footballer. Yet whatever reputation I had built up as a footballer, I was wrecking, gradually stripping away my name layer by layer with each bogus stunt.

I was respected more outside Dromore than I was in the parish. I looked at Ricey and saw him adored for what he achieved and for who he was. It saddened me, but it never bothered me. I had no regard for my reputation, or the damage it was doing to my family name. I only cared about gambling.

I was existing in a bubble. Everyone knew what I was up to, but in my head I was doing nothing wrong. Respect for me around Dromore was dwindling by the week. People were disgusted by my actions. Even my team-mates were beginning to lose time for me. They resented me. And I gave them every reason to.

I had always wanted to do a skydive. Gambling provided me with my regular fix, but I was always seeking more. I knew nothing about skydiving but jumping out of a plane and accelerating to a freefall speed of 200 kmph sounded like the ultimate rush.

To do a charity skydive, you first have to pay a registration fee and choose a charity you want to donate to. I did neither. You only get a fundraising and sponsorship card after registration, so I made up my own. I concocted a false charity, a generic cancer research project. I spotted a cancer logo online, printed it out and traced it onto my sponsorship card. I changed the heading, reworded the small detail and changed the colouring on the masthead.

When someone comes to your door with a fundraising card, the last thing you do is look at the logo. People will either give you the money or they won't. By going door to door locally, and being a well-known footballer, I knew people would sponsor me.

I went everywhere, lifting money. Everybody who answered their door to me handed over cash. Some were extremely generous. I could spend ten or fifteen minutes talking about football or whatever was going on in the community. I was asked in everywhere for cups of tea. The best china was often taken out. I was only there to scam them out of their hard-earned cash.

Before long, I had gathered over £600. I set the money aside. I wanted to do the skydive, but it was only a fantasy intention. Why else would I use a false cancer charity as a front? Where was that money really going to go?

I was hungry one day and had no money, so I dipped into the funds. That was the trigger point I had been waiting for all along to arrive. It rationalized my intention to use the money to try and win it all back, or to make even more.

I was only going to be able to suppress that urge for so long. That money was gathered for only one reason. Before long, it was all gone, lost in the morass of torn-up and beaten dockets.

Guilt wasn't my first emotion. Enterprise was. I just took up the charge again. I expanded my net, going to more houses in the locality with my false fundraising cards. The people kept scribbling their names and addresses on bogus cards. The money kept filtering into my pocket. At the finish, I had taken close to £1,000 off my own people, most of whom had always been very good to me. The slap on their face was even harder to take with me blowing every last penny.

I look back on that stunt now with crippling embarrassment. It horrifies me to think I stooped so low with my own people. I'm so ashamed that I would use cancer, a disease that is devastating this country everywhere, as a front for me to steal that money from people, some of whom had probably lost family members to the disease. It makes no sense, but all common sense dissolves once you start gambling.

The most common phrase I heard when I was gambling was, 'Will you wise up to fuck.' Everyone thought it was just a bad habit that I would eventually grow out of. I was a confused young man. I didn't know what was going on in my brain. There was no real assistance to help me process it properly. I couldn't wise up, because I couldn't recognize what was wrong with me.

Neither could those around me. Their actions often only enabled me to become worse, not better. My own teammates knew what I was up to when I called with those cards and they still gave me the money.

Eventually, the message got through to some of them. They couldn't stand for it any more. They couldn't allow me to keep desecrating my own community, to keep debasing my own name and self-worth as a person in that community.

I was sitting in my house one evening. It was cold and dark. The fire was on. I looked out the window and saw Collie McCullagh, Fabian O'Neill and Seamus Goodwin walking up the drive. I knew I was fucked.

I was good friends with Collie and Fabian. Seamus had been my football manager for years. As soon as I answered the door, I was braced for impact.

'What the hell are you at, Cathal? Do you realize what you are doing to yourself? You either cop yourself on now, or we're basically washing our hands of you.'

I broke down crying in front of them. 'I'm fucked from gambling. I need help.'

I felt a weight lifted off my shoulders. It was the first time I admitted to myself that I was sick, that I needed help to be cured. I wasn't yet twenty-one but the disease had already ravaged my body like a deadly virus tearing through my organs. Slowly, I was breaking down, dying in a different way.

We spoke about treatment. Oisín McConville had just written his autobiography, in which he had become the first GAA player to publicly speak about his gambling addiction. Seamus rang Oisín and we arranged to meet the following day in the Armagh City Hotel.

Seamus drove me there. Oisín was waiting in the lobby for us. He had already suffered the same pain I was experiencing from gambling addiction, but he had faced down his demons. After sinking into an abyss of drinking, depression and debt, Oisín could see in me the same pain and torment he once visited on himself. He had suffered similar wounds to be able to recognize the scars. And my scars were everywhere.

Oisín had gone for treatment in Cuan Mhuire in Coolarne in Galway. Since its formation in 1966 by Sister Consilio, Cuan Mhuire had treated tens of thousands of Irish people. They had nationwide centres in Cork, Limerick, Kildare and Newry, but Oisín had spent his recovery in Galway and that's where he advised me to go. 'It will be tough,' he said to me that morning, 'but you will get through it.'

Seamus rang Cuan Mhuire and arranged to get me in two days later. I wanted to go straight away, but the lads felt that I should begin that process of rehabilitation at home first. Fabian, Kevin O'Brien and Niall Colton said they wanted me to pay back the money I had stolen off people in Dromore before I left for Galway. When I did come back, they wanted me working off a clean slate, or as clean as I could make it after all the stains I had smeared across it.

I hadn't any money to make those repayments. I knew Daddy would give it to me if I asked him, but I'd put him through enough pain and I didn't want to admit what I had just done. The lads and Seamus gave me that money themselves. Fabian was the club captain at the time. He had his own plastering business and was doing well, but he went into the bank and withdrew a ball of cash to clean up a mess he had absolutely no part in creating.

I'll never forget the lads for their kindness. It was money they weren't going to get back, but the process was only beginning for me and it was humiliating. They drove me around to every person I had taken money off. Door by door, step by step, I had to hand back every penny of the £1,000 I had taken from them.

The shame was overbearing. I was crying in the car, engulfed with guilt. There was just pure silence as we made our way around the town, meandering through the arteries of the parish. Fellas who I had grown up with, who I played football with, I couldn't even talk to. It was terrible.

The fear was worse. Getting out of the car and having to walk ten or fifteen yards to a front door felt like a mile. What was I going to say? It didn't really matter, because they knew what had happened, they were fully aware of why I was there. I was just trying to control the shame and humiliation to a manageable point.

I kept it very brief. 'The skydive was cancelled, so I'm just giving you back the money you sponsored.'

Most people knew I was lying through my teeth, that the skydive was never going to happen in the first place. Yet no one had called my bluff when they should have. It was a form of communal perseverance that was doing me more harm than good.

They were afraid that I might get offended, or that my gambling habit would become so bad that I wouldn't be able to play senior football for Dromore again. Most of those who paid up were prepared to subjugate my dishonesty for the welfare of the Dromore team. In the long run, the transaction was doing nobody any good, especially me.

A fiver was nothing but the fivers added up and it was still stealing. There was a bigger picture too. Word travels quickly. The club or the parish didn't want to be associated with the stain I was leaving everywhere. I was damaging more than just my name; I was blackening Dromore's name too. Its people didn't want others thinking, 'Those Dromore boys are a shower of robbing bastards.'

Making that walk of shame was humiliating. It was important for me to do it for myself, but was it just another easy way out? The lads were bailing me out. I had blown £1,000, but it wasn't my money that I was handing back. The lads were trying to do the right thing, but were they just enabling me in a different way?

I knew the only place I could really recover was in Cuan Mhuire. Seamus Goodwin called to the house two days later and we set off for Galway. On the long road south, I was staring out the window in a daze, wondering where my life was headed. The tears were streaming down my face. I was ransacked with anxiety.

I didn't know what lay ahead for me, but Oisín McConville's words kept ringing in my ears. 'Bare your soul and leave everything down there. Put in the hard work and it will be worth it.'

I had to. I was just about to turn twenty-one. I was at rock bottom.

CHAPTER 7

COOLARNE

'This place is a fucking shit-hole. Jesus, I'm never going to
survive this ... I can't wait to get
the hell out of this fucking dump.'

Diary entry, Cuan Mhuire, Coolarne,
16 November 2009

Coolarne is in the middle of nowhere. It's about fifteen miles from Galway city, around five miles outside the town of Athenry, a tiny townland enveloped by a rolling landscape of huge farmland and stone walls. The place is only connected to Galway's main road arteries through a complex network of back roads, but in the middle of that nowhere is one of the biggest addiction treatment centres in the country.

As you enter past two big concrete pillars and black and gold iron railings, the Cuan Mhuire centre sits at the end of a long, meandering driveway, hemmed in by a wall of trees, bushes and shrubs. As the road veers around to the left, the big white building, with its Perspex reception area, instantly looms into view, like a blob of white paint dropped onto a grey and green canvas.

Seamus Goodwin parked the car. We walked up the steps to the reception area. I was embarrassed, full of shame. My head was so low that my chin was almost hitting the concrete. After giving my name at the check-in desk, I was brought down to the nurses' station, where this wee nurse took my details.

Before I was shown to my room, Seamus hugged me. 'This is the beginning of a new chapter in your life, Cathal,' he said. 'You'll be back playing football with Dromore in a few months.'

As soon as the intake process is over, the detoxification process begins. I was sleeping in a room with eight other people, all alcoholics and drug addicts, all desperately trying to deal with the withdrawal symptoms from alcohol and opiate detox.

The first night was hell. Guys were throwing up all around me. Fellas sweating and cramping, groaning and moaning. The stench of vomit and piss was repulsive and nauseating, so repugnant that it was corrupting every breath of air I inhaled.

The beds were stacked up beside one another, just one metre apart. One fella was snoring so loudly that I thought there was a train in the room. The place was freezing cold. The mood was miserable. Depressing. Pure fucking hell.

Alcohol and drug addicts usually spend two weeks in detox, whereas the detox time for gambling addicts is normally seven days. They don't suffer the same physical distress from withdrawal symptoms, but compulsive gamblers are inserted into the environment to reflect and unwind, to slow down your brain and stop it from spinning.

I didn't sleep a wink on that first night. Another six nights seemed like a form of torture, so I approached a nurse as soon as I saw one the following morning. I wanted to be moved to a private room so that I could sleep. I was tired and cranky, but my tone was laced with arrogance. 'I'm not an alcoholic or drug addict,' I said. 'So what the hell am I doing in there with all those other boys?'

Her reply cut me in two. 'I don't care who you are, or what your addiction is, but you're the same as everyone else here.'

It was her way of trying to equalize my attitude to the mindset I needed if I was to make it through this place. I was used to getting my own way. My father had always been my get-out-of-jail card. Here, there was no back-up plan or escape hatch. It was lockdown.

Everyone in detox wore pyjamas, but my head was wrecked from far more than just the clothing during that first week. I was a total mess. My world was a horror chamber. The place was dark and cold. It was November. The winter was closing in, siphoning more and more light from the sky with each passing day.

Every day seemed like the longest of my life.

'No heating on again. I'm frozen here most of the time. It takes visitors for them to turn on the heat in this place. It's a joke.'

Diary entry, Cuan Mhuire, Coolarne,
30 November 2009

After I came out of detox, my attitude didn't change much. For most of the first month, I still had the same brazen, belligerent attitude that had taken me there in the first place. I didn't want to listen. I couldn't be told anything. 'Fuck them. Fuck this place. Fuck everyone in this place.'

My ego was hardly able to fit through the door. I had won an All-Ireland with Tyrone, but I was still only a peripheral member of the panel. I was a nobody. I had only played a handful of league matches, but I still expected everyone to know that I was a Tyrone footballer. I was nearly demanding special privileges from the nurses on the back of that footballing status. My head was up my hole.

The head nurse was a lady called Mary Falvey. I couldn't stand the woman. I used to think she had an attitude. I thought she was arrogant. I hated the way she talked to me. I hated her, full stop.

I just saw Mary as a figurehead of power. I never liked people with power. I always questioned that authority, because I wanted to smash it. That was one of the reasons I never got on in school, because I looked at teachers and principals from that viewpoint.

A lot of people resist as soon as they pass through those doors in Cuan Mhuire. They want to keep doing it their own way. I did. It's only natural, because you don't want to do it any other way. It's a shock to your system. Pure hardship. Breaking addiction is never easy, but Cuan Mhuire try and break you in order to get you to see that there is another way.

I started my programme after two weeks, but it took me another while for my mind to adjust, for it to sufficiently slow down to a more manageable pace. You can't really make any progress until you begin to start thinking clearly. When I finally did, my attitude softened.

Resistance was gradually peeled away, layer by layer. You can see the benefits in what Cuan Mhuire are trying to do. You have tried to do it your way for so long and it hasn't worked. After a while, I began to see Mary for who she really was. I understood what she and Cuan Mhuire stood for, of how hard they worked to change and improve the lives of people like me. When I let all that old attitude go, Mary was lovely to me.

My mindset changed, because my circumstances allowed it to. Gambling and football was all that I had ever cared about. Being a footballer had often granted me a dispensation to do what I liked, to get away with whatever I wanted. It fed my gambling addiction even more. That was no way to live. There was no honour or dignity in that kind of life.

I realized there was far more to life. I became more sensitive. I mellowed. I was able to cast off the chains which had been tying me down like an anchor stuck to the floor of an ocean. All the pressure was gone. I had no money to spend. No phone to answer. The stress of owing money, of people coming after me, was absent from my life. The relief was liberating. For the first time in five years, I had freedom. The peace of mind was priceless.

I didn't even want to gamble any more. Gambling was just a chasing game. The chase was over.

'Had a great walk with Joe today. It was really windy,
but we kept walking and had a great chat.'

Diary entry, 7 December 2009

For weeks, I was the only gambling addict in the place. Then Joe arrived. He was a big football man, but that was initially a complete irrelevance. I was just delighted to be able to talk to another person suffering from the same addiction as myself.

Joe was in a bad way when he first came in. It was obvious how much distress gambling had caused him, of how much the disease had impacted on his life. Since nobody had been there to guide and direct me when I first arrived, I wanted to be there for Joe.

He knew who I was. Football was a natural connection. We talked a lot about football, especially about where he was from and Tyrone. We walked a lot together. That natural correlation between football and gambling strengthened our relationship.

We both had a lot of personal difficulties to deal with. Joe had a family. He was afraid of losing them at the time. We thrashed out our problems. We tried to keep positive. As the weeks and the programme progressed, we were just so happy to be alive.

Our friendship helped us in so many ways. It made Joe more open to me about articulating his difficulties, but I encouraged that openness because I had been ahead of him in the programme and I had seen the benefits that open-mindedness had had on me.

As an addict, you will only get recovery if you want it. I desperately wanted to get better, but you have to be prepared to expose yourself, and all your vulnerabilities and weaknesses, during that process. I had to leave everything on the table, right from my childhood, from everything I had seen, heard or done during that childhood, up to the crazy adulthood I had lived until the age of twenty-one.

'Bare your soul and leave everything down there,' Oisín McConville said to me. I did.

Whatever I didn't want to share in group therapy, I let out in my one-on-one counselling. No skeletons were left in the closet. It was hard. More skeletons than in a horror movie appeared. It was the first time I had ever spoken about a lot of this stuff, especially family details.

I was a closed book. I had spent years constructing this persona and image, layer by layer, brick by brick, lie by lie. I was like a beaver building its dam, trying to close off everything. I never wanted anyone to see the cracks, the weak foundation behind the impressive structure. But once I opened up in Cuan Mhuire, the dam burst and the tears and emotion flowed in torrents.

Most of the tears were pure stress and relief. I hadn't cried since I was about sixteen. I often wanted to, but I would never allow myself. Even when I was mentally suffering, I suppressed the urge and the desperate need to try and release it from my body, to use it as a conduit to try and purge the pain.

At one stage during the programme, I couldn't stop crying. Every time I spoke, every dark memory I revisited, I broke down. I was like a tap that couldn't be turned off. Initially, I was covering up the tears, rubbing my forearm against my eyes. My sleeves were damp from my sobbing. The counsellors have seen all those moves a million times, they can read you like a book. You don't have to hide from them. They want to see you stripped bare, to see you strip yourself bare.

Expressing my emotions added to my liberation, to my new sense of self. I never saw my father cry, when I'm sure the man was going through so much turmoil that he wanted to release a gallon of tears.

Crying is something that men rarely do. If a facet of your being is not being used, especially when it's hardwired into your system to be utilized, suppressing that emotion is only going to have an effect on you somewhere down the line. You don't want people bawling and blubbering over nothing, but crying is often a sign of strength more than weakness.

That's an important message to transmit in trying to promote mental health and wellness in modern society.

> *'There's more gamblers in this place now*
> *than there is in a busy bookies.'*
>
> Diary entry, 11 December 2009

Not long after Joe arrived, there must have been a gambling meltdown somewhere. Fourteen gambling addicts walked through those doors within the space of a couple of weeks. It was Cuan Mhuire's biggest ever intake of gamblers.

I tried to help those people as much as I could. I had been through the initial process. I knew how tough it was. I also understood how much your mindset at that point differs from those who have spent more time in the recovery programme.

By that stage, you have a responsibility. Apart from the nurses, a lot of the work in Cuan Mhuire is done by the residents. As you begin to get better, you have to lead by example. You have to show the way to those who find it hard to see that way forward after being blinded by addiction for so long.

Not long after Joe came in, this boy, Conor (not his real name) from Armagh, arrived. He was in a really bad way. He wasn't interacting with anyone. He wasn't even talking. I sat down beside Conor one day. I didn't say much, but I tried to say all I needed to in a handful of words.

'I know how you're feeling,' I said to him. 'I know where you have been. When I came into Cuan Mhuire, there was nobody here for me. If you want, I'm here for you now.'

I was eight weeks ahead of Conor by that stage. I had a completely different perspective on addiction by then. He needed help. By that stage I was able to provide whatever assistance I could.

You just try to get by, but every experience was also an opportunity. All those other gambling addicts had stories to tell. I could learn from them. I could absorb their experiences for the benefit of my own recovery.

Life's lessons were everywhere. There were 'open' meetings in the house every Tuesday evening. Recovered and recovering addicts from Galway, and the surrounding areas, would attend. They would tell their stories too. I grew very friendly with two of those locals – Mike and Mick (not their real names). They were big football men. They loved to chat about Ulster football. Mike was free of gambling for fifteen years. He was a great man to listen to.

The more I heard, the more I absorbed, and the more I learned. I felt like a completely new person. I was thinking like a normal person. Because I hadn't connected with that normal person in five years, I had lost him. In Cuan Mhuire, I found him again.

The primary reason I did was through telling the truth. Shortly into the programme, I decided that I was going to be as honest as possible. That alone was a solid starting point, because I had forgotten what honesty was.

My life had been a cocktail of lies and deceit. My default setting was to be dishonest, but I prayed to God every day for help to enable me to start telling the truth. I asked God every night to assist me on that journey to becoming an honest person again. As the weeks passed, I would thank God for getting me through the day, and to keep helping me to tell the truth.

In the main building, there is a wee chapel down the back. There is Mass every day, which you have to go to. I always did.

When we were growing up, Mummy and Daddy brought us to Mass every Sunday. I was never religious, but I always believed in a higher power. 'Our Lady' was always my highest power. I believe those prayers helped me get through my recovery in Galway. I still pray to Our Lady the whole time.

Before games, I pray to her even more. During the national anthem, I always say 'The Memorare', the prayer that asks the Blessed Mother for her assistance and her grace.

Remember O most gracious Virgin Mary, that never was it known that anyone who fled to thy protection, implored thy help, or sought thy intercession was left unaided. Inspired with this

*confidence, I fly to thee, O Virgin of virgins, my Mother; to thee
do I come; before thee I stand, sinful and sorrowful. O Mother
of the Word Incarnate, despise not my petitions, but in thy mercy
hear and answer me. Amen.*

When I'm on the pitch, I seem like a contradiction as I'm
going around like the devil. Nobody has sinned more than
I have, but Our Lady is always in my heart. I say more than
just that prayer before big games; I also thank Our Lady for
the opportunity I have just been given, for allowing me to
be on that pitch and to live my dreams.

Because there were many times, especially in the early
stages of my recovery, when I wondered if I would ever play
football again, especially with Tyrone.

*'I worked hard today. It was freezing cold,
but I got a lot done on the Grotto.'*

Diary entry, 16 December 2009

At the back of the main house, behind the flowerbeds and
the glasshouses, a long rectangular stone building is the
central feature of the courtyard. It is broken up into four
sections, with a door into each of those segments, each hous-
ing its own mini-department, with the craft's name written
above the door in red lettering.

Art. Carpentry. Upholstery. Pottery.

That courtyard had some unique features. The stonework
was fabulous. Benches, old relics and old machinery, painted
and jazzed up to appear of their time, further decorated the
enclosure.

When you came out of detox, you had chores to do. It

wasn't a bootcamp. The work wasn't a form of punishment. Many people learned new skills, but those crafts were to keep your mind busy and occupied as you struggled to come to terms with a new life without addiction.

I had my own craft. I was a bricklayer. There was plenty of work around the place to be done. Mick 'Stones', as he was called, did most of the plastering and stonework in Cuan Mhuire, so that was my focus instead of painting or drawing or moulding wet clay into ceramics or crockery.

I was never afraid of hard work. Mick 'Stones' was building a grotto and I threw myself into the project. I even had a few guys labouring for me as I crafted the stone and framework around the Holy statue.

I worked for five hours a day. I'd start at nine but the work was broken up by intermittent counselling sessions and group therapy. There was meditation twice a day. Before you'd know it, the day would be done, especially as the days got shorter and the darkness descended over those tall trees like a giant shadow.

Everything was coming together. I had peace of mind, but I formed a completely new level of self-discipline and self-regulation. I learned the importance of something as basic as timekeeping. Before, apart from football training, I turned up wherever and whenever I felt like.

I was finally learning how to carry myself properly.

'Today was hard. Last night was worse. Fuck, I've found the last few days wild tough. I'm not in good form. I think I'm depressed.'

Diary entry, 25 December 2009

On Christmas Eve, we had a Christmas party, even if a Christmas party in Cuan Mhuire is not really a Christmas party in the literal sense. Obviously there is no alcohol. Somebody had a guitar. There was a singsong. People were playing board games. Finger food was on the tables, a real treat in an addiction treatment centre.

I felt really low. It was the first time I had ever spent Christmas away from my family. Even after Mummy and Daddy split up, Christmas was always a big family event. Daddy would put on a big spread. He still does.

That Christmas Day in Cuan Mhuire, everyone ate together in the canteen. For a lot of us, it was very difficult. For others, it was a joyful day, a happy experience. Many addicts don't have strong family connections, mostly because their addiction has destroyed those links. That slightly altered the outlook of the day, but it didn't dull the ache.

Cuan Mhuire try their best to make the day as normal as possible. Everyone got a present. I got a shirt and a pair of black socks. You wouldn't be wearing the shirt on a night out, but I really appreciated the gesture. In Cuan Mhuire, a gift is akin to being spoiled.

The only real positive memory I have from that day was of the perspective it offered, of the perspective people tried to provide. I was only twenty-one. I still had my whole life ahead of me. Most of the other people in my company that Christmas were in their forties and fifties. Others were in their sixties. Many had washed away the best years of their lives in rivers of alcohol.

Please God I still had decades left to live that I would

survive tomorrow's generation as well. I could look at my potential new life through the prism of sobriety. And I swore to myself that I would never, ever spend another Christmas in an addiction treatment centre.

'I finally got my All-Ireland medal today.'

Diary entry, 4 January 2010

When we won our first county title with Dromore in 2007, we were promised a team holiday. It never happened. When we won our second title in 2009, the club were true to their word, albeit two years later. That winter, the Dromore senior team went to Gran Canaria for a week.

It was heartbreaking. There was no sunshine where I was. That winter of 2009–10 was the harshest in decades. When the snow started falling, it refused to stop. A white blanket was draped everywhere. The paths were like a skating rink. The building in Coolarne was always cold. During that December and early January, it was like an icebox.

I was a key part of those Dromore championship winning teams. I deserved to go on that holiday as much as anybody else. I felt aggrieved and hurt, but I also had to accept that missing that trip was a price that had to be paid for all the hurt I had caused, to the people of Dromore as much as myself.

Recovery was my priority, but football was always going to play a key part in that process. I wanted to go back playing for Dromore. I knew I would. I desperately wanted to return to Tyrone as well, but I wasn't sure if that door would ever reopen.

In the middle of week nine, my name was called out over

the intercom for me to go to the reception. I didn't understand why. When I got there, Mickey Harte was standing in front of me.

We went into the TV room to chat. Mickey took something from his pocket and handed it to me. 'I think this belongs to you,' he said. I opened this little red velvet box. It was my All-Ireland medal from 2008, the glorious Celtic Cross, gleaming and sparkling against the sunlight dipping in through the Perspex windows.

I didn't go to the 2008 All-Ireland winning banquet. I didn't even chase up the medal afterwards. I was too busy chasing the constant streams of highs from gambling to even bother. Over sixteen months after winning that medal, I finally had it in my possession.

Cuan Mhuire didn't allow visitors midweek, but they weren't going to turn Mickey Harte away. Mickey is a special person. I got a warm feeling as we started chatting. I asked him if the door with Tyrone was still open for me.

'It has never been closed, Cathal,' was his reply.

We spoke about my life, about my recovery, about how Mickey wanted to play a part in that recovery. He knew football was my life. Mickey knew I was a decent player, but he also acknowledged that I needed to help myself first before I could help Tyrone.

'If you focus on life, and on living life well, just think of all the possibilities out there,' Mickey said. 'Look at the football you were playing, with all the hell that was going on in your life. Imagine, just imagine, what you really could do if you got all of this sorted out.'

Cuan Mhuire wouldn't let me play football. They didn't

want me training. It was easy to see why. This was three months of my life. I was here to get myself well again. I needed to put my full focus on getting better. Football wasn't important while I was there. I could play football again when I got out.

In my mind though, it wasn't that simple. If I was going back with Tyrone, I couldn't just do nothing for three months and then walk straight back into the setup. Football was also such a huge part of my life though, that it couldn't be fully separated from my recovery process; it had to be part of the process. Playing football again for Dromore and Tyrone formed an incredibly important part of the journey I wanted to undertake in reconstructing my life.

Before Mickey inspired me, the rebel side of my personality had already started to show again. At the end of week seven, I asked Mike to get me a football. The next time he arrived for one of those 'open' meetings, Mike handed me a brand new O'Neills ball.

The Coolarne GAA pitch backs right onto the boundary wall of Cuan Mhuire. That wall is about ten feet high. There is an iron gate at the bottom of the courtyard, a six-feet portal into a more normal world. It looks right onto the pitch, but it's in full view of parts of the main building and outhouses. I could have jumped over that gate, but the top of the iron bars were formed like spears and I didn't want to impale myself. Plus, I didn't want to get spotted.

I knew the run of the sheds from my work and I knew where there was a ladder. One Sunday in the middle of December, I lifted the ladder out from a shed, climbed the wall, pulled the aluminium stairs up with me, and planted its legs in the wet ground at the other side.

That pitch in Coolarne belongs to Turloughmore Hurling Club. There was a handball alley behind the dressing rooms. The pitch was surrounded by trees but it was wide open, a little patch on the vast patchwork quilt of fields stretching across the vast expanse of mid-Galway.

A hurling team was training there. They looked like a junior outfit. A few of the players approached me. We started chatting. They knew I played for Tyrone and that I had to have been in recovery in Cuan Mhuire. It was a basic equation to balance. Why else would a Tyrone footballer suddenly be transplanted into such rich hurling territory?

The manager asked me if I wanted to train with them. I declined. I needed to make the most of the time I had on the other side of those four walls. I started to kick the ball over the bar, run after it, and then go again. And again. And again.

It felt so good to just kick a ball again, but the rust was caking off my limbs with every motion. My kickpassing and shooting was diabolical. It was a graphic indication of just how far behind I had fallen in my training.

Training on my own on that field became a ritual I followed every Tuesday and Thursday. I was way out of shape. I was completely unfit. I didn't know if I was ever going to play for Tyrone again, but whatever training I was doing on my own in the dark in mid-Galway was far removed from the scientific approach in Garvaghey. At least doing some training, however basic, was my only hope of matching the strides of every other Tyrone player.

When the winter hit hard, I just gritted my teeth and

drove through it. Some nights were complete misery: wet, cold, damp, with a breeze that would cut you in two. The fire was on in the house. When the snow arrived in late December, I had an ideal dispensation to break that ritual, but I never did. After Mickey arrived, I ramped up the pace a couple of notches.

I began training more. I had always walked up the driveway every day, but I started running and sprinting up and down that meandering tarmac. There is a thin grass strip between the road and the trees, so I stuck a pair of boots on and began twisting and turning to try and simulate turning sharply, or being jinked by a forward, in a match situation.

By that stage, everyone in Cuan Mhuire was aware of what I was up to. They probably knew I was scaling the ten-foot wall too and training on the pitch because Coolarne is a small country place. A new face would have raised a red flag to the locals. If a nurse didn't spot me, a local would have told her that I was running about behind their walls.

I'm not sure if turning a blind eye is the best way to describe why the nurses didn't question my approach. They could see how driven and determined I was, how focused I had become. I was eating well. I hadn't touched a drop of alcohol in months. I was doing hundreds of press-ups every day. My body was like a coiled ball of iron. My appearance was nearly a metaphor for how well my recovery had gone.

There were times when guilt kicked in. My old ways had returned. I wasn't doing what I was told, or what I was supposed to do. I was in Galway to get better, not to make myself a stronger footballer. This wasn't a three-month training camp. Technically, I knew I probably shouldn't have been doing what I was. I was still putting my body and mind under strain. I was pushing myself to the extreme when strain was the last thing I needed. But I did need it. And I justified the approach by convincing myself that staying in top physical shape had to be good for my mind.

It meant more than just football too. Joe came out with me on a few occasions to kick the ball back, the two of us scampering over a big wall on a ladder like a couple of escaped convicts.

'I'm in a really good place now.'

Diary entry, Cuan Mhuire, 12 January 2010

The more I changed, the happier I became. I was happy to be in Cuan Mhuire. I was grateful for the opportunity the place had given me. I had a totally new perspective on life. And I was excited about the prospect of living that new life in its fullest form.

I wrote very little in my journal and diary over the last few weeks I was there. I didn't need to. Much of my earlier writing anyway was only venting, expressing a level of anger and frustration stored in my body and mind for years. By now, that ball of bitterness and rage had been rubbed out like a physiotherapist would break down a ball of scar tissue and massage the fibrous material out of your muscles.

There was a payphone and we were allowed only one phone call at the weekend. I used to ring Daddy a lot. We had great conversations, probably the first time we ever hit that level in our father and son relationship. Other weekends, I rang Barry. He was in Australia at the time, but we spoke like we were in the same room.

Over Christmas, I called some of the club boys to wish them well. It was probably me craving a reconnection to a communal relationship which had snapped, but I desperately wanted to mend and restore that tear. I wanted to go back to playing football with Dromore. The boys wanted me back.

My final few weeks in Cuan Mhuire were a life of basic, simple but really enjoyable pleasures. I kept myself busy with work, beavering away on little jobs around the place. We were only allowed to watch TV on a Sunday evening. It was often harmless and banal TV viewing, but those few hours still provided precious entertainment.

The New Year was here. A new life was beckoning me from beyond those two big pillars. In the early weeks of my time in Cuan Mhuire, I walked around the place like a phantom. My scarf was pulled up around my neck, headphones on, music blaring into my eardrums, oblivious to everyone and everything else around me.

There are cameras at the front gates. They say if you take one step outside those gates, you are gone. In those early days, I often walked right up to those black and gold railings and wanted to keep going, losing myself in some dark forest in the middle of nowhere in mid-Galway.

From around week six, I would walk up to those gates every Sunday with different thoughts in my head. I was ticking off the time like a checklist.

'Six weeks done.'

'Only five left now.'

'A month to go.'

'Twenty-one more days.'

'Nearly into single figures now.'

'Nearly there.'

I was excited about going home, but that excitement was also splattered with fear. I had been locked away for three months. You don't become institutionalized in such a short time, but you are living a completely different existence from the one you are now going back to, the one you hope to return to.

Shortly before I was due to leave, one of my counsellors asked me two very basic questions.

'How do you think your family are getting on without you? Do they miss you?'

I was emphatic in my response. 'Of course they do.'

'What do you think it is that they miss?' my counsellor immediately shot back.

It stopped me in my tracks. I was a son and a brother but what did my family really miss? Over the previous few years, I had caused them huge pain and heartbreak. They certainly didn't miss all that chaos and turmoil.

Cuan Mhuire try to prepare you for your new life. You enter a new world from the one in which you inhabited for so long. Your life has changed. But so has that of your family. 'Don't expect to go back home', said my counsellor, 'and for everyone to drop what they're doing just because you are back.'

Daddy had been down to see me a few times. The first time he arrived, we hugged tightly. I broke down crying. I could see tears in his eyes too. The hurt in his face from seeing his son in rehab was also clearly visible.

Daddy was sad but he was also glad that I was finally getting the help I desperately needed, the assistance which he couldn't give me, which he was not equipped to provide.

When I thought about that question my counsellor posed, I appreciated just how much I had put my father through. However hard it was for him to see me in Cuan Mhuire, at least he finally had some normality in his life. Being free from that constant worry about me stealing had probably granted the man peace of mind for the first time in years. All that strain and anxiety connected to my addiction was no longer hanging over Daddy like a black cloud.

The day I left Cuan Mhuire, Daddy came to lift me. I was never so delighted to see him. My new life was beginning. In another form, so was Daddy's.

When we drove out those gates, past those big concrete pillars, I felt a real sense of satisfaction, of completion. I was only twenty-one, but I had gone in a broken man. Now I felt like a completely new person.

Emancipated. Free. Liberated.

At last.

CHAPTER 8

NORMALITY

National League, Round 4
Tyrone 2–15
Derry 0–12
Healy Park, Omagh, 5 March 2016

Derry had won two of their first three league matches. They had eyes on promotion. Everyone was expecting pyrotechnics after the McKenna Cup final. There were no fireworks. We just beat the shite out of them.

The build-up reflected the match. It was completely muted. All week, I never even thought about Derry or who I might be marking for one second. What happened in January was irrelevant, especially to us. We were due to meet Derry in the championship in May but that thought hadn't even crossed our minds yet. Our only focus for now was the same as it had been since the beginning of this league; we're going to walk all over anyone, or anything, that stands in our way.

We're going to win this division. So any other team that may have similar ambitions, as Derry might have had, can just fuck off.

I was out in Omagh one night when I drove past this gorgeous-looking girl. I had seen her around before, but I didn't know who she was or where she was from. I asked around and found out her name was Andrea. She was from a place about ten miles away from Dromore. I checked to see if she had a Facebook account, which she had, so I sent her a message and just asked her out.

Andrea wasn't a mad football supporter, but she knew I played for Tyrone. So did her friends and family. Her sister warned her to be wary of me. She had heard all the negative stories, of how I was only out of recovery less than six months. Andrea still agreed to meet up. She wanted to make her own judgement. On our first date, we just went for a drive. Immediately, there was this natural connection between us.

I'd never been in a serious or long-term relationship before, but I wanted to be with Andrea because I was crazy about her. I had always been a wild man for women. I was hard to tie down. When I was single, I could be texting six or seven women at the same time, playing one off the other, shagging whichever one was available whenever it suited me.

I loved women, but addiction has many forms and my promiscuity was just another strand of gambling. I always had to be texting some woman, just to caress my ego as much as wanting to be with that girl. Some of them really liked me, but I was only using them. I didn't care.

Playing women off one another and sneaking off behind their backs was just laying bets without losing money. The more women I had on the go, the bigger the buzz. I was always trying to manage and manipulate those women, but I couldn't control that stream of highs because I wasn't able to fully control myself.

Some of my actions were high risk, but I got off on that thrill.

I was kissing two Maeves at one stage. I sent one Maeve the message intended for the other Maeve. I was caught out immediately, but I just tried to lie my way out of it. When she wasn't buying any of it, I couldn't have cared less. I just moved on to the next girl.

As well as the gambling and stealing, Andrea had also heard those stories about my womanizing. Early into our relationship, one of her close friends told her that I'd never settle down, that I'd only be with her for a few weeks before heading for the hills. Her friend was wrong. I was going nowhere.

Andrea had a great outlook on life. She was an independent thinker, always positive and vibrant. She made her judgement on what she knew of me, not what she had heard.

That person was gone. I wasn't gambling. I was happy, finally content in my adult life. I used to tell Andrea some of the crazy stunts I had pulled in my life and she could never associate that madness with the person she now knew, the guy she grew to love.

When we first met, Andrea was studying to be a nurse at John Moores University in Liverpool. The distance wasn't an issue, because I just wanted to be with her. Even when

I was training with Tyrone, I would try and get over to see Andrea as often as I could. We were constantly on the phone.

I was in a great place in my life. I was far more open after Cuan Mhuire, so I could finally relate my emotions properly to someone I cared about.

When Andrea finished her college course and returned home, we became even closer. I loved this girl so much. I got on really well with her family. Everything felt right. I finally had balance and real happiness in my life. And I thought I would spend the rest of that life with Andrea.

The first night I returned home from Cuan Mhuire, everything felt strange. Even just walking into the house was weird. I was talking to Daddy and Eimheár. I was on the phone to Mummy. They were all delighted that I was back. Deep down, I knew I was in a good place, but I was still on edge.

I was still hiding. All the shame and hurt I had brought on myself and my family wasn't going be washed away with three months of recovery. Initially, I was withdrawn. I always had the head down. A couple of days after I returned, the club had their annual dinner dance, where we were being presented with our county medals from the 2009 success.

I didn't want to go, but I was talked into attending. It was only Dromore's second county senior title. There might not have been another one. It was a great relief and release when I did go, because I met everyone. They were all very kind and welcoming, but I wasn't myself. I just wanted to get the evening out of the way.

Tyrone had already played the Dr McKenna Cup by that stage. They were preparing for the national league and Mickey Harte had called me back in. At the end of the month, the squad had a fitness test in Jordanstown. I was a nervous wreck.

It was difficult to be around the people I knew in Dromore, but returning to Tyrone was a completely different and more challenging environment. It was far more public. I was still racked with shame and guilt for what I had done. Everyone knew where I had been, about the reckless pathway that had taken me there. Heading to Belfast that evening, I was fearful about how I would be received. What would the boys think of me now? Would some of those team-mates ever have any respect for me again?

I was lucky that we were only meeting in groups. Not all of the panel would be there. I hoped that would dilute my anxiety, but my fears dissolved as soon as I arrived. The first person I met outside was Enda McGinley. He had a huge welcome for me, the warmth palpable from his handshake.

Enda didn't sidestep the big issue. He asked me how I was doing, how long I had spent in Cuan Mhuire. We even spoke about my time there during Christmas. 'That must have been hard,' Enda said.

When I entered the dressing room, most of the players in the group were already there. 'Ah God, here he is,' announced Owen Mulligan, 'the wild man is back.'

It was vintage 'Mugsy'. That was his way of inveigling me back into the group, of making me feel part of the dressing room dynamic again. Everyone else had a warm welcome.

Twenty minutes later, fear and anxiety were the least of my worries as I was being pushed into serious oxygen debt from a fitness test.

Gradually, the shame and guilt I was carrying was flushed out of my system. I had made mistakes. I had screwed people over. I could never fully repay all the hurt I had caused, or undo all the damage I had done to my name, but I had a new life now and I had to try and live it to the best of my ability.

My life was normal. All the chaos was gone. The constant chasing was over. I could go out and just relax. It felt liberating not to have to constantly lie and cheat and steal. Even something as normal and routine as answering my phone was a luxury. Anytime it rang before, I'd be terrified to look at the number on the screen and see who was trying to find me. Those avoided phone calls were mostly from people owed money.

Having that peace of mind was precious. It allowed me to fully concentrate on my football. I could train and prepare properly. I finally made my championship debut that summer in 2010. I won my first Ulster senior title. I was falling in love with Andrea. I was able to focus on building a good future for myself, because I had found a new job.

The building trade had gone down the tubes. I could see that train coming down the tracks before I went into Cuan Mhuire, but I was looking for a way out anyway. I liked bricklaying. The physical side of it appealed to me. It gave my game an added edge, but it was torture during the winter when the cold and damp would seep into your bones.

I was always a good talker. I was confident in any

company, so I applied for a few sales jobs. One of those, which I didn't know at the time, was for selling advertising for *Gaelic Life* magazine, a very popular GAA weekly newspaper based in Omagh.

Anybody who had any connection to football in Ulster knew I had just come out of recovery, but I was young and people were keen to give me a second chance. Those in the *Gaelic Life* were no different. I got the job.

I finally had money that I could say was my own. I worked hard and built up a nice savings account in the Credit Union. After a year, I got a loan for a car, a 2007 Volkswagen Golf. I needed a guarantor, but Daddy had no problem providing it. He could see how well I was doing.

I was going to my GA meetings. I was playing the best football of my life. I was very content in my relationship with Andrea. Gambling was the last thing on my mind.

They were the happiest years of my life.

When I was gambling, I never bet on Tyrone because I never bet on football. It was too important for me to allow gambling to contaminate the one pure passion I had in life. Gambling took everything from me, but it never took the power away from my football.

There were times when I could have cleaned up with inside knowledge. After Down beat us in the 2008 Ulster quarter-final, everyone wrote off Tyrone. Westmeath nearly beat us up in Omagh. We only scraped past Mayo by one point. Dublin were hot favourites to wipe the floor with us in the All-Ireland quarter-final, but we were on fire in training. Tyrone were coming in completely under the radar. The odds were very appealing. I was gambling heavier than ever before, but I always resisted the temptation to go down that particular road.

Gambling just filtered into my relationship with Tyrone in different forms. Before the 2008 All-Ireland final, we got twelve free tickets and the option to buy twenty-four. I put in for the twenty-four, which amounted to over £1,000. A couple of days before the final, I hadn't a penny to my name. The £1,000 I owed the county board had been blown on horses.

I still had two tickets left. I sold them for £100. I went into a bookies on the Thursday before the final and came out with £1,200. The windfall couldn't have come at a better time. It would pay for the tickets and still leave me with a couple of hundred pounds' drinking money for the week. I didn't bother paying the board. I drank most of the money during those crazy days after the All-Ireland.

Winning an All-Ireland granted me the licence to do whatever I wanted. We were untouchable. A couple of hours after the final, most of us were blocked drunk before we even left Croke Park. The bus back to the Citywest Hotel was like a nightclub. The week was a blur. Whatever money I had left at the end of the week was blown on gambling. I paid the county board back in instalments over the following year.

Football always provided the focus that gambling tried to destroy, but without a proper football focus I was even more of a liability. A three-month suspension wrecked my 2009 season. I wasn't back until late August, though I was still training with the squad. Tyrone won an Ulster title and reached an All-Ireland semi-final. They lost to Cork, but the summer was just a personal write-off.

I was gambling every day. I had a court case hanging over me. I lost my drive for football. I was making up excuses to miss training. The same demands weren't put on me to show up, so I'd only appear once a week. I wasn't an established player on the panel. I didn't want to jeopardize my future by pulling the pin, but I still did. I told Mickey Harte that I was drawing a line under the season and I walked away.

Harte had no idea of the extent of my gambling addiction. If he felt I wasn't giving Tyrone the focus and attention the team deserved, he would have got rid of me. If Mickey knew the turmoil gambling was creating in my life, he would have tried to help and direct me on a different path. He didn't know anything, because nobody did back then. Gambling wasn't really seen as a disease or as an illness.

The only person who could help me was myself, but I didn't want any help. After I had done something reckless or crazy, somebody close to me might say, 'How can you not stop now?' It's not that you don't want to stop. It's just addiction. You can't stop.

It had this grip on me that continued to wreak havoc. I had to get more money. I continued to have the collateral and security of my father. It ensured I always had some access to cash, but there are still only so many times you can ask to be bailed out.

Our house was always full of anger. My father was angry from money being taken. Life was just a constant spiral of aggression and frustration and complete unhappiness.

I was never happy until I lost my money, because that

meant I couldn't gamble again. Of course I wasn't happy with losing money, but it granted me peace of mind for a short period of time. When that is the only real happiness in your life, it's a distorted form of reality.

I had no consistent peace of mind. I had no career path. I hadn't a clue where I was going with my life, but I still thought that playing for my county would set me up with whatever job I wanted. I was existing in a self-styled dreamland. And that place was a disaster zone.

There was no way out. If I had won a billion pounds, I would have still gambled. I would have probably been gambling in millions. And I probably wouldn't have been fully happy until I'd blown every penny.

No matter how long you spend in recovery, you have to keep working on yourself to maintain that momentum. It's like being an inter-county footballer; if you start missing training sessions, drop off your intensity, get arrogant, become complacent, it makes you weak. And vulnerable.

For two years, I was strong. When I started off working for the *Gaelic Life*, there was a bookies right across the street in Omagh. Odds On it was called. There was a betting office down the road. I never took any notice of them.

GA meetings were providing the medicine I needed to treat my illness, to maintain the impetus of my recovery. The first time you go to a GA meeting, the feeling is of such huge relief. You think you're a nutjob to have found yourself in this position, but then you realize everybody else has been trying to pull the same crazy stunts, living the same crazy life.

For a long time, I thought there was something wrong with me, that maybe a chemical imbalance or a psychological issue was the reason I couldn't stop gambling. I didn't talk to anyone, because keeping the problem hidden was just as important as trying to address it.

The mask portrayed this strong, masculine, arrogant, cocky, unbreakable individual. Concealed behind the mask was this weak little boy crying out for help. I didn't know how to ask for help. And I didn't want to either.

GA meetings showed me there was another way. They kept my willpower strong and resolute. They were a firewall to the gambling virus, but the addiction had been so rampant in my system that they couldn't wipe every infection from my hard drive.

About a year and a half into our relationship, I spotted Andrea conversing with this boy on Facebook. It was harmless chat. There was no substance to my argument, but I accused her of flirting and trying to hook up with this fella. I started loading guilt on her, a move I had perfected on my father.

Not long afterwards, this girl started texting me. She got my number off someone and didn't hide her intentions. I loved Andrea, but I still got off on the thrill of this girl's confident and casual advances. It was filthy chat, her telling me what she would like to do to me, and me responding in kind. I knew I was never going to do it, but I kept up the dialogue anyway for the thrill. I wasn't gambling any more, but this was a similar type of high and risk in a vicarious form.

I was in the shower one evening in Andrea's house when she stormed in and cut loose. She had been on my iPad and had spotted the stream of filthy conversation. I had never even met this doll, but I tried to lie my way out of the situation. Then I threw it all back at Andrea. 'What the fuck are you on about? Sure, you were at the same craic a while ago.'

I had never texted another woman while I had been with Andrea, but that was the first sign of a crack appearing. I wasn't gambling, but I was beginning to slightly lose control, even in our relationship. From that moment on, Andrea's trust in me was partially broken. If I was sitting at home with her, texting somebody, she would be suspicious.

I hadn't gambled in three years. I was down at our family house one day and the car was low on fuel. I put £30 of diesel into the tank from one of Daddy's pumps. I had often topped up the tank at home, out of convenience as much as anything else, but I had always paid for the diesel. If Daddy wasn't around, I'd leave the money on the kitchen table. Aside from the honesty issue, it was my way of keeping myself disciplined, of doing things right since I'd come out of Cuan Mhuire.

That day, I kept the money in my pocket. 'I'll get him later,' I said to myself. Without knowing it, a switch had flipped in my head. I believe that was the start of me gambling again.

My behaviour and attitude were leaving a constant trail of evidence to suggest I was about to crack: arrogance, cockiness, telling lies, taking chances, not being true to myself, not being truthful with Andrea. Not doing the right thing, full stop.

I got complacent. I broke away from the circle of recovery

and I was back to doing it my way again. I thought I knew best. I was weak and I was vulnerable.

Mike, who I had become friendly with in Coolarne, rang me once a week for two years after I left Galway. He didn't call as often afterwards, but anytime he did, he always asked the same question. 'Are you still going to your GA meetings?'

Even though I wasn't gambling, I had stopped going to those meetings. I would tell Mike I was, but he knew I wasn't. It was audible in the tone of my voice in trying to answer his questions. I'm sure Mike knew I was on the verge of relapse before anyone else.

Gambling addiction is such a complex disease that only a compulsive gambler can read the signs of another compulsive gambler. It's like looking at yourself from the past in the mirror.

If I sit in a GA meeting in the morning with fourteen or fifteen other compulsive gamblers, I can read all those signs myself now. Each one of them is just like how I used to be. It is so obvious. The evidence is everywhere.

But at that time, I couldn't see it in myself.

CHAPTER 9

SELF-DESTRUCTION

National League, Round 6
Tyrone vs Armagh
Healy Park, Omagh, 26 March 2016

Mickey Harte approached me in the dressing room before we went out onto the pitch.

'Are you alright, Cathal?' he asked. 'How is your mind?'

'I'm fine,' I replied. 'I'm good to go.'

I thought I was. I wasn't. When I was gambling, when I was up to my eyes in debt and trouble, football was a form of escape. This was completely different. A different kind of storm was brewing. Bad news about me was about to break. And this typhoon was carrying all kinds of shit and debris.

The previous day, I got a phone call from my solicitor Adrian O'Kane. The Tyrone PRO, Eunan Lindsay, had just called him. Eunan had been contacted by a journalist from the *Sunday World* newspaper, asking if he wanted to comment on a story they were running two days later about me being involved with a fifteen-year-old girl.

Friday and Saturday was a mad scramble. I told Mickey Harte. I explained the situation to some of the players. I just told the truth. Mickey wasn't worried. 'Look, Cathal,' he said, 'you'll get over this. You have been through a lot worse.'

Mickey and the players were fully behind me, but we didn't want this to get out. We tried to get an injunction passed to stop the story going to press, but we weren't going to know if we had until after the match. I had been selected to play. I wanted to try and take my mind away from the anxiety.

I'm training to be a counsellor now. I'm telling people to let stuff go. But that's easier said than done when something this big is threatening to blacken your name, to destroy your life.

Again.

I don't know what it is with me, but sometimes I just can't help myself from pressing the self-destruct button. It's not an excuse, but it is part of my addiction. It is a defect in my character that I sometimes crave attention. It's a weakness that I have to keep working on.

I love my current girlfriend Niamh Delahunt, I really do. I first met Niamh in October 2014, on a night out in Athy. She hadn't a clue who I was. Niamh likes football. She plays herself. Niamh follows Kildare occasionally, especially during the summer, but she wasn't immersed enough in the game to know anything about Tyrone, or that I played for them. We got chatting. We exchanged numbers and I texted her the following day. I asked her if she wanted to come for a drive. She said she would. Before I arrived at her house, her sister filled her in on who I was, on what I had done, and why I was living in Athy. It was a huge amount for Niamh to process in a handful of minutes. She decided to meet me anyway. As soon as she sat into the car, Niamh told me that she had just found out about my past. It was inevitable that she would but I was totally honest with her. I told Niamh everything. The stories she heard were all true. That was who I was. That was me when I was sick. Now, I was better, or at least trying to get better. That process was still ongoing but this was me now.

I wasn't asking Niamh to trust me. I knew well enough by now that trust had to be earned. I was just lucky that Niamh was willing to give me that chance, to try and get to know the person I now was, not the one who she had heard, or read about. Niamh and I grew close very quickly. She was the first girl I fell in love with since breaking up with Andrea. She means the world to me but, like most men, I love looking at beautiful women. I always have.

In October 2015, I was on Tinder, a location-based dating and social discovery app. I had no need to be near that service but I just was. Why? Temptation. Curiosity. The hunt for a high that gambling normally provided. It's not an excuse. That's just the truth.

I was on Tinder for a few weeks, matching and conversing with women who were interested in meeting up. I never met any of them. It was more the thrill of the chase than anything else. Addiction. Pure addiction.

Eventually, I decided to meet one of them. I was texting

this girl from Kildare. We arranged to meet that night in Kildare town. I was on my way to a GA meeting in Athy.

I know. The contradiction is ridiculous.

The girl said she drove an old-style Jaguar. She sent me a picture of the car. I think it was red. She said she was in college doing a business course. She mentioned how her course was wrecking her head and that she was thinking about packing it in. I told her about my job. It was harmless online chat. When we met, she looked at least nineteen or twenty.

Two weeks later, I was at my desk in work when a call came through my office line. I was surprised, because most calls came through my mobile. As soon as the other person spoke, I could instantly detect something was definitely wrong.

'Is this Cathal McCarron?'

'It is, yes.'

The man on the other end of the phone then cut loose. 'You know what you did,' he roared.

I recoiled, because I couldn't pinpoint who, or where, it was coming from. 'What are you on about, sir?' I asked him. 'Who are you?'

'You know who I am. You met my daughter recently.'

Then the penny dropped. 'Yes, I did.'

'Well, do you know she is only fifteen.'

Oh, my good God.

A weakness came over me. I started shaking with fear. I asked the man if I could call him back on my mobile.

I couldn't believe this. I tried to compose myself. I went outside and rang him back. 'We made contact on a dating website,' I said. 'Your daughter told me she was in college. I thought she was over eighteen.'

I wanted to ask him if he had spoken to his daughter about what had really happened. I couldn't. I was in shock. I also felt I hadn't the right to say anything to the man. Part of me could understand his anger.

A week later, the Gardaí called me. They said an allegation had been made against me. They asked me to come into the station in Kildare to be interviewed. I fully co-operated. I told the two Gardaí the truth.

The whole country is on Tinder. I know a lot of the Tyrone boys are. So are boys on other inter-county teams. Most of those fellas rarely get out because they are living like monks, so what the hell are all the other people who have no commitments at?

It is still dangerous stuff. Tinder has a separate platform specifically for users aged between thirteen and seventeen. The app limits users' potential matches to those younger than eighteen, but the profile information, including photograph and age, is voluntary information. There is no way of verifying if users have provided their real age.

I have a way of walking myself into trouble, but my journey always seems to have twists and turns. The day I was interviewed by the Gardaí was the same day as the All-Stars function in the Convention Centre in Dublin. I had a great night but the worry was hanging over me all evening.

It still is. Even more so, now that the *Sunday World* had reported it. I don't want this or need this. If I end up in court again, everything from my past will be dragged up. I made a mistake, but this was the most innocent misjudgement I ever made.

If this does go to court, we will do everything we possibly

can to prove my innocence. We will go to the ends of the earth to show log record analysis along the path of transmission to confirm and corroborate that innocence. There were times in the past when I was in court and I knew I hadn't a leg to stand on. I was guilty. No question. This time, I'm not.

I do accept that I let myself down. Badly. I brought more shame and embarrassment on me and my family. The fallout was humiliating for Niamh. It threatened to destroy our relationship and everything we have together.

Niamh has always stood by me. When the whole country was judging me, when Niamh's friends and family were advising her to stay away from me when we first met, she judged me for who I was, not what I had done. Niamh had to deal with all that grief at the time, but that was her choice because she wanted us to be together. She didn't deserve to face more grief this time around.

I am angry with myself for putting Niamh through that heartbreak and distress. It was all my fault, but I'm just as angry with the *Sunday World* for continually trying to make my life a misery.

The article itself said very little. It stated that I had been questioned by the Gardaí and that a file had been sent to the DPP. But it was a front-page story, emblazoned with the headline 'Tyrone Star Quizzed Over Girl, 15'.

In modern society, perception is everything. A bad name follows you around like a bad smell. My reputation and history adds to the whole stink. In many people's eyes, I've already been lined up against the wall and condemned.

I have my faults. I have done some terrible things. I have hurt people deeply. The illness of addiction was the primary reason, but you can't keep blaming addiction either for serial mistakes. You have to do something about it. And I am. Every day. Every single day.

There are often times when it takes a big event in my life for me to change the path I am on. There have been so many of those big moments that you'd wonder how I even define them now. Have I learned anything? Am I ever going to learn?

I even wonder at times how Niamh sticks by me. How much more will she take? She always tells me that she knows the good person I am. I just don't always show it. A lot of people never see it. More just never want to see it, or believe that I am capable of showing that goodness.

Tyrone 0–13
Armagh 1–10

Armagh scrambled a draw with the last play. They had laid siege to our goal throughout the last ten minutes, desperately searching for the score to provide them with some lifeline in their attempts to stay in this division. We were swarming bodies like bees around a honey jar to protect our goal until Tony Kernan launched a high ball into the Tyrone square and Niall Grimley palmed it to the net.

It was almost an appropriate end to a shit night. The weather was atrocious. We were useless in the last twenty minutes. We left Armagh in a game we should have long closed out. My own performance was poor, with Gavin McParland causing me problems. I was yellow-carded late on, which was no surprise. My head was up my hole.

When I entered the dressing room, Eunan Lindsay told me that the story was out. It had already appeared on the *Sunday World*'s website. 'It's not that bad,' he said. 'It doesn't say much.'

'It will say enough,' I replied. 'Especially with my history.'

That was the least of my worries at that moment. Niamh knew nothing. I hadn't even told her I had been questioned by the Gardaí. Concealing something that big wasn't healthy in a relationship, but I gambled. I was hoping I wouldn't have to tell Niamh, that there was nothing more to this story. Now I had to tell her everything before somebody else did; or before she read about it.

Niamh was at home with my sister in Dromore because she had been up for the match. When I arrived in the driveway, her car wasn't there. She and Eimheár had gone to pick up a Chinese takeaway. Daddy and his partner Eileen were in the sitting room.

Eileen is a great woman. She is very level-headed and measured. I knew she would be a calming presence around my father when he heard the news, so I just came out and broke it.

'Ah, for God's sake,' said Daddy, 'what have you gone and done now?'

'Look, I didn't do anything wrong,' I said to my father. 'The only thing I did wrong was I shouldn't have been on the fucking thing when I was with Niamh.'

The main concern of my father and Eileen by then was Niamh, and how this news would impact on her. Shortly afterwards, her car pulled up outside the house. As soon as Niamh and Eimheár came in the door, Daddy and Eileen intercepted Eimheár, pulling her aside to take her out of the firing range. They all went upstairs. It was just the two of us left in the room. My stomach was heaving. My mind was like putty.

Niamh had just put her food out on a plate. She hadn't eaten all day. She was starving, but I couldn't wait any longer. I inhaled deeply.

'I've something to tell you.'

'What's wrong?'

Anxiety and worry was smeared all over Niamh's face. 'Eat your food and I'll tell you afterwards,' I said.

'No way,' she replied. 'I can't even look at food until you tell me what's wrong.'

So I did.

Niamh broke down. It's not easy to see the girl you love physically and emotionally dismantled by your wrecking-ball actions. The pain is even more acute by the level of distrust and deceit attached to those actions.

The lyrics in the Miley Cyrus song, 'Wrecking Ball', could have been written by Niamh: 'All I wanted was to break your walls / All you ever did was break me / Yeah, you wreck me / It slowly turned, you let me burn / And now we're ashes on the ground'.

I thought we were. I was sure I had torched what we had. Niamh got up and stormed out the door. I went after her. She wanted to go for a drive. I wouldn't let her. If anything had happened to her, I'd never have forgiven myself. We sat in the car talking for half an hour. She still wanted to leave.

I had to let her go. 'Be careful,' I said.

It was well after midnight. Niamh didn't come back for

another two hours. I was out of my mind with worry. She was driving around back roads in Tyrone, not knowing where she was going. It was her way of trying to filter the pain, of processing the anguish.

'Why did you do this to me?' she asked again when she returned. 'Why did you do this to us?'

The betrayal Niamh felt was exacerbated by how public my infidelity was. Having a potential court case associated with that infidelity enhanced the frustration. The potential implications of a court case were enough to push her over the edge.

Niamh's parents and family are great people, but it was very hurtful for them too to see their daughter that distressed by my actions. I texted Niamh's mother to apologize, but there has been no other contact. I accept their frustration. I have no defence, but I just hope they can understand that I am still in recovery, and that every day is still a challenge for me to try and overcome.

More than anything, I hope they understand that I really do love their daughter. Deep down, I think they do. It's just up to me now to keep proving that I am worthy of having their daughter.

It has been tough for Niamh to rebuild trust in me, but I am prepared to try anything to ensure she does. I have no privacy any more. Niamh checks my phone regularly. Messages and internet history are constantly monitored. In the past when she looked for the password on my phone, I wouldn't give it to her. Now, those digits are encrypted onto her brain. It's not ideal in a relationship, but if that is what Niamh wants, it's a price I am fully prepared to pay. I love her. I don't want to lose her. I think we have something special. And I am prepared to fight for it.

Everybody wants life to be perfect. It never is. And even if it was, you'd probably be looking for some kind of excitement or devilment to shake it up. Sometimes, people unconsciously go searching for that sprinkle of madness. At times I can't help myself. That self-destruct button is often too appealing not to press.

I have done some crazy stuff. My story is news. I accept that it has to be reported. I don't hold a grudge against anybody who has written about me. Reporters have a job to do, but the *Sunday World* have consistently hounded me as if I have killed somebody. I've been a front page story on their paper more often than mass murderers.

The latest article is about the sixth they have done on me, all by the same reporter. I know my actions have impacted on the lives of others, but have I destroyed those lives to such an extent as to merit the kind of public opprobrium and vilification those stories have sparked?

I will always hold my hands up and admit that I have been wrong. My addiction is never a good enough excuse to expect absolution or demand understanding, but does that reporter realize how sick gambling can make somebody? Of how hard recovery can be? Does he appreciate for a second the impact his stories have had on my life? Of the hurt and pain it has caused my family?

My addiction was putting me and my family through enough hell without more petrol being poured on the flames. After the porn incident, I felt suicidal. When I was in recovery

in Newry afterwards, word reached me of the constant bom-
bardment, of consistent follow-up stories. I could very easily
have taken my own life over that relentless barrage of bad
press. I wanted the pain to end. I was trying to get better, but
the reporter never relented. How would he have felt if I had
killed myself?

He is still on my case. At this stage, it's as if he is trying to
defame my character, to absolutely destroy my name. Have I
really done enough to deserve that? If he responds at all, he
is likely to say, 'Look, you put yourself in that position, I am
just doing my job.' However, it is my experience, over a long
number of years, that if a person is offered an opportunity to
comment before publication, and his comment is included,
he is unlikely to complain.

Front page news stories will always form opinion. Serial
front page stories on the same person will absolutely confirm and cement that opinion. Whatever I do in life now, a
large share of people will always have a certain perception of
me, a hardened conviction of who I really am. They believe
everything they have read. Many of them want to believe
it because they want to see you fall; many of them are your
next-door neighbours, your own fellow county people.

I can only keep going, to keep trying to live my life
the best I can. Recovery is never easy, but I am trying to
change, trying to get there. It's just a daily struggle. Two
steps forward are often followed by three backwards. I'm
always going to make mistakes, but I am learning to try and
think like a normal person does.

Because that is my daily reality.

CHAPTER 10

SURRENDER

I loved Kauto Star. He was my favourite horse from the time he won his first Cheltenham Gold Cup in 2007. Kauto was the first horse to regain the cup, in 2009, after losing it in 2008 when seven lengths behind Denman. Kauto tried for three more years to win the race again, but the best placing he could achieve was third behind Long Run in 2011.

The horse had already won the King George VI Chase a record five times when it made one last charge for the Gold Cup in 2012. Kauto got injured a month before the race, but intensive physiotherapy restored his fitness. After taking part in a gallop at Wincanton, Kauto was declared fit for the Cheltenham showpiece event.

Something as minor as that information still hammered against the wall in my mind like another swing of a wrecking ball. The dam I had erected was heavily creaking. Leaks were springing up everywhere, the wall was coming apart with crevices. It was only a matter of time before the dam burst.

I hadn't placed a bet in almost three years, but two weeks before Cheltenham began, I started googling betting accounts. I knew I was dicing with danger. I didn't want to throw away all the good work I had done on myself, but I just couldn't arrest the compulsion. I deleted the detail and information on the accounts from my phone, but the imprint was tattooed onto my brain.

A few days later, I went back online and opened up an account. I didn't lodge any money, but Cheltenham was only days away and the countdown to my descent back into that world, to me finally breaking after three years, had begun. It was inevitable. I couldn't stop it.

When I finally lodged some cash into the account, I was shaking with fear. I tried to convince myself that this was the last pathway I needed to take. I transported my mind back to those cold, hard days over Christmas in Cuan Mhuire in Galway. I swore that I would never return there but, no matter how hard I tried to stay off that path, I was already back on it.

Trying to convince myself otherwise was futile. I thought of how people in the club had warned me that I was on my last chance, that if I went down that crazy path once more, I might never play for Dromore again. Even when I was in a good place, Daddy used to issue me with regular warnings to prick my consciousness; that if I screwed people around again, there might be no way back this time.

I was aware of the grenade I was holding in my hand, but

I still pulled out the pin. The wee devil sitting on my shoulder just kept prodding the sharp prongs of his fork into my flesh, encouraging me to throw the grenade. Before I knew it, I had placed a £200 bet on Kauto Star. Detonation was imminent.

I was overcome with guilt and shame. Two hours later, all those worries and inhibitions had long faded into the background. The narcotic was driving through my bloodstream. The feeling was better than ever. Every other race during that Cheltenham festival, I had money on a horse.

I couldn't go into betting shops around Tyrone and Fermanagh, because everyone knew I was in recovery. I didn't need to. Online gambling was a whole new world. I didn't even have to get off my chair. I could gamble at work or in my car. Nobody needed to know.

Not having to deal in cash granted me an even greater licence to take risks. I had saved a few thousand pounds while in recovery, but I put most of it into that online account. I looked at it like fake money, like a game of Monopoly. I wasn't betting in £10 and £20 notes any more, I was dealing in hundreds.

Experts say that if a compulsive gambler stops, and then relapses after a period of recovery, the addiction goes to a new level. I had hit that level. Very quickly, I was starting to lay bets of £700 and £800.

Progressively, I got worse. I started taking more chances, risking more money. I did a £1,300 treble one day on three Premiership soccer matches. The first two results came in. Everton, who were playing in a later game, were on a hot streak having won six Premiership matches in a row. They were drawing with Aston Villa in the ninetieth minute when they bagged the winner. That goal netted me £16,000.

When you win that big, there is never enough time to do what you want to do with the money, what you should do with that kind of windfall. You want to buy a car, go on a swanky holiday, treat your girlfriend to a fancy meal, spoil her with some flashy jewellery. It's just your mind chasing again, where the chase will always ultimately lead you back to the same place. You don't have time for anything else. You don't want to do anything else.

I could have put a down payment on a house, or bought a brand new car with just the stroke of a pen, but my mind didn't want that security. I wanted the money close to hand to allow me to keep feeding the addiction. Anyway, that money is not your money until you withdraw it. And I didn't want to.

Andrea knew something was up. She was concerned. She could see that my mind wasn't as settled as it used to be. Andrea had never seen me as a gambler. She didn't know how to look for the signs, but it was clear to her that I wasn't myself any more.

I had become a master at concealment, but my front began to slip. When I was doing well in recovery, I was always in good form after GA meetings. I was keen to talk about what had happened. I wanted to share and transmit the good vibes with my girlfriend. Now, all Andrea saw when I walked in the door after a GA meeting was a ghost.

I didn't want to engage with her as much. I'd say very little. I'd say even less if I had lost money that day. If Andrea tried to ask me about the meeting, I'd shoot her down straight away. If she probed, I'd immediately go on the attack, shouting at her that I didn't want to talk about that dark stain on my soul. It was another form of manipulation which I had mastered on my father.

I thought I would manage but, deep down, I knew I couldn't. My presence at GA meetings was diminishing by the week. The odd time I did go, I was hoping something would break the addiction, that some emotion deep inside me would put a halt to the impending onslaught. I knew nothing would snap me out of my mindset, because the only emotion I was chasing was the high from gambling.

Fighting the urge was pointless. I was back inside a world of lies and chaos and deceit, and it had me by the balls. I'd walk out of a GA meeting, return to the car and start gambling again straight away on my phone. After a while, I stopped going to the meetings. I was out of control again.

Andrea soon stopped asking questions. Deep down, she knew I had relapsed. She just didn't want to admit it to herself. Andrea loved me. She didn't want to lose me. She was desperately trying to hold on to what we once had.

Andrea didn't understand how crazy addiction is, because she had never been exposed to its perils. When Andrea feared that the addiction may have taken a hold of me again, she didn't have the knowledge, or the experience, to try and help me treat the disease.

I loved Andrea but when gambling overpowers all your emotions, those closest to you merely become a resource to keep feeding the habit. I was working every day, but I had no money. When I'd drained everything out of the

Credit Union, Andrea was the easiest option to source more funds.

I didn't have the same easy access to cash that I had enjoyed, and exploited, with my father, but a similar opening was still within reach through my relationship with Andrea. And I only needed the tiniest crack to expand it, in my mind, into a canyon of enterprise.

I knew the PIN to Andrea's credit card because she had often asked me to take money out of her account. It had never crossed my mind before, but now that I was back gambling again, it was a stonewall opportunity that I couldn't resist.

I lifted Andrea's credit card out of her wallet one day and withdrew £300 out of her account. I went straight to the bookies and lost it all in the space of twenty minutes.

It was one of the lowest means of theft possible. Andrea worked hard. She clocked long hours as a nurse to earn every penny, but I had so little regard for that effort that I wiped out the bulk of her week's wages with six taps of my index finger.

The chase was on again. I wanted to get that money back into Andrea's account before she found out it was missing, but there was only one way of doing so. I took her card again and lifted another £300. It was the same mindset as the first time – gamble the money, double it and then put it back before Andrea noticed it was missing. I lost that £300 just as quickly as the first time.

This was the girl I loved and this is what the addiction was doing to me, doing to us. It was destroying what we had and I couldn't stop it. I had taken £1,200 from Andrea's account by the time she found out.

She rang me on the phone and confronted me. 'I'm missing £1,200 and I know you took it.'

Andrea had gone to the shop and asked the owner to see the CCTV footage from the camera above the cash machine. I was cornered but I still tried to lie my way out of the mess. Who was I fooling? The evidence was damning. I eventually had to confess. I broke down on the phone and started crying.

Andrea threatened to leave me if I didn't try and deal with my addiction, but she also wanted to help me find my way back on that journey of recovery. She forced me to return to GA meetings. She wanted to help me because, despite all I had done, she still loved me.

I went back to those meetings for a few weeks, but it was purely for show. As soon as I went in the door, I just wanted to get out again. Baring your soul is the only way you can really cleanse it, but my soul was at the mercy of the devil. I was worshipping at his altar, with money, or the desire to get money, draped all over it.

I was a compulsive liar, telling everyone in the circle that I wasn't gambling when it was the only focus in my life. I wasn't just lying to myself, I was lying to people in recovery who were only there to try and help me. They don't care how much pain you have caused, all they want is for you to be truthful. No matter how many times you fall from gambling, no matter how much destruction you have wreaked, the one place that will always take you in again is a GA meeting.

I understood that empathy, but it held no appeal for me any longer. I couldn't tell other people the truth, because I didn't like what it revealed. I saw myself as a total failure, a complete disappointment. I was on the road to destruction. There was no turning back. Nothing could turn me back.

I told Andrea I was still attending meetings when I had long stopped. She believed I was being truthful, because she probably wanted to believe me. Just like my father, Andrea was trusting me too much. She needed to be harder on me. She needed to check and see if I actually was attending meetings. Unknowingly, she was enabling me, and feeding the monster even more.

The monster grew new claws. It became more destructive in its pursuit of survival. We booked a holiday to Egypt to get away. Andrea gave me £500 to pay for her half of the trip. I had already saved £650, which she knew I was putting aside, but I blew the whole £1,150. I told Andrea that the travel agent went out of business and that we just had to suck up the loss.

It wasn't acceptable or rational behaviour, but I had set out with completely different intentions. I thought I could double Andrea's £500, and my own £650, which would effectively allow me to purchase the holiday for free. I'd hand Andrea back the £500 for spending money. She would love me even more. I was only codding myself. Even if I had quadrupled my money, I'd have kept going until I blew it all again.

Good intentions always crumbled like wet sand against the tidal wave of my gambling addiction. The buzz controlled everything. I couldn't get a handle on it. Even when I had won a large amount of money, I wasn't able to stop and just enjoy those earnings.

Happy all together. Barry, Eimheár, Daddy, Mummy and I pose for a family photograph on the day of my First Holy Communion.

The three Amigos. Barry, Eimheár and me.

Blues Brothers. Barry and I get ready for school.

Butter wouldn't melt in my mouth. Posing for a photo after my Confirmation.

The first is always the sweetest. Outside our house in 2007 with the league and championship trophies won by Dromore for the first time

Chasing Benny. Trying to stop Down and Mayobridge star Benny Coulter in Dromore's maiden Ulster club championship match in 2007.

We've done it! My elation is obvious as the Tyrone bench runs to embrace our team-mates after the 2008 All-Ireland final win against Kerry.

'The Dromore Four'. Left to right: Ryan McMenamin, Collie McCullagh, myself and Seán 'Snowy' O'Neill at the homecoming after the 2008 All-Ireland final.

Protect the prize. Guarding possession with Conor McManus coming in to challenge against Monaghan in the 2010 Ulster final.

Meat in the sandwich. Fighting to win possession between Dublin's Eoghan O'Gara and David Henry in the 2010 All-Ireland quarter-final.

You cannot be serious ref. Arguing the decision by Maurice Deegan to award a penalty to Mayo in the 2013 All-Ireland semi-final.

Total focus, no distractions. My comeback game with Tyrone in 2015.

The storm awaits. My first match back for Tyrone in 2015 and the cameras were waiting for me.

Where do we go from here? A dejected bunch of boys after Donegal hammered us in the 2015 league.

Up close and personal. Squaring up with Danny Heavron and Niall Toner in the championship against Derry in May 2016.

No way through. Tackling Meath's Donal Lenihan in the 2016 league campaign in Navan.

Breaking free. Bursting out past Kerry's James O'Donoghue, Johnny Buckle and Stephen O'Brien in the 2015 All-Irelan semi-final.

Blood boiling. Getting ready to go for Derry manager Damien Barton during the 2016 Dr McKenna Cup final.

Bullet the blue sky. Marching behind the band before the 2016 Ulster final against Donegal.

Please go over. As soon as my late attempt at an equalising point in the 2016 All-Ireland quarter final left my boot, I knew it was tailing off.

The heavens can't help us now. Darren McCurry and I know that defeat is imminent in the 2016 All-Ireland quarter final against Mayo.

Surrounded by love. Sharing the Ulster final success with Mummy and Niamh in Clones immediately after the game.

My rational self was computing the right information to my brain. 'Cathal, you've done well, let's go now.' Then the addiction, that insatiable craving, continued to overwrite everything. 'No, stay. You might win more.'

That voice kept roaring into my ear. And I couldn't drown it out.

A month before I laid that first bet on Kauto Star, I nearly ended up in prison. After appearing at Strabane Magistrates Court, I admitted assaulting a traffic warden during an argument over a parking ticket. A fucking parking ticket.

I pleaded guilty to charges of common assault, using a motor vehicle without insurance and driving while disqualified at Bowling Green in Strabane a few months earlier. A further charge of dangerous driving was withdrawn.

I lost my temper over something I should have been able to control. I popped into the Credit Union in Strabane to discuss an advertising sale for the *Gaelic Life*. I was back at my car inside five minutes, but a traffic warden was writing out a ticket for parking on double yellow lines.

'You're not giving me a ticket, are you? I'm only here five minutes.'

'No, you're not,' he said. 'You're here three minutes. I was counting.'

I lost the head. 'Go way to fuck. Have you nothing better to do than count minutes for people trying to do business in this town?'

He tried to put a ticket on the windscreen of the car, but I stopped him. I didn't physically lift a hand to the traffic warden, but I stood in his way to prevent him from sticking it under the wiper. 'Get you to fuck out of my road,' I roared.

The traffic warden made a complaint to the police that I assaulted him. I was arrested and brought to the police station for questioning. A court date was set for February. If I was convicted, I was heading for prison because the previous suspended sentence imposed by a Crown Court for credit card fraud would have been activated. I got lucky. The case was thrown out.

I was still sober from gambling at that stage. I was still trying to do the right thing, but the complacency I had shown towards my rehabilitation was being reflected in my life. I hadn't renewed my car insurance. I had been disqualified for driving after passing the quota of penalty points. All that saved me on that offence was that I hadn't been notified of the disqualification because of a mix-up with my solicitors.

I got away with it, but the wheels were coming off. And after laying that first bet, I was on a collision course with the wall.

CHAPTER 11

BROKEN

I was in Cookstown one morning in January 2013, in a Protestant part of the town. I was driving around waiting to call into a customer when I got restless. Circling around a town in mid-Ulster was never going to dull the ache of boredom. I decided to slip into the bookies, where nobody would know me.

I went with £100 and ended up blowing £2,500 in the space of four hours. I spent every penny I had in my bank account. I still had some other savings in a Credit Union, so I decided to use that as collateral against advertising money I'd gathered that day.

I withdrew another £300 and won £1,000. I was as high as a kite. As the day went on, I started to deflate like a balloon, each wasted bet like another release of air. When I was down to £300, I knew it was time to leave. Staying put was crossing a dangerous threshold. I still had work calls to make anyway. I rang the clients and told them I wouldn't make the appointments I had made. An hour later, I hadn't a penny in my pocket.

I wasn't giving in. I had £1,000 in my Credit Union account. I tried to withdraw the whole lot, but I could only take out £500 with my cash card. There was evening racing on the TV. I blew the whole lot.

The vicious circle had started all over again.

After my sacking from the *Gaelic Life*, I should have been unemployable again in the world of sales, especially in any business where money was changing hands. Yet the *Gaelic Life* had been so embarrassed by what had occurred that very few people outside their office were aware of what had actually happened. That granted me the licence to go searching for a new job.

I knew John Jordan at *The Dealer*, a 'free-ads' paper based in Donegal but which covered most of Ulster. I rang John and asked him if the paper was looking for anyone in sales. He told me to call down for a chat. I started work for *The Dealer* in October 2012.

I had only been unemployed for three weeks, but that reality had splashed cold water over my face. I had gone back to GA meetings. I had stopped gambling again. Andrea and I were doing well. That stability again in my life was probably evident when I sat down with John Jordan.

He was a lovely man, a big football supporter from Donegal. If John knew anything about my past, if he had heard any rumblings in the sales world about why I had left the *Gaelic Life*, he might have reasoned that my profile with Tyrone would still bring in a lot of business.

Initially, I did. I was selling advertising around Tyrone and Fermanagh, with one day a week spent in Derry. I had a nice company car. Being free from gambling allowed me to put my whole focus and energy into work. I was on a full commission salary and was taking home between £600 and £700 a week.

I thought I had flushed the demons from my system, but they were only lying low, just waiting for the right moment to pop their heads back up. And that day in Cookstown, after being sober from gambling for nearly four months, I just blew the horn to sound the invitation for the demons to return.

Automatically, the chase had begun again. I began lifting money everywhere. I'd get £200 and £300 from businesses to place their ads in *The Dealer* and march straight into the bookies with that money. I was conniving in everything I did. I'd go to betting shops where nobody knew me. I started to transfer money into top-up vouchers which allowed me to bet online and cut off any trace to my account.

It was a constant game of dangerous roulette. I'd spend the clients', and my boss's, money but I still had until Friday to try and win it all back and balance the books. It was scandalous behaviour, but it wasn't even about money for me at that stage. It was just about getting that constant fix of gambling. The repercussions and the fallout were only an afterthought.

I had to gamble. Every day. I just had to have that buzz. Every single day.

As soon as I hit the slope, I couldn't stop sliding. I had

no focus on work any more, because it was only a means of facilitating and advancing my real focus. My commission was down to half what I had originally been earning. John called me into the office one day and asked if anything was wrong. I put up the front again. Everything was fine. Business was just slack.

John Jordan had always trusted me. We had a good relationship. We always had great chats about football. If I was down a few hundred pounds at the end of the week, I'd tell John that some guy didn't pay up, and that I'd get it sorted the following week. He believed my lies, or maybe he just kept giving me another chance, which bought me time to survive the constant game of roulette for another couple of months.

Along with playing football for Dromore and Tyrone, my mind was constantly racing and chasing; getting money, spending it, then ringing the people who paid me to try and stop them complaining why their ad wasn't in the paper. It was lies heaped on top of more lies.

'Your ad is put back a week.'

'There was a mix-up in the office, but it will be sorted next week.'

I was trying to manipulate everyone. I had a guy who always cashed cheques for me. I made up a story that the company preferred to deal in cash rather than lodging cheques, so he was a constant source of betting currency when I didn't have enough hard cash collected.

I was a professional liar. I was lying so often that I hardly even knew the difference between truth and lies any more. I don't know how people believed me, but they did.

*

On the bus journey to the 2013 All-Ireland semi-final against Mayo, the match was the last thing on my mind. I was standing in quicksand. The money I owed was like a weight on top of my head, pushing me straight to the bottom even quicker. This was my first All-Ireland semi-final. Tyrone hadn't reached that stage since 2009. We were playing a team which had reached the previous year's All-Ireland final. It was the biggest game I'd ever played in, but I ran out onto the field in Croke Park that day as if it were a challenge game down in Dromore.

We lost by six points, but I was one of Tyrone's best players. I didn't give Andy Moran a kick. He was taken off scoreless with fifteen minutes remaining. How the hell did I manage to play that well with all the turmoil raging inside my head?

I had no nerves. Zero inhibitions. I attacked every ball like a fanatic. I was just so happy to get out on that pitch and get away from the stresses and pressure stalking me like a virus. I hadn't time to be thinking about debt or the accompanying headaches. It was just a pure release to be chasing Mayo boys all around Croke Park.

It could have all gone the other way. We trained as hard as anyone else that season. Boys on our team were living like professional athletes, doing everything to give themselves, and the team, the best chance possible to win an All-Ireland. All those boys were depending on me and here was I off the fucking rails, a potential liability.

I survived because it was the only way, or life, I knew. When the final whistle blew, I lay down on the Croke Park pitch, my right arm stretched back against the turf, my left elbow resting against my bent left knee, teeth gritted, eyes darkened. A photograph captured the moment. The anguish in my face was obvious, but it had a deeper meaning than just the disappointment of losing an All-Ireland semi-final.

I wasn't free any longer. The real world had just arrived back. Bang.

I knew the squad would go drinking for a few days. I only had a few pounds, but I had enough to last me until Monday. The drunken haze in the meantime was a means of suspending the inevitable. That reality hit me like a sledgehammer by the time I was sober on Monday afternoon.

I was desperate. I needed money but I also wanted to keep drinking to keep deflecting what I couldn't avoid. I was home in Tummery. I called over to see Stevie Fitzpatrick, my close friend and neighbour. There was nobody there. A window was open. I didn't hesitate for a second. I climbed in and prowled around the house. I found a chequebook belonging to Stevie and stuck it into my pocket. I wrote out a cheque for £700, forged Stevie's name on the bottom line, and made my way into Omagh. The guy who always cashed cheques for me when I was scamming *The Dealer* handed me over the cash.

I couldn't have sunk any lower. The Fitzpatricks had been like a second family to me all my life. Stevie had been a great friend. The addiction had just poisoned everything about me. Every last shred of self-respect had rotted away. I was completely toxic.

I genuinely am so sorry to anyone I took money from when I was gambling. That was not me. That was not how

I was brought up. If I wasn't gambling, I would never have been in that position. I won't say it was like an out-of-body experience, because I knew exactly what I was doing. I knew it was very wrong, as bad as anything I had ever done before. I just couldn't stop myself.

Repercussions were unavoidable, but my mind was able to suspend any of those concerns in the interim. I could relax and drink and gamble in my alternative world for a few days. Anxiety and stress would come in its own good time. It usually arrived when the money ran out.

On the Wednesday, three days after the Mayo match, Stevie's van screeched into the driveway as he pulled up outside the house. He had contacted the police. The trail had been traced back to me. Stevie was, understandably, full of fury, anger and hurt.

Daddy appeared and tried to reason with Stevie. He didn't want to hear of it. He wanted to press charges. I pleaded with him. 'Stevie, I'm fucked from gambling. I need help.'

Those pleas made no difference. 'I don't care,' he said. 'This is going on far too long.'

Despite our close connection and deep interwoven history, Stevie's attitude towards me was the same as everyone else in Dromore. They didn't give a fuck about me any more. They were sick and tired of me and my actions.

Dromore people didn't look on my gambling addiction as a serious problem. They just saw me as a gambler and a thief, a selfish bastard who just needed to cop himself on, but who wouldn't.

*

Daniel McDonnell and I grew up together. We had been friends since primary school. I always had a great time with Daniel. He played football for Trillick, but the rivalry between our clubs hadn't affected our friendship.

I often called over to Daniel's house for a cup of tea and a chat. I arrived one day and there was no sign of him. The door was open. I shouted in, but there was nobody there. I closed the door and left.

One Monday shortly afterwards, I was driving around our home area, going nowhere in particular. I was supposed to be working, but I'd no interest in making a sale. I was just killing time, but that vacuum was a dangerous place for my mind. In that mental state, addiction fuelled my whole thought process.

Rationality didn't exist in that world. I thought about calling in on Daniel, not for a visit, but to see if the door was open, and if any loose cash might be lying around. Even a few sporadic coins might add up to a fiver to get me started. That's how desperate I was, reduced to scraping coppers off a friend's floor.

I opened the door and did a quick surveillance of the house. When I didn't find anything, I left. I returned the following day. The door was locked, but I found a key under the mat. I went in again with the same intent.

What I didn't know was that I was being watched. Daniel's neighbours and cousins, the McLoughlins, had seen me around the house the previous day. Trillick were playing championship at the same time I was now in the house. They knew that I knew Daniel wouldn't be there. They were waiting for me.

A bank card was lying on the counter. It was no good to me. I only wanted cash. I kept searching. I was in a bedroom when I heard two cars tearing down the lane, the screeching brakes a clear indicator of haste and resolve. The door flew open. Shane, Ryan and their father, Philip McLoughlin burst in. I was overcome with fear and trepidation. I was half hiding in the room, but staying there would have been a complete admission of guilt because I could hear them searching through the house.

I came out of the room. I could see Shane puffing and panting, in a fit of rage and adrenaline.

'What the fuck are you doing here?' he roared at me.

I didn't know what to say. I knew I was caught, but I tried to wrangle my way out of the web. I said I was there to play a prank on Daniel, to hang a Dromore flag above his fireplace. I just didn't have the core evidence of the flag to back up that claim.

Playing some kind of a prank on Daniel had been on my mind, but it was only a loose excuse for me to draw on, to use in case I was cornered. When I look deep into myself, I was there to steal money from my friend. I didn't take anything, but if there had been cash lying around, I wouldn't have hesitated for a second in taking it.

The McLoughlins were understandably angry. Shane was aggressive and was stuck in my face. Ryan was walking around behind me, recording everything on his iPhone as evidence. I told Shane to get out of my way or I'd put him on his ass. Philip McLoughlin was trying to keep some order, probably fearing there would be a free-for-all.

I had no right to be behaving the way I was, but my

arrogance had kicked in by then. I was ready to take the head off this boy. 'You think you're a big man,' I said to him. 'Go on ahead and see where it will get you.'

If I'm being really honest, I was half hoping he'd throw a punch. I was spoiling for a row. I never liked Shane McLoughlin. I knew he didn't think much of me.

I had no defence, but the McLoughlins knew I had a serious problem. They were fully aware that I had an illness. Within an hour of leaving that house, the whole of Tyrone seemed to know what I had done.

That was their right. They were entitled to stand up for their cousin, but there were other ways of dealing with my predicament. They just wanted to hang me out to dry.

It was a front page story in a national Sunday newspaper a few days later. 'Red Hand Star Caught Red Handed' screamed the headline.

As soon as I arrived home, Daddy stormed out of the house. 'What the hell have you gone and done now?' Philip McLoughlin had rung him.

I tried to play it down but Daddy gave me the hard truth straight between the eyes. 'All the good you have done, all the strides you have made in recovery, you've just thrown it all down the drain.'

A few hours after that confrontation with the McLoughlins, I travelled to a Tyrone players and management meeting in Kelly's Inn in Ballygawley. It was a review of the year, with some loose structural planning for the 2014 season. Some players spoke. I was one of them. There was authority in my tone. I probably spoke about honesty and integrity. Even though I could have been arrested or questioned by the police at any stage that evening, I carried the air and appearance of somebody without a care in the world.

What was I thinking? A lot of people in the area already knew what I had been up to. I'm sure Mattie Donnelly and the other Trillick boys in the squad were fully aware of what had just happened between me and the McLoughlins. After trying to rob one of their club team-mates while he was playing a match, what must they have thought of me? What kind of a Tyrone team-mate did I look like to them? Who in the name of Jesus would trust someone prepared to stoop that low?

On the way home, a man called. He wanted to meet. He needed to talk to me. As soon as I saw his face, I knew something serious was up. His expression spoke a thousand words.

'You're fucked here lad,' he said. 'You've gotta get out of the country.'

This wasn't just advice. He was carrying a threat from the IRA. He told me that if I didn't leave, I'd be shot. He said they were coming to the house that night to carry out their threat and shoot me.

Dromore is a big Republican town which always had an IRA presence. We were always aware of that presence growing up. When we were young, we got off on IRA bravado. It was just youthful ignorance: 'Up the IRA. Up the green, white and gold. Fuck all Protestants.'

We all knew how it worked. There was no messing about around Dromore. If you were, you could be shot. There was no antisocial behaviour or drugs in the town. Boys who were messing about or doing drugs were put in the back of vans and knee-capped. The son of a well-known local business-man was knee-capped and left in a field to die.

We always carried that fear of the IRA in Dromore. That's the way we were brought up. I never had anything to do with the IRA, but you knew if you were involved in anti-social behaviour that you were fucked. In the minds of some IRA people around the town, I had gone too far. I needed to be taught a lesson. Those people wanted to seriously hurt me.

I knew that the man was uneasy, that he felt uncomfort-able passing on such a shocking threat. This was nothing to do with him. These people knew he was close to me. They had rung him and told him to deliver the threat. He said he tried to put them off, but I couldn't take the chance that he had succeeded.

After he drove off, I sat in the car and cried my eyes out. 'What the hell has happened to me? How has my life sunk this low?'

At that stage, I wasn't even sure if I had much longer left to live. I was still in tears when I got home. I told Daddy that I had to be out of the country as quickly as I could. I cried and cried in front of my father. I didn't know what to do, but I wasn't hanging around to explain myself to a gunman.

I don't know if the IRA fully intended to carry out their threat, or if it was designed just to scare me, but I couldn't take any chances. Daddy didn't want to either.

I should have gone back into recovery, returned to Cuan Mhuire in Galway, or booked myself into their place in Newry. Daddy and Barry wanted me to go back into recov-ery, but the warning was to leave the country.

Forcing me to return to Cuan Mhuire would have been a more reasonable way of handling my situation, but those people don't think in those terms. I had already blown some collateral anyway. I had been in recovery and was worse now than ever. In the eyes of the IRA, there was only one way I was ever going to learn my lesson. That's the way they normally deal with these issues.

There was no excuse for my actions, but I was sick. The Provos were flexing their muscles, but those people who wanted me punished had no clue about my level of addiction. Threatening to shoot me, or running me out of the country, wasn't going to treat the problem.

I rang Andrea. She was at work, in Derry.

'I'm sorry Andrea, I have to get out of the country straight away.'

'What? Are you winding me up, Cathal?'

'I'm not. I have to go.'

Andrea couldn't get her head around what I was talking about. I had to tell her the IRA had threatened me. The shame of uttering those words alone was nearly as overbearing as the fear gripping me.

Andrea was hysterical. 'What did you do? Is it really that bad that you have to go? What the hell is going on here?'

'I just have to go,' I said. 'I'm so sorry.'

'Are you not even going to say goodbye?'

She was crying. I was crying. I loved Andrea, but I had to leave her without even saying goodbye.

Andrea was the biggest casualty in the whole saga. I couldn't believe this was happening to me. I cried so much that I eventually cried myself to sleep. The IRA didn't carry out their threat. I was still alive but I wasn't hanging around Dromore any longer.

Barry and I spoke on the phone very early the following morning. He would meet me after my flight landed. I was going to stay in London with Barry until I got a place myself. I could also detect an unease from my brother. He felt that London was the wrong place for me to try and get better. I didn't care. The flight was already booked.

Before I left, I hadn't even spoken to my mother or sister. My company car from *The Dealer* was still outside the door. That was another mess Daddy had to clear up, but I was leaving far more than just debt behind; my family, Andrea, my friends, Dromore, Tyrone. I had had a great season with Tyrone. I had just been nominated for an All-Star. Now, I wasn't sure if I would ever play for the county again.

When Daddy dropped me at the airport, tears were flowing down his cheeks. I had caused him unforgiveable hurt and heartbreak. I could see that pain in his eyes, but I could also see that unbreakable love a father has for his son.

'Good luck, son,' he said as he wrapped me up in a hug. 'Let's hope you can turn your life around now.'

As Daddy turned and walked away, anguish was smeared all over his body language. He was creaking with pain. It surely crossed his mind that he might never see his son again.

Because I certainly wasn't sure if I would ever see my father again.

CHAPTER 12

RELENTLESS

National League, Division 2 Final
Tyrone vs Cavan
Croke Park, 24 April 2016

All week, the media has been raving about this new Cavan scoring machine. About how they are the highest scoring team in the top three league divisions, of how much their goalscoring record has improved, of how impressive their scoring spread has been with twenty-one different scorers throughout the spring. Cavan are a decent side, but when there's a cup to be won, Tyrone turn into a different animal.

We didn't finish top of the group to get beaten in the final now. Cavan seem to think that they're going to come and shock Tyrone. They're not. We're ready for them.

So am I. Whoever I'm marking on Sunday, whether it's Seánie Johnston or Eugene Keating, I'll be all over them like a rash. Seánie has scored 3–16 in this campaign. Keating is a decent player as well. If you give players of that quality time or room, of course they will pick off points. I will be doing my best not to give those boys a second.

Gearóid McKiernan has been brilliant so far in this campaign. He is Cavan's top scorer with 1–24 from play. He's a good player, but we have the boys to do a job on McKiernan. I don't even know if Harte will put a man-marker on McKiernan to disturb him out on the field. Maybe Mickey will just leave our pack the way it is and McKiernan will have to come through it. Best of luck to him if he tries.

McKiernan is the face of a new Cavan ever since he captained the Under-21s to the 2011 All-Ireland final. Cavan went on to win four Ulster Under-21s in a row afterwards. Cavan are entitled to think that their time has come, but we will see on Sunday what these boys are really made of.

As soon as I landed in London, I met my brother Barry. I can't even remember if it was the airport or some Tube station. My head was all over the place. Barry wrapped me up in a big, warm embrace. He and his wife Mary were house-sharing with another couple. It wasn't ideal for them, or the other couple, to have me parachuting into their orbit, but I had no place else to go.

Barry took a few days off work to help me get settled in a new city, but the time we spent together was also his way of trying to get through to me. It hurt him to see me having been run out of my own home, our home place. Barry was worried about me coming to London but, now that I was here, he tried to set certain conditions: I couldn't gamble and I had to go to GA meetings twice a week.

In those early days in London, we went for long walks around the city. It was our way of reconnecting again, of rekindling the flame that distance and gambling had quenched over the previous few years. I promised Barry that I would stay faithful to all his requests.

I started looking for work. I contacted Tír Chonaill Gaels, the top Gaelic football club in London, who were based in Greenford. The boy I rang nearly dropped when I told him I was keen to play with the club. He promised me the world. Then I never heard from him again.

Tír Chonaill Gaels weren't the only ones that backed off. Word had filtered out as to why I was in London. I was an inter-county player that had just been nominated for an All-Star, but that was an irrelevance now. I was bad news. Damaged goods. Clubs wouldn't touch me.

I was just looking for a new start. Some people were prepared to give me that chance. Eoin O'Neill, a big Tyrone football man from Round Towers, rang me. He had contacted the chairman of the club, Kevin English, who went out of his way to sign me up. Kevin did everything to make me feel welcome, to try and kick-start a new life for me. He put me up in a penthouse in Wimbledon with his two sons. I had no rent to pay. He got me a job bricklaying. I was on the ladder. Now I just had to keep climbing.

The first two months in London were really positive. I was working hard, keeping my head down, going to my GA meetings. Mickey Harte rang me close to Christmas to ask how I was. He wanted me to come back. I didn't want to. Mickey tried again. This had nothing to do with football.

'Look Cathal, this problem can be fixed,' he said. 'Come home, so we can get you into proper recovery.'

I didn't want to go into rehab again. It was too tough. I couldn't face another three months of that hardship. Deep down, I knew it was what I needed, but I was doing everything in my power to avoid it. Anyway, what had I to return home to? My life had been threatened. Dangerous people didn't want me around. Was that threat just going to be written off after two months away? Anytime Mickey rang, I kept putting him off. When he called again in early January, I told him that I was taking a year out.

I threw myself into football with Round Towers, the only GAA club in south London. All the players were aware why I was in the city, but they still welcomed me with open arms. In those early months, I gave them whatever I could. I started taking training sessions. I'm a driven bastard when it comes to football, so on the pitches of Mitcham and Carshalton Rugby Club that winter, I ran the Towers boys into the ground. They had never trained like it.

Towers had some good players, but they weren't a big name on the London scene. They hadn't won a senior championship in over fifty years. They had only come up from the intermediate grade a few years before. I wanted to try and elevate that status through my own involvement and input into team preparation, but that possibility was gradually reduced. After eight weeks of not gambling, I cracked again.

GA meetings had kept me back from the edge, but boredom eventually tipped me over. I was working six days a week. I was training hard, but the weekends were a dangerous vacuum. Barry had his life to live with his wife. I didn't have any close friends in the city. The football season hadn't kicked off yet. There weren't any matches to play on a Sunday, so I didn't have any real focus. I had too much time on my hands. Then again, I was only looking for an excuse to scratch the itch that had been tearing at my skin for months.

I don't know whether it was a new environment or what, but once I started gambling again, I moved to a whole new level entirely. Not in terms of the amounts of money I gambled, which had spiked when I first relapsed, but more through the intensity of how I gambled. If I could have gambled for twenty-four hours in the day, I would.

The craving was relentless. I got paid on a Friday evening, but I'd wait for the money to lodge into my account with the same ravenous hunger of someone who hadn't eaten in a month. Then as soon as the money dropped, I wanted to gorge myself.

I'd sit up until 2am for live US basketball games to begin. Fucking basketball. I knew nothing about the game, but it was the sport I gambled on most around that time. The timing of those matches, and the opportunity they afforded me to sate my craving before the morning arrived, was probably the main contributing reason why I laid so much money on a game of hoops.

Basketball was a complete nightmare of a game to gamble on. The team you backed could be fifty points clear. You'd be counting your money in your head and then the other team could suddenly get on a run and take them. I could never understand basketball. How could a team destroy another side for that long in a match, and then the opposition turn things around that quickly? That added to the frustration, but it still didn't stop me laying thousands on basketball matches.

I rarely won. Normally by 5am, I'd be left with just £100. I'd get two or three hours' sleep before rising again for work. What was the point in even getting up? What was I working for? Nothing.

I'd be skint for the next week, jumping barriers on Tube stations to get to work, starving while I was there. And yet the only hunger I had was for gambling. It was a relentless carousel returning me to the same woeful spot. It was a miserable existence.

I spent that Christmas completely on my own in London. It was a lonely time. I rang my family on Christmas Day. I spun a story that my counsellor advised me against going home. I wanted to be there, but I couldn't. I hadn't the balls to go back anyway. I was happy to isolate myself from my family, but even if I had wanted to be with them, I hadn't the money for a flight.

I hadn't the money for anything. Christmas dinner was sausages and beans. Dessert was a bar of chocolate. The only reason I had food was because my flatmates had left it lying in the fridge. I was so broke that I texted my solicitor Adrian O'Kane in desperation. I tapped out a pack of lies on my screen, telling Aidy that I was doing well but that funds had run out. He probably knew why, but Aidy still sent me £300.

The money arrived a few days later. On 29 December, I travelled over to west London, where Chelsea were playing Liverpool. I went to Stamford Bridge looking to buy a ticket off a tout. I couldn't find one. The game was on ten minutes when I tracked down a tout. He wanted £400. I offered him £250. He wouldn't take it.

That money would have fed me for three weeks, but I was still prepared to throw it all away on two-thirds of a match involving teams I had no real interest in. Why? Because I wasn't thinking straight. I had got money. I would get it again. I went to the bookies the following morning and blew everything in one hour.

I was existing day to day. I hadn't the money to pay the rent. I couldn't go on nights out with the lads. If I did, I'd get a cheap carry-out, but the drink would only get me half-smashed because I didn't have enough of it in my system.

Football held zero interest for me. Playing for London had never even been on my radar when I signed with Round Towers. It held no appeal to me, but it was always only going to be a matter of time before Paul Coggins, the London manager, called.

I hadn't the commitment to play or train when Paul did call. I said no, but Paul kept calling. He wasn't taking no for an answer. Eventually he sat me down. 'Look, you're one of the most high profile players we've probably ever had here,' he said. 'You were an All-Star nominee last year. You cannot be over here playing club football and not be playing for London.'

I had no interest in playing Division 4 football but I put a deal on the table to Paul. I wanted to get off the building sites. The winter had been hard. The cold was killing me. I said I'd play for London if Paul got me an office job. He said he would try. I just had to give Paul time to try and get me sorted. In the meantime, I joined the squad.

No disrespect to those teams in Division 4 but I just wasn't used to playing at that level. We beat Waterford and drew with Carlow, which was a half-decent league campaign for London. The team actually got to a Connacht final later that July, but we got the shite leathered out of us by a few teams that spring.

I played most of my football in the half-back line and half-forward line. Coggins didn't want me man-marking fellas. He had me up at centre-forward. The only time he gave me a man-marking assignment was against Clare. David Tubridy is a very good player. Coggins told me that he had caused London desperate trouble in the past and he wanted me to put a stop to it. I hardly gave Tubridy a kick. He only scored one point from play, but Clare won by ten.

Six months earlier, I had played in an All-Ireland semi-final. Here I was now, playing in Division 4. Whatever little interest I had in playing for London was slowly being drained away by every one of those disappointing results. The only game we won, against Waterford, I was carried off in an ambulance after being half-killed in a collision.

I was well used to the guerrilla warfare of the Ulster championship, but playing football in London was a different kind of combat. My first game for Round Towers was a disaster. The weather was awful. The game wasn't even on a pitch, it was played in some park that seemed more like a bog. I was a big name with a big target on my back. I got the shite kicked out of me. I asked the referee at one stage, 'Are you going to do something here, or are you going to let these boys keep writing me off all day?' He didn't want to know about it. I used to think the refs in Tyrone were bad. In London, they were horrendous.

The London players were a credit to themselves. They were committed when it was anything but easy to be committed. Getting to training alone was an ordeal for most of the players. You could be forced to change trains in six different Tube stations to get to Ruislip. You'd normally get home at midnight. You didn't get expenses. Profile was almost non-existent. All to play Division 4 football.

I do regret not committing more to the London cause. I didn't even give them 50 per cent. My lack of commitment was a complete slap in the face to those London players. I was only training when I wanted to. Matches were almost an imposition on my time. And not having an increased focus on football like I had in Tyrone widened the vacuum for gambling to fill.

I was taking days off work just to go around the city gambling. One day, I won £10,000 in three different betting shops. I had done so well that I swore to myself that I was finished gambling for that day. I decided to go on a shopping splurge. I spent £1,000 on clothes. I was walking home, weighed down with all these bags of designer gear, when I passed a betting shop. I couldn't help myself. I lost £4,000 in half an hour.

The chase had already begun. I took the following day off again, because I had to get that £4,000 back. By that evening, the remaining £5,000 was gone. I contemplated returning all the clothes and asking for money back. I would have done, only the receipts stated no refunds unless the clothes were damaged.

The money was disappearing so quickly, because I went from betting in hundreds to thousands. When I first started working in London, I was on site six days a week. I was taking home nearly £1,000 a week. I had no rent to pay, no bills. I should have been living like a king, but one swipe on my phone, just one online bet, was all it took for me to exist like a pauper.

The flipside to the increased risk was the increased windfalls when I did win. I did a double one day and ended up with £13,000. I bumped that lump sum up to £25,000 the following day. I went into a gambling frenzy and lost £22,000 in a matter of hours. I thought I had only £3,000 left, but I was gambling so much I didn't know who or what I was betting on. I was doing so many £1,000 doubles and trebles that I couldn't keep track of them.

I woke up the following morning and logged onto my betting account. There was £68,000 sitting there, like a gold bar wrapped up in ribbons. The winning bet was a £5,000 treble. I can't even remember what the fuck the treble was. I think it was a tennis match, a handball game and a volleyball game. I stopped looking at one of the matches, because the team I had money on was getting tanked. I just wrote off that £5,000 and put another bet on a double.

Seeing £68,000 sitting in my account was like coming back from the dead to win an All-Ireland. I was ecstatic. I didn't go near work that day. I took off for a walk down town. I passed a travel agency and spotted a summer deal emblazoned across the window in big white lettering: 'Three weeks at the [soccer] World Cup [in Brazil], with tickets for three games, all for just £8,999.'

I walked straight in the door. I would have paid for the trip straight away but I couldn't. The money was still lodged in my betting account and I knew it would take me three days to withdraw it. I had £500 in my wallet, so I slapped that down on the counter as a deposit. I told the girl behind the desk that I'd pay the rest of the money three days later.

For whatever reason I couldn't withdraw the money from the betting company's system. I tried to withdraw £5,000 online and for some reason it couldn't pay it out.

I blew the full £68,000 in three days.

Losing that vast amount of money in such a short time was a sin. How I blew it was a form of insanity. The bottom line of why I blew it was purely down to illness.

I was betting online on women's volleyball, on teams like South Africa and Saudi Arabia. If Dromore had a women's volleyball team, I'd know fuck all about them. What the hell did I know about teams based in Riyadh or Cape Town?

That knowledge was irrelevant. Any bet that was even money, odds-on or odds just slightly below evens, I was all over it.

No matter which team I backed, any double or treble I tried, nothing was coming in. I had burgled a room in the huge betting company's House a few days earlier with my big win, but the House had now hit back. The House always wins. And now the House was giving my ass a right good kicking.

When I was down to my last £5,000, the realization hit me. 'Holy Jesus, I have just lost £63,000 there.' The only smart move in the middle of such a losing streak is to walk. Only having £5,000 from where I started from was a disaster, but at least I still had £5,000. It was better than nothing. 'Get the hell out of here,' I said to myself. I couldn't. The £5,000 was gone in a couple of hours.

Initially, it was devastating. A few days earlier, I had been hungry. I was depressed for a couple of days afterwards, but that black cloud didn't linger for very long. My positivity soon kicked in. I had won £68,000 before. I could win it again.

I still thought I had access to some money to get me started again. I returned to the travel agency and told the girl that I couldn't pay for the trip to Brazil now. I asked her for the £500 deposit back. She wouldn't give it to me. The deposit was non-refundable.

I lost the head with her. 'Give me that fucking money back, you bitch, it's my money.'

I was lucky I wasn't arrested.

If I had been able to withdraw that lump sum of £5,000 when I had initially tried, at least I'd have had a trip to the World Cup to look forward to. Now, that money had gone, too.

The whole gambling vortex will suck you in and just spit you out, like a piece of discarded chewing gum. In the state I was in I felt that I meant no more to the gambling companies than that soft substance stuck on the grubby carpets of their offices. If that substance clings onto the bottom of the shoe of a gambling company, they'll just scrape it off and fire it into the bin.

A month later, I tried to put a bet on and I couldn't. My

account had been closed down. Maybe the company did a background check.

Tyrone 1–17
Cavan 0–15

I remember reading where Seánie Johnston had scored 1–5 against Armagh. He'd been on fire that day, just like he had been throughout the league, but I soon let him know that I was the fire engine ready to put that blaze out.

'There will no 1–5 today, Seánie,' I said to him early in the match.

Seánie was taken off after forty-six minutes. He didn't get a kick in open play. He only managed one point from a free. When my head is right, when I am fully switched on, no forward is going to burn me.

Eugene Keating replaced Seánie. Keating scored one point off me. He played a ball into Martin Reilly and as he was going for the return pass, he clipped my legs as I was chasing back in front of him. I ended up in a heap on the ground. I got up as quickly as I could to try and hunt Keating down, but he had bought himself the couple of seconds he needed to get the shot away.

I lost the head with him afterwards. Words were exchanged. When Mattie Donnelly was sent off for a second yellow card five minutes later, myself and Keating got stuck into each other again. I hit him a dig. The linesman spotted it and the referee showed me a yellow card.

I don't know whether that incident drew attention to me

or what, but the Dublin crowd on Hill 16 started jeering me as the referee was taking my name. When I won a breaking ball a minute later, the crowd started jeering me even louder. As soon as I released the ball to Richie Donnelly, I hit the deck with cramp. When I got up, Richie played the ball back to me. I was in bits. I could hardly stand but Padraig Faulkner and Killian Clarke were trying to dispossess me, so I had to try and wiggle my way out of the trap. As I was in possession for those few seconds, the Dubs on the Hill were booing me.

Maybe some of them thought I was faking injury a minute earlier. Or maybe the penny dropped as to who I really was, and what I had done in London. Maybe more of them had read that front page story in the *Sunday World* a few weeks back. More than likely it had something to do with my personal life rather than football, because some of those guys on the Hill wouldn't know a football if it jumped up and bit them on the leg.

It didn't bother me. We won. We played well. And we sent out another loud message about how serious our intentions were for this season.

CHAPTER 13

APOCALYPSE

I woke up in my apartment in Wimbledon early one morning in late March 2014. It was a beautiful day. The sun was already out. You could sense a spring crispness in the air. The days were getting longer. Every place already appeared brighter. And all I wanted to do was descend into the blackness of a betting office.

I had drained every penny from my bank account, but I had put £150 to one side as an emergency revenue stream. I swore that I wouldn't gamble that money, but it was burning a hole in my pocket and I couldn't stop myself. I was in the bookies by 10.30am. Before a single horse race had even started at 12.45pm, I had lost everything.

I had blown it all on virtual horse racing. Pure madness. Some betting offices show races from these non-descript meetings from years ago, where you haven't a clue who is running. A jockey's colours might sometimes tell you who is steering a horse, but the odds are so mixed up that you haven't a clue if you're backing one of Sheikh Mohammed bin Rashid Al Maktoum's stallions or a useless nag that wouldn't win a donkey's derby.

When you're betting everything in your pocket on virtual horse racing – cartoon racing I call it – you know you're in a bad way. Your brain has to be messed up. That morning, this fella was roaring on his horse as if he was at a live meeting at Sandown Park. He was winning but the horse in second just steamed past and charged over the finishing line. The boy picked up the chair and fired it at the TV.

The chair rebounded off the screen and crashed against the window. I don't know how it didn't smash. The bookie behind the counter lost the head. He ran the man out the door, telling him never to come back. I was shaking my head. 'That boy is fucking nuts,' I said to myself.

I was worse. At least he was being honest with himself and showing his emotions. I wasn't. I was lying to myself and then believing those lies.

That boy nearly smashed up a bookies. Big deal. A few days later, I was about to do far worse.

When I went to the porn company the following week, I hadn't a bean in my pocket. I had no way or means of getting money. Since I didn't want people to know I was gambling again, I wouldn't ask for money. Anybody I knew wouldn't give it to me anyway, because they knew where it would end up.

I was homeless in every way bar having a roof over my head. I couldn't pay for electricity or heat. I was starving.

I was feeding myself through shoplifting from a supermarket. I'd walk around and slip a ready-made meal into my gear bag. I went past the security check one day and was convinced the security guard was on to me.

Another day, after lifting food, I heard the beeper going off as soon as I walked out the door. I didn't look back, I just sprinted down the road and ducked into an alleyway. When I heard police sirens a couple of minutes later, I was convinced they were on the hunt for me. I was paranoid beyond belief.

It was humiliating to have to steal to eat. The circumstances inflated the guilt and shame. There were times when I could have had thousands of pounds in my pocket, but I'd starve myself because I wanted every penny for gambling. Hours later, I wouldn't even have fifty pence for a packet of chewing gum to quench the stench on my breath from hunger and dehydration.

I didn't even care about no longer having the money to feed myself. I could live with the humiliation of stealing food. It got me by. Gambling was the only nutrition I wanted. One bet was like a five-course meal in a Michelin star restaurant.

Still, I needed money to take my seat at the gambling table. When I initially said to the company that I might be interested in doing porn, I got £180 alone for just filling out a form. I couldn't grab the pen and the piece of paper quickly enough. It was a list of questions, basically asking what I would be up for: gang bangs, threesomes, anal sex, oral sex, every kind of sex the industry has to offer when you click onto a porn website. Any of the boxes I ticked were all related to having sex with women. The only category which included a male was a threesome with a woman.

When the call came to come in again, it was like the devil was working his magic. I was completely desperate. I couldn't keep risking jumping barriers on Tube stations, so I couldn't go anywhere beyond Wimbledon. It was the first time in my life that I felt so helpless. That phone call was like hearing the sound of pound notes rubbing together.

When I landed in and they said they wanted me to have sex with a man, I didn't want to do it. I couldn't. But there was £3,000 on the table. I would be given the money immediately afterwards, all in cash. Could I really survive for much longer like I had been?

Could I do this? Could I really get away with it? Could I really, really bring myself to do this?

I cracked.

Before the filming began, they brought me into a room with a camera. The director was standing over a whiteboard. Sitting on a chair with my green and black London GAA hoodie, the director asked me what I expected to see in a gay porn scene. I made suggestions. He wrote six headings on the board, ranging from kissing to sucking to fucking. 'Now,' he said, 'you're going to do all of that today.'

I composed myself.

'You ready?' he asked.

'Yeah,' I replied. 'Let's do it.'

I was introduced to the fella who I was going to have sex with. I didn't even get his name. I didn't want to know anything about him. We struck up a brief conversation. He was straight. He was getting married in three months' time. He and his fiancée had actually booked their honeymoon that very day. How fucked up is that?

The video was heavily edited. It was made to look as if I was having the time of my life. I had to stop five times. My stomach was heaving the whole way through. I felt like throwing up every few minutes. I wanted to stop. They wouldn't let me.

'If you stop now, you won't get paid,' they said. 'The form you signed explains how you have to finish before you can be paid.'

They were ruthless bastards. They were going to town on my vulnerabilities. They knew something wasn't right with me. I had probably dropped my guard when initially asking on three separate occasions how much money I was getting, long before I knew they had a gay scene in mind. I was just a piece of meat, ripe for eating by a pack of wolves.

I couldn't maintain an erection. I had to be given Viagra twice. It was pure misery. Horrendous. I tried to transport my mind elsewhere, to make it feel like an out-of-body experience. I was somehow trying to make myself think I was somebody else. I despised what I was doing. It was absolute torture. It was making me physically sick, but I just had to try and get through this. 'Just block this out,' I kept saying to myself. 'Keep blocking this out, so I can get the fuck out of here as quickly as possible.'

When it was all over, the guy I just had sex with asked me how I found the whole experience. 'Do you want the truth?' I asked him. 'Fucking disgusting.'

He sniggered. I walked straight past him. I just wanted

to shower and get home. As I was standing under the water, I felt filthy. Stained. Soiled. Polluted. Defiled. And, deep down, I knew all the water in the Atlantic Ocean couldn't remove those stains on my soul.

I was standing at the door waiting to be paid. The director came out with a wad of cash, £3,000 in £20 notes, slowly counting them out in front of me like a dodgy second-hand car salesman.

I felt horrible. I wanted to go home. I've no idea how prostitutes feel after their first time selling their body for money, but it's a dark, dark place. Some prostitutes don't have any issues dealing with the mental baggage associated with their trade, purely because it is their trade, and because they probably like sex anyway. But everything I did completely railed against my instincts and sexual desires.

I felt weak. Broken. And then, all of a sudden, the addiction overwrote all those negative feelings and emotions. 'Sure, I'll do a bet here to take my mind off all this shit.'

Gambling had taken me to this place. And now that I had money in my pocket, gambling certainly wasn't going to give me time to process what I had just done.

Addiction doesn't allow your mind to settle. If I wasn't an addict, I wouldn't have done what I just did. On the other hand, addiction enabled me to suppress those negative feelings during those couple of hours afterwards as I went chasing that next high.

I was starving, but I wouldn't even allow myself time to get food. I bought a Yorkie bar in a shop to stave off the hunger and marched straight into a betting office. I was in my element. I was back in my world, doing what I really wanted, firing those £20 notes into betting machines again.

The first bet I placed was a £200 double on some team I knew nothing about. As I was sitting there watching the game unfold, I was euphoric. 'This is the best,' I thought to myself. The narcotic was flowing through my bloodstream again. The drug was so strong that it initially erased the turmoil from my mind from just moments earlier.

That high lasted for a while until the euphoria became more staggered. I was getting flashbacks. The images were so graphic and so fresh in my mind that they were nearly making me sick. You can't just wipe something that seismic from your memory with a ball of paper decorated with the Queen of England's face.

Going home on the Underground that night at 10.30, the magnitude of it all hit me. I couldn't believe what I had just done. I was looking at the person beside me on the Tube, wondering what they would think of me if they knew what I had been up to. 'Do you know what I just did? Do you know that I just had sex with a man for money?'

It reaffirmed how little you know about the person beside you. I could have been sitting in a seat across from an axe murderer. How the hell does anyone know what the next person has ever really done that day?

I had only half the £3,000 left. All I was thinking about was getting up early in the morning and winning that £1,500 back straight away. I thought I was the big man. I wasn't worried that I had blown half the money I got for my sordid actions. I still had £1,500 left. That opened up a whole new world of possibilities. By 7.30pm the following day, most of the money was gone.

I had sold my body. I had blackened my soul. All for just two days of gambling.

I wasn't destroyed by guilt. I wasn't tortured by what I had done, because I wasn't thinking about it. I had done my best to erase it from my mind. I had to. I had to stay positive. If I didn't, I'd have been lying in a room in London, rotting away, just existing, or finding a way to exist, until my next bet. If I didn't have that false positivity to cling on to, I'd probably have ended up killing myself.

The guilt and shame only arrived five days later when my grandmother passed away. Granny Maggie, my father's mother, had been suffering from dementia for years. It was an ease to her when she finally passed, but the news triggered the emotions I had tried so hard to suppress. I was engulfed by guilt and shame when I thought of Granny looking down on me, wondering if she knew how low I had sunk, possibly aware now of how much I had degraded and demeaned myself.

Daddy rang Barry and me to tell us the news. We arranged to fly home together. It was an uneasy journey. Barry and I weren't getting on well at the time. We'd had little or no contact while living in the same city. He suspected that I was back gambling again. When I told him how well I was doing, Barry's reaction told me how much he could see through my lies and deception. He knew me well enough by then to be able to read my moods and actions.

I put on the same positive face when we arrived home,

but I was lucky I had been able to construct that front. I had kept £400 of the £3,000 I got for the porn movie, purely to survive. I wasn't working. I couldn't keep stealing. That money was saved for gambling, but the timing of the funeral meant I still had the cash to buy a flight home.

My grandmother had spent the last few years of her life in a nursing home in Enniskillen. Andrea and I had often visited her there. I texted Andrea to let her know that Granny had passed and to see if she wanted to come to the funeral. I hadn't seen her for months, but I was desperate to meet her.

I had been with other girls in London but it was purely for sex, nothing more. Andrea had been out on a couple of dates. She was trying to move on with her life. The hypocrite in me didn't want her with any other fella, but I was just delighted to see her. I still loved her, surely.

Granny was waked in our home house in Tummery. After everyone had passed through the house for the funeral, Andrea and I sat down together. Our chat was a stark reminder of how much gambling had taken from my life, of how it had forced me out of my own home, prevented me from playing with Dromore and Tyrone, reduced me to sexual depravity. And how it had deprived me from being with the girl I loved.

We spoke about London, but everything I described was one giant lie; I had stopped going to GA meetings; I wasn't enjoying my football; I said I was doing well at work, but the only money I had to my name was the few quid in my back pocket.

As for the dark secret I was carrying, I was taking that with me to my grave.

I wanted to stay with Andrea, but I couldn't. I had to leave Dromore again. That Sunday, London were playing Antrim in Belfast in the league. The match was just an imposition on my time, but it was dead handy because I could return to London with the team and I didn't have to pay for my own flight.

I always want to win when I play, but I had zero interest that day. On the bus journey to Belfast, I was gambling like hell on my phone with the few pounds I had left. I scored two points, but Antrim beat us well. Some of the Antrim boys took pleasure in sledging a Tyrone fella who'd had his problems.

'You're only a gambling bastard, McCarron.'

'You're a thieving fucker, too.'

'You're only kicking football with this crowd now because your own don't want you.'

It wasn't nice. But I had to suck it up and take it. Anyway, it was only a mild breeze compared to the tornado coming around the corner.

I often wondered who was the first person to see me in that porno movie. Was it a gay footballer or hurler watching gay porn who suddenly recognized that Fergus was Cathal McCarron, the Tyrone footballer? Whoever it was, or who-ever posted the video on social media, those few taps on the screen of a phone or a computer were like detonating a massive explosion.

The video went viral. It was trending on Facebook and Twitter. Every football team in the country was apparently sharing it on their WhatsApp group.

Even though I knew what I did was crazy, that it was high-risk stuff, I still convinced myself that I was insulated from the apocalypse. 'This will never get out,' I said to myself so often. 'That footage is going to the USA. Nobody will ever see it.'

Yet at the back of my mind, there was this underlying fear. 'Jeez, imagine if anybody here ever saw that?'

Now, the four horsemen of the apocalypse had just come over the hill with their swords and spears at the ready. It felt like the end of the world.

And there didn't seem to be any place left for me in this world any more.

CHAPTER 14

RAGE

16 May 2016

Dublin city centre. The place is buzzing. The sun is high in the sky. Tourists are everywhere. The summer is two weeks old, but the sporadic rain and cold of restless early May days have passed and there is finally a sense of summer sweeping across the River Liffey.

I've just come from a GA meeting in Teach Mhuire on Gardiner Street. Teach Mhuire was the first of Cuan Mhuire's extensive network of temporary emergency accommodation. The building also provides short-term accommodation for up to sixty homeless males who have completed a drug, alcohol or gambling programme and who are in early recovery. It is a holistic response to an inner city need which is characterized by extensive substance misuse and related issues.

I chaired the meeting. It was powerful. Ten people were present. Most of them bared their soul, including myself.

In GA meetings, you talk about stuff that you would never bring up with your best friend. Niamh, Barry, my dad, my mum, Eimheár, they can try and understand my addiction but they will never have the same grasp that those ten people sitting around me have. They understand my mind, and how it works, because they have lived that life. They are still living it every day.

Two guys had just come off the street. Both were extremely raw. They opened up on the journey which had led them there. Their stories are what I call my medicine. It returns me to that life, of how tough it was, and how much I never want to go back there.

One of the guys had been destroyed from gambling. He admitted that he thought his life was over. His wife had left him. She was already in counselling to try and deal with the destruction her husband's gambling had wreaked on their lives. 'My wife doesn't know me any more,' said the addict. 'She doesn't seem to understand me.'

I tried to offer him some insight through my experience. 'Your wife doesn't understand that guy who is gambling, but you are still the same person that she married. If you stop gambling and get into recovery, you will find yourself again. And so will your wife.'

The other guy who had come off the street was dealing with drug, alcohol and gambling addictions. So you think I have it bad?

Their stories are harrowing, but it is still great therapy for me. It is even better again when your own story might be of some help to the people sitting around you. I can feel their pain. I understand it, because I was exactly where those guys are now. I was in an even worse position, because my case was so public. A million people were aware of my problems. At least these guys have the privacy to try and deal with their addiction that I wasn't afforded.

Dealing with addiction is always a struggle. One of the guys at the meeting admitted that he didn't see any way back from an offence he had committed. 'I can't believe what I did,' he said. I don't know what he was up to, but maybe my story might offer him a different perspective. If he read up on the stunt I pulled, and the abyss of pain and shame it plunged me into, it might make him realize that there is a way back. I'm still on that journey. It is never easy, but at least I'm getting there, or am trying to.

If I can help people in any way, I will. I always share as much as I can. This evening, I spoke about something as trivial as my phone, and how something that basic has impacted on my life. Lately, I've been edgy again. Really edgy. Angry. My head is always racing. I can never seem to switch off my mind. My personal phone is also my work phone and I always seem to be on it. Clients are ringing me in the evening after I have finished work. I'm still checking emails at 10pm.

My head is wrecked from the device, but there's another part of me that can't do without it. I love social media. I'm always on Facebook. I had 30,000 followers on Twitter at one stage, but most of those people were just watching and waiting to see when I would press the self-destruct button next. I deleted my Twitter and Facebook accounts immediately after the porn incident, but I've reappeared in the last few months and am constantly locked into what everyone is sharing and exchanging in the new global communities and networks.

I told my counsellor last week that I thought I was addicted to my iPhone. 'I'd love to fuck the thing away,' I said to him.

'Why don't you just get rid of it?' he asked.

'Nah, I couldn't. I'm on loads of WhatsApp groups: Tyrone GAA, Dromore GAA and a handful of others.'

My counsellor didn't see any issue with maintaining that connectivity if I got rid of my smartphone. 'Are you telling me that you won't be able to receive a text message from any of those people if you don't have an iPhone?'

Part of me didn't want to get rid of it. I was looking for excuses not to. Was that a sign of something coming down the tracks? I've noticed wee traits surfacing again in my personality. I've always had anger. I always play with anger. That's the type of footballer I am.

Players like Paul Galvin, Ricey, Noel O'Leary from Cork, those boys were all angry, passionate, primal footballers. It was part of their game. That personality made them the great players they were. They wouldn't have been as good without that anger. I feel the same, but I am more concerned with taming that animal within me off the pitch rather than on it.

In recent weeks, that beast has been roaming wildly outside the four white lines. Four days ago, a handful of us in my class went out after we finished college. I only had the intention of drinking water but I got this wild notion for a few glasses of wine. At 11pm, me and a classmate, a respectable man married with kids, decided to amble up to Temple Bar.

We were in this place in Anglesea Street for two hours. My friend was drunk but he wasn't causing any harm. He wasn't hassling anybody. I went up to the bar and ordered a couple more glasses of wine but the barman refused to serve me. More to the point, he was refusing to serve my classmate any more drink.

'How can you be serving a boy and then not serve him any more?' I asked. 'He's drunk alright but he's not doing any harm to anybody. We're just out having a few sociable drinks.'

The barman raised his hand. 'Don't talk to me any more,' he said.

I kinda fucked him out of it under my breath but loud enough to let him know I wasn't impressed. Before I knew it, a bouncer had come up behind me, grabbed my arm, and shoved me towards the door.

My friend tried to reason with the bouncer. 'What is happening here?' he asked.

'The barman said that this guy has to go.'

'On what grounds?'

'For being drunk and disorderly.'

I was only wearing a T-shirt. As I was trying to break free, I could hear the material stretching and ripping. As he went to push me out the door, I turned around and grabbed a hold of him. The bouncer tried to wrestle me to the ground. Bad move. Wrong move on his part. I chopped him down with a box on the side of the head.

A scuffle ensued. More bouncers arrived on the scene. The Gardaí were called. They began asking questions. I gave my take on events. 'We were having a few drinks and next thing I knew I was being man-handled.'

I was cross at this stage. My tone was loud. My temper was boiling. I was probably over-aggressive.

One of the Guards must have known who I was. 'Ye footballers think ye can get away with whatever ye want.'

I wasn't taking that shite. 'Hold on a minute here, what the hell has that got to do with anything? What did I actually do wrong to get thrown out of that place?'

I half-fucked him out of it in the process. Before I knew it, I was inside in the Garda car. My friend was still trying to plead my case when they arrested him too. We were charged with being drunk and disorderly. We spent two hours in a cell before being released. We have a court appearance somewhere on June 8th.

I did hit the bouncer. It's not good when you end up decking someone with a punch but I felt I was standing up for myself. He was man-handling me. I wasn't going to take that shit lying down. That bouncer has a job to do but, in my opinion, he had no right to behave towards me in the way that he did. Maybe it was my dislike for authority resurfacing but I wasn't going to let him walk all over me. If this becomes an issue down the line, I'll request the CCTV footage in the place as evidence in my defence.

I accept that this is more personal anger issues. I got too angry but I also acknowledge that this is part of who I am. Most people would have just walked away. It would have been the sensible thing to do. Maybe I should have but I just don't like being walked over.

When I'm wrong, I'll hold my hands up. When I'm right, I'll fight my corner. It might sound hollow and fake when I repeatedly say I'm trying to make myself better, but I really am. There are people out there who will always cause trouble, who will always want to cause trouble. They have no interest in changing. They don't want to change. I do. It's just a daily struggle trying to get there.

I was conscious of containing that fury over the following weeks but I still seemed to be finding battles everywhere.

A couple of days ago, I pulled into a garage just on the border for diesel. A lady was ahead of me in the forecourt. She filled her tank, paid for it and then struck up a conversation with this fella. I was on the way to Tyrone training and didn't want to be hanging around. I sat for a minute, but the frustration was bubbling inside me like a rattling saucepan about to boil over. I started shaking my head. She spotted me and made some remark. I waved my hand in a gesture for her to get moving. Then, the lady decided to have a staring contest. The lid came off.

I rolled down the window. 'What the fuck are you doing? Will you get out of my fucking way.'

She drove off, letting fly with a burst of expletives as she went.

I tore on up the road, cursing and swearing, draining my body with nervous energy over something completely pointless. I was still in plenty of time for training. That one extra minute sitting on the forecourt made no difference to my journey time.

For me, anger is another form of addiction. I can suppress it, but it will always be part of my make-up. That is fine, as long as I can control that fury. For years, I couldn't. When I first went into recovery, I learned how to manage that volatility better, working with a counsellor on it for years. Then about seven months ago, I took a break from engaging with that counsellor on dealing with those anger issues. I had other counselling commitments. It was only meant to be a break, but I never went back.

I'm always a different animal on the pitch, but is that one of the reasons I went to war with Emmett McGuckin and Damian Barton in January? Did it contribute to me needlessly verbally abusing that lady the other day? I don't know. Either way, it's time for me to start visiting my counsellor again to try and control whatever angst is raging inside me.

Addiction has so many forms that it requires so much self-regulation. I can never, ever get complacent. I know that when I'm not firing 100 per cent, I'm liable to do anything. An iPhone and constant access to the internet is a huge temptation. If I was having a really bad day, the devil could tug my tail and prompt me into having a bet. I don't need that temptation.

I have had to be honest with myself a lot lately. In my relationship with Niamh, I'm not sure if I was always 100 per cent committed. Now, I know that I fully am. I know my mind and my moods oscillate wildly at times, but I have to try and always keep a clear head. I know I have so much to gain by staying on the right path, by continuing to do the right thing. Just one step on the other path could lead me back on the road to nowhere.

Life is for living. I want to live it to the fullest of my capabilities. When life isn't going well for me, I'm dangerous. It is more dangerous for me than anyone else, because I am a compulsive gambler. That's why any form of temptation has to be wiped from my line of sight.

At lunchtime today, I went into the Carphone Warehouse shop in Santry. I asked the girl behind the counter for the cheapest and most basic phone she had. She looked at me as if I'd landed from the moon. 'Do you not want a new iPhone? I could get you an upgrade with all the mod cons.'

I had gone in looking for a SIM card-only contract for a reason. 'Give me the cheapest thing you have,' I repeated.

She produced this small yoke that looked like a miniature block. It could only make and receive calls, along with sending text messages. The phone only cost €40, with a contract of €35 per month. Niamh certainly won't have any difficulty keeping track of me on this thing. Only a handful of people now have this new number.

It's enough.

We are playing Derry on Sunday, but GA meetings are still the most important thing in my life right now, far more important than football. The game means everything to me. I'm as dedicated as anybody, but if I'm not well, nobody benefits. If I'm not well, everybody suffers. Mickey Harte will suffer. So will my team-mates.

I have played great stuff before when chaos was tearing my life apart. The 2013 All-Ireland semi-final against Mayo was a prime example. That performance was a form of escapism, but there is no stability or reliability in that source. If I went off the rails again, I might not be there to play for the boys. I might not even turn up on the day of an All-Ireland semi-final. I could have done something crazy and been arrested. I could be in recovery. Or maybe I would play in those circumstances and I'd cost Tyrone the game.

I need to get to those GA meetings, because I need to keep taking my medicine. If I said to Mickey Harte in the morning that I couldn't train because I had to go to a GA meeting, he wouldn't blink. He'd tell me to go to my meeting. That's the kind of man Mickey is.

Those meetings are also about perspective. Some players, especially the younger guys, construct their whole lives around playing inter-county football. They dedicate their lives around Tyrone GAA. Their focus is on getting themselves up to the highest level on every aspect of preparation: fitness, conditioning, skills. Yet the one thing constantly strained is mental health.

When they are dropped, or they get injured, those players sink into depression. You can see it in their body language. They're lounging around training rooms, just desperate to play and train because that is all some of them know. I saw it in one of our boys last week when he got injured. He's out for a while and I know it's going to hit him hard. Missing weeks like these is killing him. I can see it a mile off. He needs to be minded.

I was that player once. When I wasn't gambling, the rest of my life revolved around playing for Tyrone. I used to work myself up into a frenzy. I made myself too nervous. Now, I just go out and play. Life's lessons.

Championship weeks are always special, but Sunday is just another game to me. I couldn't be any better prepared. Tactically, I know what I have to do, but I'm not going to overthink or overanalyse. Whatever happened between Emmett

McGuckin, Damian Barton and me in January is irrelevant. If Derry intend targeting me, to try and spark a reaction, they're wasting their time. I'm ready. Tyrone are ready.

A lot of commentators are speaking about a potential ambush. Tyrone have never beaten Derry in Celtic Park. Derry know all about this Tyrone team after already playing us three times this season. They may be planning an ambush, but we are primed to repel everything they throw at us. To defeat your enemy, you have to know your enemy. We know them inside out. The video analysis we did on Derry over a two-day training camp at Johnstown House last weekend has us even more prepared.

It's a derby game. Anything can happen in those matches, but we believe if we stick to what we do best, we'll take them by seven or eight points. It might take fifty minutes. It could take sixty, but we're taking these boys out.

Celtic Park, 22 May 2016
Tyrone 3–14
Derry 0–12

In the fifty-eighth minute, Connor McAliskey played a quick sideline ball into space for Ronan O'Neill to run onto. Derry were chasing the game. They were forced to push men forward. Prairies of space had opened up in their defence, so I took off on a support run. As O'Neill turned inside Danny Heavron, I was coming off his shoulder and he popped the ball through. I was thinking, 'Score on here.'

The thought was only in my head for a second before

James Kielt came across and cut me down. I lay on the ground for a couple of seconds, but it was more to catch my breath than fake injury. Kielt bent down and said something over me. As soon as I got up, Danny Heavron arrived and hit me in the chest with his shoulder.

I squared up to Heavron. I put my arm around his neck. Our heads came together. We were grappling with one another when Niall Toner got involved. The linesman arrived, broke it up and cleared me.

I couldn't help myself. I turned back and pointed up to the scoreboard. 'Look, lads, ye are going home.'

Harte took me off five minutes later. He knew they were trying to rile me. It didn't matter at that stage anyway, because the game was over. Our full-back line was never in bother. I think there was only one ball kicked in all afternoon. Derry were trying to run the ball, but they were only crashing into Tyrone walls everywhere they turned.

They couldn't lay a glove on us. We will face much tougher challenges down the line, but our defence is playing well. Teams will sporadically kick long-range points against us, but they are mostly going to have to attack us in numbers, and hope they can hang onto the ball. And if they don't, we will hit them hard on the counter-attack.

Even Dublin don't break as fast as we can.

CHAPTER 15

NEWRY

When I was in recovery in Cuan Mhuire in Newry, I did most of my chores working alongside a man named Colm (not his real name). He had already been through the recovery programme in the house. When Colm finished the programme, he got a job with Cuan Mhuire as a handyman. Colm was a big football man from Armagh and was still playing club football at the time. Similar to Joe in Coolarne, our deep love and passion for the game fostered a natural bond and affinity between us.

'You'll be back playing with Tyrone some day soon,' Colm would always tell me.

I didn't believe him. He probably didn't believe it either. He was just trying to keep my spirits up, to help me to think positive again, to aim towards an attainable goal, despite how unattainable that target appeared at that time.

I hadn't seen Colm in over two years. I was at a GA

meeting in Athy recently. I was walking through the hall when I suddenly spotted him in one of the rooms.

'How are things, big man?'

'Not good,' Colm replied. 'I'm back doing the programme again.'

He had fallen off the wagon. The alcohol addiction which he had battled for so long had taken hold of him once more. He was clearly suffering. When I knew him in Newry, Colm had been in a loving relationship with a girl. Now, the girl was long gone.

When he was sober, the man was a rock. He was always supportive, honest, helpful. When I was broken, Colm helped me put the pieces back together. Here I was now trying to offer him the same assistance he had so graciously provided me two years ago.

The wheel of addiction keeps turning. Three weeks into my recovery programme in Newry, I got a visitor call one afternoon. It was Conor from Armagh, the boy who I had helped when he first arrived into Cuan Mhuire in Galway.

'Cathal,' he said, 'I'll never, ever forget that you were there for me when I was at my absolute lowest. The least I could do is to come here and see you now.'

The wheel of addiction just keeps on turning.

Mark Gottsche is a great guy. I played with him in London. He was a good player and lined out for Galway in early 2008, but Mark was always far more than just a footballer; he was completely ingrained in London GAA through his position as the London county board's full-time secretary and treasurer.

I'd love to speak to Mark some time, if only to ask him how I appeared just hours after the news of the gay porn film had broken. Did he even know the story by that stage? After I left the Tube station in Wimbledon Park, where I had gone to try and kill myself, Mark was the first person I spoke to.

We had arranged to meet that morning at 10am for me to pick up a compensatory cheque for £700. I got wrote-off in a league game against Waterford the previous month, so I couldn't work for a couple of weeks. As it happens, I wasn't working anyway but I put in for the recompense and Mark told me that the money was there for me.

After the story broke, I was paranoid that he wouldn't turn up but he did. I'm not sure if Mark knew. If he did, he never let on. I certainly didn't give him any indication anything was up. A couple of hours earlier, I had almost killed myself. During our discussion, I behaved like I was on top of the world.

I was loitering around Tooting Broadway Tube station in south London, lost in a haze of terror and trepidation. My phone had been ringing relentlessly all morning. Eventually, I answered it to Barry. I wanted to let him know I was still alive.

'Where are you, Cathal?'

'I'm fucked, Barry,' I replied. 'I need help.'

'Don't worry, we will get you help,' said Barry. 'Just don't do anything stupid. You need to go home today. You have to go back into rehab today.'

He continued, 'Don't move. I'll meet you shortly. I'm going to book you a flight home first. I'll ring you back as soon as I have something sorted.'

All along, I had resisted recovery and rehab. It was too hard. I didn't want to face another twelve weeks of a recovery programme, but I couldn't avoid it any longer. I knew I needed help. For the first time in years, I wanted help.

While I was waiting for Barry to call back, Paul Coggins rang. For some reason, I answered.

'Where are you?' he asked.

'I'm going home, Paul. I just have to get out of here.'

I told him where I was. 'Stay there,' he said. 'I'm coming to meet you.'

I didn't want to meet or talk to anyone, but I had such respect for Paul that I agreed. He wasn't taking no for an answer anyway. I knew from the tone in Paul's voice that he was gripped by the same fear as Barry; he was afraid that I was about to kill myself.

I was still one of Paul's players. Football was the last thing I wanted to do in London, but Paul was such a decent guy that I didn't want to let him down when he asked me to play. I had given him very little commitment while I was there, but that was irrelevant. All Paul was concerned with now was trying to help me.

I sat in his car. We never spoke about the incident, but Paul was fully aware of what had happened. I only heard afterwards that somebody in the media had already contacted Paul that morning looking for him to comment on my situation.

Paul knew that I had a serious addiction. It was obvious. The GAA is a huge community, but that community can still often have the dynamic of a small village. Small minds will have their say. People are often quick to judge, but Paul had a greater empathy and understanding of my problem because somebody he knew had also spent time in recovery from addiction.

'Everything will be okay, Cathal,' he said. 'You might not think it now, but if you put your head down and put the work into yourself, you will get better. This will all be soon forgotten about.'

Paul wanted to know my next move. At that stage, I didn't have one. I needed to go back into recovery. Returning to Cuan Mhuire in Galway was the logical next step.

Paul rang them from his phone. He tried to get me booked in that night. There seemed to be an issue. Paul didn't relent. 'This is one of my players here,' he said. 'He needs to get into recovery now.'

I think they were already aware in Cuan Mhuire of my predicament. They advised me to go to their centre in Newry. I wanted to return to Galway, but I wasn't in any position to dictate anything. I could hear the lady on the other end of the line. I looked at Paul and nodded my head to him in agreement.

I got out of the car. Paul hugged me. 'It will be alright Cathal,' he said. 'I promise you, it will be if you put the work into yourself.'

Barry rang me back. He had a flight booked. I was to meet him at Clapham Common Tube station in an hour. I returned to my apartment and packed my bags. The only possession I had that was worth anything was a TV I had bought. I just left it there.

When I saw Barry, he wrapped me up in a big hug. We spoke honestly. I told him what had driven me into this abyss of depravity and degradation and humiliation. There was deep sadness in the conversation. As children, we had been inseparable. I had always looked up to Barry. He was my own flesh and blood, my only brother. Yet while we had been living in the same city, we had been worlds apart.

Barry never wanted me to come to London, because he never believed it was the right place for me to get better. It wasn't. Barry and I didn't speak very often. Anytime we did, my brother knew I was lying. And living out that lie only caused us to drift further apart.

Before I got the train to Heathrow airport, Barry gave me some money. He told me to get some food. I had two bags, a suitcase and a gear bag. Barry couldn't remember if he had booked on one bag or two, so I just left the suitcase with him. I put whatever I needed into the gear bag.

We embraced again. I was crying. So was Barry. I was going home, but what was I returning to? I couldn't see how I could extricate myself from the train wreck that I was now entangled in.

From the moment I left Clapham Common Tube station until I landed outside Dublin airport, I had my hood pulled up. In the departures lounge at Heathrow, I met this boy who knew me from playing football in London. He was mad to chat. He obviously didn't know the story. I basically just ran away from him.

I cried the whole way home on the plane. I was paranoid beyond belief. I thought everyone was looking at me. When we arrived in Dublin, a queue of people were waiting at the far side of the departures gate to board the same plane.

Three or four of them seemed to be staring at me, as if they had copped who I was. Maybe it was just me being paranoid.

Ricey and Niall Colton had rung Daddy and said they'd lift me from the airport. I had just disembarked from the flight when they called to tell me where they had parked. I had known those two boys all my life, but the unease I felt before getting into that jeep was unnatural.

My hood was still up as I opened the door. I just wanted to roll up into a ball and hide.

'Alright, lad.'

'Alright, lads.'

Like, what do you say?

There were no hugs, no handshakes, no real warmth in the welcome. It was just business. Uncomfortable business. The lads were there to do a job – to drive me to Newry, no more.

I don't think they fully understood that I was sick, that I needed help. Their mannerisms and tone suggested that I wasn't deserving of any sympathy for what I had done.

The first half hour of the journey was painful. Then the two boys started cracking jokes to try and slice the tension. It would have taken a machete to cut the edginess in the air.

I wasn't laughing. I was in tears, with my hood still up trying to hide my shame.

As the car edged closer to Newry on the M1, Ricey and Colty tried addressing what I'd done in London in a circuitous way. 'Lad, it's okay to tell us if you are gay. It's fine with us if you are.'

What the f . . . 'Ricey, Colty, how long do you know me now? Do you honestly fucking think I am gay? Come on.'

When we finally struck up a tiny flow of conversation, Ricey echoed what Paul Coggins had said to me earlier that day: it would work out if I fully threw myself into recovery. In my unimaginable state of darkness and despair, I felt that his words didn't carry the same tone of compassion or understanding as Paul's. I am probably being unfair to him, but at the time I felt that their real meaning translated to: 'If you don't sort yourself out this time, there is no coming back.'

Few words were exchanged as we pulled up outside the Cuan Mhuire centre on the Dublin Road in Newry. I lethargically walked up the steps to the front door of this brand new building. It was late at night. They normally don't take admissions at that hour, but they made an exception for me because my case was so high profile.

I was shaking with fear and shame when I was met at the door by Pat McGinn, a great GAA man from Armagh, who works at Cuan Mhuire as a volunteer. He brought me in and sat me down. Pat was talking in a really low voice, but his dulcet tones were trying to put me at ease.

'Everything will be alright, Cathal,' he said. 'Look, did you kill anyone?'

'No.'

'Well, it's alright then. It can be fixed.'

The only person I had done damage to was myself. I had nearly killed myself. But I was still here.

Pat McGinn said that some media hounds had been sniffing around my impending arrival in Newry. A couple of journalists apparently knew what flight I had been on from London. They even had the flight number. It suited Cuan Mhuire for me to arrive as late as I did that night. They didn't want a circus outside their gates the following morning.

The programme was similar to Galway. My first week was spent in detox, another vat of puke and vomit and piss and misery.

I was depressed. How would, or could, there be an end to the darkness closing in around me? Where did I go next? I had blackened my name so badly this time that it was charred to a cinder. If I got through this programme again, what was my next move now?

Most people in the house didn't know who I was, or what I had done, but news gradually began to filter through the place from information on the outside. The story was so big that visitors were carrying it in with them. I didn't want to know what was being said or written, but it was impossible to close your ears off to so much thunder. At one stage, somebody told me that there was a semi-naked picture of me on the front page of a tabloid.

Holy Jesus.

I was an amateur GAA player, but this story transcended far beyond my footballing status. In 2010, a Wexford Intermediate hurler, Greg Jacob, appeared in a heterosexual adult movie, filmed in a caravan in Limerick with a well-known UK porn star. Jacob spoke openly about the incident afterwards. He had no regrets. He admitted to making money, but it was only some fun, a dare from his friends. He still ended up splashed all over the front page of the tabloids.

Nobody knew Jacob. He was just an ordinary guy, doing something millions of people do every day, in a global industry. Yet his connection to the GAA world was enough to create a media frenzy.

I hadn't a chance. I was well known. I'd played for Tyrone in an All-Ireland semi-final the previous year. I'd been nominated for an All-Star at the end of the season. Now I was appearing in a homosexual adult movie. Who even knows somebody who has appeared in a porn movie? No one. A gay porn movie? Holy fuck.

The tabloids were salivating over my story like a hungry lion standing over the juicy meat of a freshly killed gazelle. It provided enough food for headline writers for weeks, because the tabloids kept picking away at the story's carcass.

I was supposed to be insulated from all that turmoil within the four walls of Cuan Mhuire, but there was no escape anywhere from the torment. I had enough chaos going on inside my head, but being aware that people were talking about me inside the house tormented me even more.

I didn't want to meet anybody. I didn't want to talk to anyone. I would go to my room and sit there on my own, crying, for hours. I cried for five full days.

It was horrendous. I was weak. Numb. Then I'd be at the other extreme – trembling with fear and anxiety. I regularly had heart palpitations. Looking back on it all now, I was having a breakdown.

I was lying on my bed one evening, in floods of tears, when James (not his real name) entered the room. He was probably the only person I had any connection with during those early days in Newry. James was a good guy. I liked him. He could see how low I was. In trying to console me, he offered me the use of his phone.

Phones were forbidden in the house, as Cuan Mhuire don't want you interacting with the outside world. You can only recover within their world, where there are no distractions, where the only focus is on getting better. Yet that outside world had intruded into my grim existence to make it even grimmer.

James had sneaked in a phone because he wanted to keep in regular contact with his partner. He had to be very careful and discreet when making calls, but he let me borrow the device to send a text message.

I was desperate to contact Andrea. On the morning the news broke, she texted me in London. She was seething with anger. It was also humiliating for her, but Andrea acknowledged and accepted that I was sick from addiction. She knew something must have snapped inside me, for me to do what I did.

I thought we might still have a chance to rekindle what we once had. I really wanted to but Andrea extinguished that hope in a handful of words in a text message sent that evening to the St Joseph's ward in Cuan Mhuire.

I still loved Andrea. I wanted to be with her. I was craving to even hear her voice, but part of that longing was for some form of comfort in a world full of desperation.

I had effectively lost Andrea as soon as I returned to London, but my latest actions had fired a torpedo straight through whatever tenuous relationship we still had. I was still absolutely desperate. I didn't want to give up on what we might be able to salvage from the wreckage. I was still hanging onto the flotsam and jetsam. A few days later, I wrote Andrea a long letter.

Andrea wrote me back shortly afterwards. There was compassion in her words but a firmness in her conviction that our relationship was over. She had actually watched footage of the incident to convince herself that it was really me. Physically, she could never be with me again.

Andrea even suggested that I should have stayed on in London to build a career as a porn star. It was her way of introducing some light humour to such a dark tale, but Andrea's thought process probably reflected my own – there didn't appear to be any way back from this in Ireland.

It was another devastating hammer blow. What was the point in all of this? Where was my life going? Even if I made it through the programme, what had I to live for afterwards? Why didn't I just throw myself in front of that train?

More salt was piled into a gaping wound when James was kicked out of Cuan Mhuire a couple of days later. They found the phone. He broke the rules and he was gone. Another blow. The cloud of depression hanging over me only got darker by the day. I knew I had to break that cycle of desperation, but I couldn't. I didn't want to. I still had an attitude. It was a defence mechanism in a world where I thought everybody was against me. I'd snap back at everyone. I never listened to anyone. I continued to do whatever I wanted.

There was a gym in the house, which I began to use after about two and a half weeks. We weren't supposed to take any food or drink or substances outside of what we were given from the kitchen, but I got my mother to sneak me in some protein and fruit because I wanted to start lifting heavier weights.

Mummy didn't want to do it. I convinced her on the basis

that my life was miserable and that working out in the gym was one of the few releases I had. It was the truth, but it was still against the rules. Everyone was continually tested for any traces of alcohol or pharmacological ingredients in their system. Room searches for contraband took place once a week. All that testing and searching was part of the routine, but I still wanted to do everything my way.

One of the counsellors, Andrew, found the protein in my gear bag. He immediately confiscated the tub. He even took whatever fruit I had in the bag. I went nuts.

'What the fuck are you doing taking that from me? I play with Tyrone. I need that protein to train and to keep fit. And taking fruit off a man? A few bananas and oranges? What the fuck kind of a place is this?'

Even though I was probably never going to play for Tyrone again, I still had that attitude of purporting to show myself above everybody else.

'You're too arrogant for your own good,' said Andrew. 'You need to lose that attitude or you'll never recover.'

I wanted to pull the head off him. He was a small little guy who I could have swatted against the wall like a fly. I wanted to splat him into mush, but I just stormed off.

'Fuck this place,' I roared back to Andrew on my way out the door.

Similar to Coolarne, I had begun my chores working as a bricklayer. There were plumes of smoke billowing from my ears when I arrived back to where Gerry and Killian (not their real names) were working. Gerry, like Killian, had also been through the programme in Cuan Mhuire before being offered employment there.

As we were clearing concrete slabs and moving stones, I vented my anger. I was telling the boys how I had been wronged. It was a form of release, but the more I thought and spoke about the incident, the more questions I began to ask myself. Had I really been mistreated? Rules are rules for a reason. Was I above Cuan Mhuire policy?

Suddenly, all the anger just left me. It was a huge light-bulb moment.

Andrew was right. I was too arrogant. I had to change. I needed to change for my own sake, especially now that I was in recovery again.

'From now on, whatever way they want me to do things here, I'm going to do it,' I said to myself. 'Take whatever shit is going. If people are wrong, just take it. Say nothing. Keep your mouth shut. Just do whatever they want me to do.'

My self-discipline had completely evaporated over the previous two years. I needed to get it back. I needed to get it back even more because Newry ran a far stricter programme than the one in Coolarne. There was no TV. No radio. Unlike Coolarne, men and women were completely separated into different houses.

It was a strict regime. A military operation. But that culture was exactly what I needed.

Tom Herron is a psychotherapist, sports psychologist, asthma care practitioner, hypnotherapist, neuro-linguistic programming practitioner and trainer. Mickey Harte brought him in with Tyrone in 2009. Much of Tom's work in asthma care focuses on breathing techniques, which he tried to introduce to us to help increase our performance. Those techniques weren't always easy to develop or implement in a sport like Gaelic football, but some of the players took them on board. Anytime I see Aidan McCrory out of breath now, he recovers through Tom's methods.

Outside of my family, the first person who came to visit me in Newry was Tom Herron. He gave me a big hug. Tom told me everything would be okay. He gave me a meditation CD to help me relax, which I regularly began to listen to. I'll always be grateful to Tom for the kindness shown to me that time.

That visit was one of the few positives in the first month, but the blinding darkness gradually began to lift. My attitude had changed. The stories circulating about me had died down. Other addicts in Cuan Mhuire gave me my space. The summer had arrived. The increasing daylight and brighter and warmer sunshine was an apt metaphor for my improving mood.

I also threw myself into my work in the backyard with Gerry and Killian. Sister Consilio had a big Mass coming up in the house. A wall had to be built at short notice and I took it on. I started laying bricks one morning at 8am. It was a scorcher of a day and I bulled into the work. I didn't finish until 9pm that night when I had the wall built. Some of the counsellors were concerned with how hard I was working, at the pace with which I was belting into the job. I just kept going. I wanted to stay going. I didn't do it for praise. I did it for myself. To me, the wall was a symbol of how strong I had become, mentally as much as physically. My life was gradually being reconstructed, brick by brick by brick.

I had a different peace of mind to what I had in Coolarne. After about eight weeks, the gym was closed down. A weight fell on top of somebody and a claim was made. Management made a decision to shut the doors. Everyone was giving out stink. Nobody was more entitled to feel aggrieved than me, but I didn't care. When I was in Coolarne, maybe I didn't give myself the proper chance to fully recover. Maybe I let football cloud my mind and upset my focus. This time, I forgot all about football. At that stage, I didn't even care about playing the game again.

My only focus was on getting better. I tried to stay positive in everything I did. I convinced myself that I wasn't going to gamble again. I wanted to have a good life, whether that was in Ireland or somewhere else. I didn't know what the future held, but the immediate future was coming hard and fast around the corner.

From week nine on, my peace of mind was disturbed. A sense of fear and dread filtered back into my thought process. It was inevitable that I would soon have to face the outside world again. I was gripped by a similar strain of anxiety before I left Coolarne, but this was a whole new departure. Before I left Coolarne, I was a footballer recovering from gambling addiction. Now I was a footballer who had done male gay porn. There's a world of difference between both perceptions.

Every fear, every worry, every projection was like another stone being fired into a tranquil lake, the ripples getting wider with every throw. In my own mind, there was a squall coming.

I wasn't ready to face it. When my twelve-week recovery

programme concluded, I didn't want to leave. Cuan Mhuire knew it too. I was approached by Andrew, who asked me to stay on.

Every now and again, the Cuan Mhuire houses have to pass certain assessments to qualify and avail of state funding. At that time, Newry was up for review. They wanted the place looking in top shape for the assessors. As a tradesman, I was handy to have around. But Cuan Mhuire also knew I needed to be around.

I immersed myself in the project, almost as a form of gratitude to Cuan Mhuire for providing me with the shelter I needed. We had the place looking immaculate. The gardens were like a scene from the Chelsea Flower Show. You could eat your dinner off the floor in any of the buildings. It was a pleasure to be in recovery at that time. The summer had arrived. The weather was great. Everyone was in good form. Especially me.

I knew I was only suspending my assimilation back into society, but I didn't care. This enclosed little world was where I wanted to remain for now. I was happy and content here.

The outside world could wait.

CHAPTER 16

ATHY

Ulster Semi-Final
Tyrone 0–16
Cavan 3–7
St Tiernach's Park, Clones, 19 June 2016

Holy fuck. Tyrone hadn't conceded a goal in eight championship matches and then we go along and leak three in seventy minutes. We had the match won, when Cavan scored their third at the end. Tyrone normally don't allow that stuff to happen, but the chaos and mayhem was in keeping with the apocalyptic skies all afternoon.

Two days from the longest day of the year, the light was as grey as late November. The old market town had been hammered by incessant rain before the game. Conditions were treacherous. We left ourselves wide open, but we still should have put the match out of reach before David Givney palmed Cavan's third goal into the net.

Seánie Johnston never came near me. Killian Clarke, the boy who plays full-back, arrived into the full forward line before the game began. We were prepared for high balls and big men, but we weren't expecting to see Clarke in that role. Cavan's first five attacks were long balls lamped into the full forward line. I won one and broke two more away. Clarke won one, but nothing came of that possession.

Cavan's first goal came at the end of a run from Martin Reilly. Mickey O'Neill saved, but Givney scrambled home. The ball went past Richie Donnelly and Ronan McNamee. I was on the line with Colm Cavanagh, but I couldn't see the ball when Givney kicked it, so it went between my legs and over the line. The second goal also shot past me before I knew where the ball was. A long range free by Ray Galligan dropped in a forest of arms and legs around the Tyrone square and one of the Cavan players got a flick to it. I put up my arms to try and catch the ball, but it whizzed past my head, hit Conor Moynagh on the leg and squirmed over the line. We scrambled the ball back out, but the umpire had the green flag raised.

It was one of those games where everything, and everyone, was all over the place. I'm normally used in a man-marking role, but when Clarke drifted away out the field after the first quarter, I played as a sweeper on the edge of the D. I pushed up on Cian Mackey and Martin Reilly on a couple of occasions when they drifted into my zone, but I was always trying to get back in front of McNamee. We were still in control for most of the second half. We reeled off six successive points before we lost concentration again for Cavan's third goal. We played shite but still should have won by six or seven points.

We're probably better off that we didn't. We'd have learned nothing.

We could kid ourselves and say that we should have still won when we were useless, but by our high standards that performance wasn't acceptable. Prior to this match, Tyrone had only conceded three goals on two occasions in fourteen seasons under Mickey Harte. Both of those other games were draws which Tyrone emphatically won in a replay. All we can do now is go along and beat Cavan, and beat them well, in two weeks' time.

The whole day was a pain in the ass. I got an accidental knee into the hip from Givney in the first half. A blast of freeze spray at half-time numbed the pain, but I knew I was going to be fucked afterwards. I was, but at least we were still alive.

The first time I returned home to Dromore, I didn't leave the house. I couldn't go into town because of the shame. Word soon filtered out that I was home for the weekend, but by the time a handful of visitors arrived at my door, I was gone again. I drove south, to Athy in Kildare. Around the time of the Cuan Mhuire assessment in Newry, I sat down with Liam McLoughlin, head of the Cuan Mhuire house in Athy. I knew I couldn't stay in the house in Newry indefinitely, but I still wasn't ready to face the outside world. Liam knew it too, so he suggested that I spend the remainder of my time in Athy, that it would be a more conducive environment to help slowly assimilate me back into the outside world. The drug rehabilitation unit were always looking for volunteers. Liam felt I would provide the ideal fit.

When I arrived in Athy, Liam was waiting there for me. The house is located just north of the town, a beautiful picturesque location, much different to the more urban surrounds of Newry, set in the vast flatlands and huge farmlands of south-west Kildare. The house had so much to offer. The drug unit is one of the best in the country. Working there would provide me with a whole new experience, and offer a totally different perspective on addiction and overcoming it.

I knew the insight and advice of Sister Susan would be invaluable on the next stage of my recovery. She always believed it took a gambler's mind at least eight or nine weeks to settle down after entering into recovery. She was right. I had been in rehab for over three months by this stage and my mind, and train of thought, were only beginning to slow to normal pace. New surroundings, a whole new environment, gave me a completely different and fresher outlook. I had my own room in the house. I felt great. I had complete freedom. I could walk down to the local shop without fear or shame taking hold of me. Apart from a few local football diehards, nobody knew me in Athy. If I walked around Dromore or Omagh, I'd have been a target of a thousand opinions. I hadn't a care in the world in Kildare. I was working as a volunteer in a drug unit from 8am to 4pm. I would supervise chores, sit in on group therapy. It was a liberating experience. I wasn't getting paid, but I didn't have to worry about rent or food. I had everything I needed.

Three months earlier, my body and mind were shrouded in unimaginable darkness. I couldn't even see a pinprick of light in the distance. Now, I was staring into an orb of light and promise. The people in the house energized me. Nicola Kelly was a brilliant counsellor attached to the Cuan Mhuire house in Athy, who became a great friend. I learned so much more about recovery too from Finbar and Johnny (not their real names), two guys who transformed their lives from heroin addicts into two of the most inspirational people I've ever met.

They went through the drug unit in Athy before becoming two of the best counsellors I've ever worked with. There is a picture on the wall in the drug rehab unit of Finbar and Johnny from their time there as addicts. Their gaunt and pale-skinned faces are unrecognizable from the vibrant and vivid features that now light up a room. Johnny is married with kids. Finbar got married in 2016. Every day was an education. I was so happy. I had complete peace of mind. It was summer time but there was that fresh, feel-good scent in the air every day. There was a gym in the house where I worked out most days. I bulked up a lot because I lifted so many weights, but those workouts were designed for my wellness. They had nothing to do with football.

It wasn't that I had fallen out of love with football; I just wasn't sure if it had a place in my life any more. Maybe the mental pressure and stress associated with football inflated my gambling addiction. I wasn't sure, but I didn't want to take that chance again. I went to Athy to do more work on myself. If football had a place in my life again, it would find its own level, in its own good time.

I was sitting outside the house one day, writing out notes on a board for Sister Susan, when Joe Kelly, Nicola's husband, passed by. The Kellys are big farmers around the town. They have land right beside the house and have always had close connections with Cuan Mhuire. Joe introduced himself. He knew who I was. He said, if I wanted, or whenever I felt ready to make that step, that I was more than welcome to come and train with the Athy senior team.

Joe said that Athy had a game against Moorefield on the local pitch the following evening. He asked if I wanted to go. I said I would. As soon as I drove through the gates of the Athy GAA grounds that evening, a massive sense of fear enveloped me. The place was packed. With so many supporters, I knew someone was bound to recognize me. It was the first time in my life I had a panic attack.

I had never known what anxiety was. I had played in front of 60,000, live on TV, and never gave it a second thought. This time I couldn't get out of the car. I was just paralysed. People were walking past and I was hiding out of fear that I'd be recognized. I kept ringing Joe. He wasn't answering, which further heightened my anxiety levels. I was trembling. I had my head in my hands when Joe finally rang back. The unease lifted slightly, but I still wasn't comfortable. I didn't want to go near the stand. I was projecting what other people might be thinking.

'That's your man McCarron, the Tyrone footballer who appeared in the porn movie. What the hell is he doing down here?'

I hadn't a clue what they were really thinking, but it was pure paranoia. I have since learned that much as a counsellor: when you think somebody else is judging you, you are really only judging yourself. It's a real truth, because you're only assessing the situation through your own eyes, nobody else's. By the time I met Joe, I was physically shaking. He asked me if I was alright. He tried to calm me down. 'You'll be fine, Cathal,' he said. 'It's all good GAA people here. You're in among your own.'

I walked into the stand and really enjoyed the game. The experience was nowhere near as tough as I thought it would be. I went to Liam McLoughlin, who was also my counsellor, the following day and told him about the whole experience. 'That's great, Cathal,' he said. 'That is one small step. Maybe the next step could be a training session with the club.'

That was my next step. Shortly afterwards, I went down to the clubhouse and met the Athy senior management and players. Pascal Kelleghan, the former Offaly player, was the manager. He welcomed me with open arms. You couldn't have met a better bunch of boys than those Athy players.

They didn't know at the time – and probably still don't – but the Athy boys played a hugely positive part in my recovery. Loads of them helped me in their own unique way. With Cuan Mhuire so close to the town, they had an understanding of how young people my age often find themselves going through hard times. They judged me for who I am, not for what I had done, or how I was perceived. I'm sure they had a set impression of me in the early days, but I think I changed everyone's perception within a week. I was a genuine person, someone with a good heart, who just enjoyed good company and playing football.

My love of the game soon returned. I was full of energy. I was playing with a freedom that I never had before. I was playing out of my skin every evening in training. All the while, Tyrone were moving on without me. Nobody from the management or team had made any contact with me during 2014. I didn't have any interest in speaking to them. I was only focused on getting better. Deep down though, I couldn't suppress that raw desire to wear the red and white again. I was in week twelve in Newry when Pat McGinn took me out of the house to watch Tyrone play Monaghan in the Ulster quarter-final. You're not supposed to leave the house, but Pat understood my connections to the team and it was a form of reward for how well I had done in recovery. Tyrone were beaten. I was disappointed for the lads, but I said to Pat afterwards, 'I'd love to get back there some day. I don't know if it will ever happen, but I know I can do it if I really want to. There is loads left in me.'

I knew there was.

Tyrone limped out of the 2014 championship. They stumbled past Down in a replay in Ulster before Monaghan took them out. Armagh finished them off in the qualifiers, a dire performance where Tyrone only hit 0–10 and failed to score for the last twenty minutes. That match was played in Omagh, but nobody seemed to even get excited about it. Only a crowd of just above 10,000 turned up. It was a world away from the previous decade when Armagh and Tyrone were kings of the footballing world and their relationship formed football's defining rivalry. This was the grim without any of the fascination, and Tyrone seemed to be going nowhere.

The team clearly needed to be reinvented. I had no doubt that Mickey Harte would rebuild Tyrone into a force again. I wanted to be part of that journey. Well, I hoped I would be. I still wasn't sure if that was the right pathway for me to take again in my life. Yet even if I convinced myself that it was, I wasn't sure how I could take the first step back on that pathway.

I didn't know if I would ever play for Dromore again. I doubted I would. There was still a lot of bad blood towards me in the parish and in the club. What I did was completely wrong. I had treated people really badly. I still didn't think I deserved to be run out of my home, but when nobody from Dromore came to visit me in Newry, I wasn't sure if I was wanted back in my community. Dromore wasn't even on my radar anyway, because I was so immersed in my training with Athy. The lads were always slagging me off. 'We will bring the transfer forms the next night for you to sign,' they would say. I always batted the veiled suggestion away, but I didn't rule out the possibility either because I was so happy in Athy.

Its people were so good to me, especially the Kellys. Joe and Nicola farm over 800 acres in south-west Kildare. Their land stretches all the way across the Laois border, hugging close to the village of Stradbally. Some of their land is used as an access point for the annual Electric Picnic festival. The Kellys get a share of free tickets every year and Nicola handed me one that September. I hadn't sipped a drop of alcohol in six months. I had been living like a monk all summer and I didn't want to drop that barrier between myself and the big bad world beyond Cuan Mhuire and Athy GAA club. I was still afraid of meeting people. I didn't want someone to see me drinking and enjoying myself at Electric Picnic and have them thinking that I accurately fitted the perception they had formed of me – that I had no remorse for what I had done in London. Even if I had drink in me, how was I going to behave?

Despite everything I had done in my recovery, knowing what I had gone through, the hardest part to change – even to this day – is worrying about what other people think of you. I have worked so hard at removing that insecurity but, no matter how hard I try, it's still difficult after leaving myself so exposed to public opprobrium. Nicola eventually persuaded me to go to Electric Picnic. She said I deserved the reward, that I needed to unwind. I was so glad I did. I had a blast. I went with a crowd of Athy boys. We carried crates of beer over our shoulders. It was a fucking deadly weekend. It was exactly what I needed.

We had our own tent. Our own crew of boys stuck together. The craic was deadly and I really enjoyed the music. Some people spend their summers going to music festivals, but those couple of days represented the first socially normal period in my life in almost a year. On the Sunday of that weekend, Dromore played Omagh in the Tyrone county semi-final. I'd had no social media interaction over the previous seven months, but I changed my Facebook profile that day from a picture of myself to the Dromore crest. I don't know why. Despite being so disconnected to Dromore at that time, I suppose it was just my own way of reconnecting to something that was still so close to my heart.

I used to go home every third weekend, but I was a ghost around Dromore. I was invisible because I didn't stray beyond the perimeter of our home place. I was still too scared to be among my own people. The only real contact I had with the boys was through Teamtalkmag Tyrone, who streamed all the club championship matches. I listened to Dromore's quarter-final win against Clonoe when they had come from eight points down to win by one. The day of the semi-final, Dromore were two points up against Omagh with time almost up when Omagh sucker-punched them with a late goal.

There was madness going on around me at Electric Picnic, but I was in shock for about half an hour. I felt for the boys. Initially, part of me didn't want them to win. Even though it was exhilarating for me to listen to the boys reel in Clonoe in the previous game, I had those same feelings afterwards because I didn't want them to win a county title without me. That selfishness was probably exacerbated by the hurt I felt from my disconnection to the club, but it vanished as soon as they lost to Omagh. I was genuinely devastated for the boys. I could feel their pain. I could picture them going back to Dromore after losing a big game, because I had made that journey so often. At that very moment, I said to myself, 'I'm going back to Dromore next year.'

Ulster Semi-Final replay
Tyrone 5–18
Cavan 2–17
Kingspan Breffni Park, Cavan, 3 July 2016

Peter Donnelly, our strength and conditioning coach, told us recently that our GPS stats for our top running speed had increased by 10 per cent over the last three years. My top running speed is around 9.3 metres per second, which is at the high end of the squad, but one of our younger lads on the panel broke 10 metres per second recently. That pace is off the charts.

A lot of our training focuses on those intense bursts of speed. The full-back line do shorter sprints than the boys out the field, but we're all still primed to take off. I might often make a burst up as far as midfield, but we usually just let our speed machines around the middle-third just drop the pedal and leave everyone else in their vapour trail.

It took us twenty minutes to break Cavan but when we did, we smashed them. They couldn't live with our pace on the counter-attack. Peter Harte scored two goals and blazed another chance over the bar. Connor McAliskey nailed our third goal on a three-on-one break. Rory Brennan walked our fourth into the net. If we'd needed more goals, Tyrone could have scored eight or nine. We knew we could blow these boys away. In fourteen seasons under Harte, Tyrone have won replays by an average of ten points. We won this by ten points, but it would have been twenty if we hadn't taken our foot off the gas in the last quarter. Cavan got two goals, but they didn't get any when they needed them.

I had a great vibe beforehand. The changing room was buzzing. We're like Wimbledon FC, the old Crazy Gang, with music blasting away before going to war. Some of the boys put the playlist together. I don't know what half of the stuff is. It's mostly just beats; jungle music, the mad sort of shit that sounds good anyway. I'm sure there was a time when Mickey Harte wouldn't have had his eardrums assaulted with that kind of noise. Peter Canavan, Brian

Dooher or Conor Gormley would hardly have tolerated tunes in the changing rooms. But these are changed times and Harte appreciates the importance of keeping up to date with the trends of a new generation.

A lot of the young players on this Tyrone squad are stylish boys. They like their clothes, and some of them are such wizards with the hair gel that they could get a job in a hair salon. Appearance means a lot to them, but they are serious footballers who back it up on the pitch.

The bright lights are beckoning. The big show of the Ulster final is just two weeks away. Bring it on.

CHAPTER 17

COMEBACK

I was sitting in my room in Athy one evening watching my small TV when an interview with Gareth Thomas came on. He had captained Wales in both codes of rugby, but Thomas had wrestled with his sexuality throughout that career. Keeping it a secret was destroying him. When Thomas eventually came out to his wife, Jemma, she left him three months later, although they remain good friends. Not knowing where to turn, Thomas thought he had reached the end of the road.

Feeling weak, deceitful and dangerous, Thomas had come to despise himself and who he was. He decided to take his own life. Choosing a dark tie, tightened in a Windsor knot, Thomas wore a well-cut grey Welsh Rugby Union suit before slipping into a pair of black, patent leather lace-up shoes. He felt the least he could do for those whose love he had betrayed was to have a decent death. The ending would be clean and easy; a box of pills washed down with a bottle of vodka would easily facilitate drowning himself in Thomas' own swimming pool.

When he couldn't follow through with this suicide, Thomas tried again. He used to go for long coastal walks, in stages, for up to six hours at a stretch. One of those trails took him close to steep cliffs, pitted by a series of small caves, towards the outskirts of Llantwit Major. Thomas noticed a small path down towards a promontory overlooking the Bristol Channel. A plan began to form.

It took Thomas several clandestine visits before he plucked up the courage to return to that ridge. Thomas leaned into it, undressing slowly and deliberately. The wind muffled his apologies to his grandparents before his attempt to leap 200 feet onto rocks.

Thomas stood there for twenty minutes in his underpants. Standing on the edge of the cliff, everything seemed so easy. A single step would release the pain. No more loneliness. No more causing chaos for the people he loved. It was simple. Thomas would close his eyes, and never have to open them again.

The detail brought me right to that moment in London when I was so close to ending my own life. The platform had been my cliff edge. The train was my jagged rocks. I was lonely, disorientated and in pain. I wanted it to stop. I wanted to stop causing so much chaos for those I loved. It was that easy; one jump and I could close my eyes, and never have to open them again.

Similar to Thomas, I couldn't do it. I wanted to live too, but Thomas' story appealed to me on so many more levels.

His predicament was different in how he came out about his sexuality, but I was gripped by the same tranquilizing fear of how I would be perceived after such a seismic public event in my life.

Rugby and high-level sport played a huge part in Thomas' journey. All his fears and anxieties finally left him once he told Scott Johnson, his former coach, that he was gay. Johnson subsequently got Thomas' Welsh team-mates Stephen Jones and Martyn Williams to talk with him at the Wales team hotel. Rather than reject him, which he feared they would, they embraced Thomas.

His world was clearer afterwards, but a huge part of my own world was still clouded in a shade of darkness. I had come a long way in my recovery, but sport was still probably the only means of removing the blackness eclipsing my journey back into broader society. My identity had always been framed by football; I didn't want it to be defined by a moment of weakness and madness in a London studio.

Could I come back though? Thomas was just being himself. The men who he respected most had accepted him but, after what I had done, would my team-mates want me back? Would they ever respect me again? Would management? Would Tyrone supporters really want me representing the county any more? Was I a negative image that Tyrone people didn't want to be associated with? Even if I did come back, how would the media portray that return? Would it really be of any benefit to the team? Was I better off just staying away altogether?

I read Thomas' book, *Proud*, shortly afterwards. It gave me huge inspiration. He showed massive strength of character and mental strength to play rugby after coming out. If he could do that on a world stage, surely I could do it playing Gaelic football in Ireland?

The first contact I had with anyone from the Tyrone senior team in almost a year was a text message sent from the coach, Gavin 'Horse' Devlin, in October 2014. 'How are you feeling for 2015?' he enquired. 'We need you back.'

I thought about it for a couple of seconds before tapping thirteen words onto the screen in response. 'Well Horse, I suppose if I was asked back, I would go back.'

About a week later, I returned from the gym one night to see a missed call on my phone from a number I didn't recognize. I rang it back. Mickey Harte answered.

We just spoke in general for ten minutes. Then Mickey said Horse had mentioned to him that I might be open to returning with Tyrone in 2015. I said I was. 'Well, we'd love to have you back, if you want to come back.'

The door which I thought was forever closed was now ajar.

This wasn't just a step. This was crossing a canyon. As well as going back playing football at that level, I would have to deal with the media and public scrutiny around my return. Everything about my past would be excavated for even more detail. I wasn't Cathal McCarron the footballer any more. I was Cathal McCarron who had done gay porn. Did I really want to create that circus? Could I survive inside that big tent?

I confided in my counsellors. Oisín McConville, who had returned to play for Armagh after going public about his gambling addiction, was a great sounding board. I didn't want to be remembered for what I had done in London. I wanted my life to mean something, for me to have some positive impact in life, whether that was through football or counselling or something else.

Football had always framed such a huge part of my identity that it was only natural to want to reconnect with the game, but my family weren't convinced that it was the right path for me to take. 'Do you really need all that shit again?' Barry kept saying to me.

My mother wanted me to walk away from football too. She thought it had put too much pressure on me in the past. Did I need that stress again now, when my life finally had some semblance of normality? Had that pressure associated with inter-county football only inflated my gambling addiction? My family were only interested in my own welfare, but I loved the game too much for me to dismiss it on a hunch that returning might do me more harm than good.

I was at home in Dromore in early November 2014. Daddy and I were watching the Ulster club championship quarter-final between Omagh and Crossmaglen Rangers on TG4. Mark Harte, Mickey's son, was doing the analysis. Omagh caused a huge upset when defeating Crossmaglen. It was a massive victory for Tyrone football and they interviewed Mickey afterwards.

The presenter Mícheál Ó Domhnaill said the word on the street was that I was coming back. He asked Mickey to clarify the situation. I can't even remember what Harte said, but I thought it was funny that my potential return was being discussed on live TV.

To me, that was a positive indicator. I didn't feel any negativity. In any case, my mind was made up by that stage.

I was going back.

I was in the house with Daddy one day when he asked me to go into town to the local butcher and pick up some meat for the dinner. I refused. He pleaded with me and I still wouldn't relent. The fear of seeing people in my own community was still crippling me. I was imprisoned inside my own house, but I never looked on it in that manner because I was only going back to Dromore to see my own family. I didn't want to see anyone else.

That went on for five months. I was completely disconnected from Dromore. I had a new life in Athy. My new girlfriend Niamh was from there. I had comfort and peace of mind in Athy. I had no money, but I didn't care. I was on the dole, getting €180 a week, but I never felt richer.

I was extremely comfortable within my new community. A part of me thought that my new life, my future, was in Kildare, not Tyrone. I could see myself playing with Athy, not Dromore. I heavily debated about joining Athy. At one stage, it was 60:40 in my mind that it was the right move.

Hurt was swaying me away from my own people. I was devastated when nobody from the club came to see me while I was in Newry. Boys I had grown up with all my life didn't come near me. I could understand their reasoning to a point, but I still struggled to reconcile it in my own mind. When I spoke to some of the lads afterwards, they said they were torn about what to do. They weren't sure if I wanted visitors. They didn't know what frame of mind I was in at the time. Did I want to see anyone?

That vacuum though, inflated all my old insecurities and fears about returning home. The longer I spent away from Dromore, the more dislocated I felt from the place and its people.

Athy had given me a whole new perspective, on life and on football. When I wasn't sure if I would ever play the game again, the Athy club took me in and rekindled my love of football. Their spirit crackled with electricity. It lit up my life again.

I tried to give something back. I was helping out with the Athy Under-21s at the time. I had trained with a lot of those boys who were on the club senior panel, who lost the county semi-final. I felt they were missing something. I tried to instil that mean streak in the players that clubs like Moorefield and Sarsfields had, and which was stitched deep into the soul of Dromore footballers. It just wasn't easy to immediately transfer one culture onto another. Athy got to the Under-21 semi-final and lost that too.

I still thought my future was with those players, and in helping to change their culture, until one of my best friends in Dromore, Seán O'Neill, rang me. He was club captain that season in 2014. He had heard I might be returning to Tyrone. 'If you're going back playing for the county,' he said, 'I hope there will only be one club you'll be playing for.'

I still wasn't sure if I would. 'Of course I want to play for Dromore again,' I said. 'But if there is any bad blood there, if there is still any opposition to me coming back, I won't be returning. I won't be coming back just because it's my club. I'll only be returning if everybody wants me there.'

Seán was emphatic that my own people did want me to return. 'Everyone in the club wants you back,' he said.

I still wasn't sure. Did they really? Was their judgement influenced by them narrowly losing the county semi-final, knowing the difference I could have made? Was that them just being clinically minded?

I appreciated how much of a delicate subject I was. I'm sure some boys didn't know where to stand on my possible return. Some of them probably didn't want me back. They might have felt uncomfortable being around me. Given my history, I'm sure not all of the Dromore boys trusted me any more.

I heard shortly afterwards that a players' meeting was called to discuss my potential return. I never asked what was said. All I do know is that Eoin McCusker, one of our most experienced players, apparently had the last word. 'Boys,' he reportedly said, 'McCarron's coming back and that's the end of it.' Then Eoin got up and walked out the door.

Seán O'Neill rang me afterwards to confirm what he had already told me. 'We want you back,' he said. 'Everyone wants you back.'

I was gradually beginning to convince myself that the time had come to return home. The threat from the IRA had been erased from my mind, because I had been away for so long. I knew some people within Dromore had always been very uncomfortable anyway with how that whole situation had been handled. I was sick. I needed treatment. Now that I had got it, the people of Dromore were aware that I was trying my best to get my life back on track.

Finally, I took that first big step. I was at home one weekend when I went into a shop in the town. I was absolutely petrified. I was projecting what others thought, of what they would think, or say, when they saw me. The experience was far easier than I thought, or expected, it to be. I drove away wondering what all the worry and anxiety had been about. I remember thinking about Gareth Thomas and the words he had spoken in that TV interview.

'All the darkness I imagined there would be, all the hatred, all the negatives, just didn't materialize. People didn't judge, they accepted me. I can see now that my fear was something I'd created.'

I practise visualization a lot. There were times when I thought I would never play for Dromore again. I could always see myself back in the red and white of Tyrone, but I knew my footballing journey wouldn't be complete until I was back wearing the blue and white of Dromore St Dympna's.

I began to visualize myself walking back out in Gardrum Park again.

And it felt good. It felt right.

Recovery is all about taking new steps. One foot after the other. Again. And again. And again.

The first, and biggest, public step in my life was going to a players' meeting with Tyrone in late November 2014. It was held in Kelly's Inn in Ballygawley, where we had always met. I was sick with worry.

Niamh came down the road with me. She had never classed me as a shy person, but she saw how vulnerable and helpless I was to my predicament that day. I was so nervous that I was shaking like a wee child.

I didn't know how I was going to be received by my teammates. This time was completely different to the previous time when I had come out of recovery. Mugsy broke the ice that day, but he had moved on and nobody was going to make a joke out of what I had been up to since I last stood in a room together with those boys.

Shame and embarrassment had left me completely exposed. I was defenceless. As soon as I got out of the car, my head was down. I didn't know where to turn.

I was early. So was Seán and Colm Cavanagh, the first two boys I met. Big Seán gave me a hug. The sincerity of Colm's welcome was reflected in the strength, yet warmth, of his handshake.

We were the first three in the door. We sat up the front and began chatting away as the rest of the boys started filtering into the room around us. My conversation with the two lads became more staccato as the room began to fill up. I was distracted. I wasn't fully concentrating. I could nearly feel the hot breath on my neck from the conversation between boys just behind me, but I was too embarrassed to turn around. I just wanted the meeting to be over.

Mickey Harte showed his class that day by something as basic as not even acknowledging me. I was the same as everyone else. It was as if my past was irrelevant. Harte's way of slowly inveigling me back into the group was obvious. It immediately settled me down.

When the meeting was over, all the boys came up and welcomed me back, each in their own way. I didn't feel any hostility or awkwardness, but I knew that the mood or attitude towards me couldn't be gauged by a quick exchange in a packed room. I would have to prove myself to those players, but I was more than ready to undergo that process.

Niamh had remained in the car working on her laptop while the meeting was on. When I sat back in beside her, I was like a new person. She could see the relief in my face. A completely different energy was audible in my voice.

The first step was taken. The next one though, was a much bigger leap. A players' meeting with Dromore was scheduled for two weeks later. I had grown up with all those boys, but I felt like an outsider now. I hadn't spoken to most of them in over a year. I was even more nervous than I had been before the Tyrone meeting.

It was held in St Dympna's primary school in the town. A new management was in place, a joint-ticket of Audi Kelly and Paul Rouse. They were obviously trying to make an impression. The talk was of a new journey and they brought me into the conversation. They asked me to speak. I didn't want to, but I was put on the spot. I couldn't say no. I muffled something about what it had been like to win championships in the past with Dromore, but I felt really uncomfortable.

The whole evening was awkward. Given all that had gone on around Dromore, I felt far more unease than I had around the Tyrone players, who were more detached and distanced from the localized feeling towards me.

My close friends welcomed me back with open arms but I think some fellas were afraid to speak to me. Some might have been embarrassed that they had made no contact with me while I was in Newry and Athy. Other lads might have been intimidated by my presence again. I don't know, some fellas might just not have been comfortable around me knowing, and probably having watched, what I had done.

I had always been vocal at team meetings. I was considered a leader in Dromore, but I didn't feel I was entitled to that status, or that I could exert that influence, at that time. My head was still down. My confidence around my own people was still on the floor. I went home to Tummery afterwards before heading back to Athy.

I had to earn my respect back, both with Tyrone and Dromore. I'm sure a handful of boys in Dromore weren't happy that I had returned. I'm certain that I had to prove myself to some of them before they started to become comfortable being around me again. That all took time.

I just put my head down and worked hard. Gradually, I felt that I was earning the respect of the management and the full squad again, that I deserved to be back playing with Tyrone and Dromore, purely from doing what I love doing best – playing football.

Going back with Tyrone was always going to be far more mentally challenging than it would be physically. My fitness would quickly return. It wouldn't take me long to hone my football again, but I knew I would have to harden my mind, to make it strong enough to withstand the firestorm coming.

To prepare myself for the inferno, I jumped right into the middle of the flames. I would go online, into chat rooms and onto discussion boards, type in my name and wait for the poison to flow.

I was shocked by some of the stuff written and said about me but uploading that stream of invective was my way of shock-absorbing my mind if that stuff was directed at me in a public arena, which I knew it inevitably would be on a football pitch.

It's always going to be out there, especially in chat rooms where guys can hit and run and hide. I just have to deal with it. After Donegal beat us in the 2015 Ulster championship, I spotted this discussion thread, the thrust of which was that Tyrone would have no problem negotiating the back door with me showing them the way. You just have to laugh at that kind of shit.

Some people will always want to have a go, just as others will always want to lend support. After the porn incident went public, some GAA fans set up a webpage titled 'The Supporting Cathal McCarron Page'. In its early days, the page clocked up more than 7,000 likes as supporters posted messages of solidarity. However, the site was trashed by trolls spewing homophobic abuse at me.

It was ironic that people were logging onto the 'Supporting Cathal McCarron Page' when support was the least of their intentions. That is standard behaviour, because some people are always far braver behind a computer or laptop than they are face to face.

One fella, who I know, and who clearly doesn't think I saw his poisonous tweet at the time he posted it, goes out of his way to be nice to me whenever I meet him. I don't waste a second thinking about him. He probably had the same mindset as all those other brave keyboard warriors who were sticking the knife into my back when I was on the ground; they thought that I'd never get back up, that my wounds were terminal for my football career.

You just have to move on. No matter how hard you try anyway, some people will continue to form the same opinion of you. A lot of them still think I am gay. Every day, I still get online approaches, or some form of social media connectivity, from the gay community. It's embarrassing when some man asks to meet you, but I don't look on that as a negative.

Some gay men seem to look upon me as a kind of gay icon. That's how I was tagged on some LGBT community websites and discussion boards. When the video went viral, some of those forums were laced with comments from gay men about how much they wanted to have sex with me. The last thing I am is gay, but I'll take those comments above vile, vitriolic, homophobic and personal abuse any day of the week.

I completely respect the gay and lesbian community, because I always really appreciated their messages of support when so many others wanted to bury me.

The first match Gareth Thomas played after publicly announcing his sexuality was a Heineken Cup game for Cardiff Blues against Toulouse – Thomas' old club – in December 2009. Thomas described it as 'the first day of the rest of my life'.

The unwavering support of his team-mates had made him feel secure and ultra-confident. Their attitude and response towards Thomas had signalled acceptance. Thomas felt ready for whatever the day threw at him. And then, the squad left the hotel.

It was only a short walk to the bus, but the players had to file through an entirely different type of scrum. Cameras were waved in Thomas' face. Flashbulbs exploded all around him. The nature of Thomas' exit from Toulouse had been messy. He understood the ferocity of the club's mentality. If they wanted to make Thomas' life hell, it would have been second nature. On that familiar journey to the Stadium Municipal, Thomas was waiting for hell to be unleashed upon him.

Once he stepped into their cauldron though, the Toulouse tribe embraced Thomas. They gave him a standing ovation. The applause was respectful, rather than raucous, but time stood still. Thomas was frozen to the spot, unable to take in the magnitude of the compliment he was being paid.

My first game back was always going to be a massive step. It was against Armagh in the Dr McKenna Cup in January 2015. The rivalry between the counties defined Gaelic football in the middle of the last decade. That gripping tension between those two groups of players had fermented for years, deepened by the maturing of outstanding footballers around at the same time, as two counties jousted for the right to become great. Tyrone ultimately prevailed by winning three All-Irelands.

After Tyrone defeated Armagh in the 2005 All-Ireland semi-final – probably the greatest game of the decade – the counties continued to share the same relentless ambition, but the relationship was never the same again. Old warriors had moved on. Scars from past battles had healed.

Armagh–Tyrone became more a local skirmish than all-out war, but the game between both counties still always means something. That day in early January 2015, a massive crowd of 8,463 turned up at the Athletic Grounds and the throw-in had to be delayed by thirty minutes.

On the bus journey into Armagh, it was obvious how big the crowd was. A big game for me was getting bigger by the second. When I got off the bus, a nest of photographers was waiting for me. It was like the Cathal McCarron circus. Darren 'Dazzler' McCurry was beside me as I walked to the changing rooms. He would be fond of the spotlight. 'Fuckin' hell lad,' he said, 'I'm going to stay alongside you here. I might get some coverage.'

Dazzler was trying to lighten the mood, but I felt terrible. You'd imagine I had killed somebody. I didn't have to deal with the same frenzy that Gareth Thomas had to face, but the tribal and localized fervour attached to the game heightened my anxiety. I certainly wasn't afforded the opportunity to slip quietly back into the inter-county scene on the first week of January, when the public normally have minimal interest in the matches. This was full-on already. The delayed throw-in time exacerbated the stress. Was my comeback part of the attraction? Was this my reality now?

Mickey and 'Horse' Devlin came over to speak to me beforehand. They reassured me that everything would go well but, until you go through that experience, you never know what's facing you in that public arena. I didn't know how the crowd would react towards me, or how the Armagh players would respond to me being on the pitch beside them.

Initially, the reaction was very positive. We got a massive

reception when we arrived onto the pitch. If anything negative was said from the crowd, I didn't hear it. The Armagh players were dead-on. Those who shook my hand said they were glad to see me back. Nothing negative was said to me during the match. I was near the sideline at one stage and I heard a few really encouraging comments.

'Aboy McCarron, great to see you back.'

'We missed you last year, McCarron.'

I was cautious during the match. I didn't want to spark a reaction from anybody. When a bonfire of bad blood was lit ten minutes into the game, it all kicked off. A brawl erupted, but I went nowhere near it.

It was a combustive match. Nineteen cards were handed out, including four reds. It was like the old days again, when Armagh and Tyrone matches felt like the centre of the universe. It suited me just fine. People had plenty of stuff to be talking about other than me, or my return to Tyrone.

Playing that match was a completely liberating experience. I felt welcome again. Comfortable. At ease in such a public arena. I had taken another massive step, especially when this step was one I doubted I would ever make again. There was still a great distance to go, but the journey, the great adventure of life, had fully begun again.

CHAPTER 18

ECSTASY

Monday 11 July 2016

Before I went to bed last night, I checked my phone. I had a missed call from an unknown number. The caller had left a voicemail. 'Hi Cathal, this is Garda—, can you give me a call back tomorrow in the office anytime after 12pm?'

It was the lady Garda I had been liaising with over the case with the underage girl. As soon as I heard her voice, my heart started beating louder and faster. I didn't know what she wanted to speak to me about, whether it was good or bad news, or just an update on where the case was at this moment with the Director of Public Prosecutions Office.

A wee bit of panic set in. I tried to flick the switch and return to what I have taught myself to do in these situations – don't worry about anything you can't affect. I tried to put it out of my head. But I couldn't.

I didn't sleep great. The impending phone call was hanging over me all morning like an obscure fog. At 12.30pm, I inhaled deeply as I tapped the digits into my phone and rang the lady back.

'Hi Cathal, good news,' she said. 'The DPP have sent back the file. They didn't think there was any case to answer. There won't be any prosecution against you.'

As soon as I heard the words 'good news', all the stress and tension within my body drained out of it like a sieve. The relief was overpowering.

This whole episode has been constantly on my mind since that day I was questioned by the Gardaí. No matter how hard I tried to dislodge it, or shove it out of my consciousness, that fear was always there. If this had gone to court, I've absolutely no doubt that I would have been cleared, but the last thing I needed was another media storm.

It was a wild accusation to be facing anyway. Jesus, if I had some Judge Dredd character as a judge, and I'd somehow been found guilty, I was looking at jail.

I told the Gardaí the whole story from the moment they first made contact with me. They didn't think this would go to trial, but they still had to follow full procedure. The truth will win out most of the time, but you still don't know how these situations will roll.

I rang Niamh straightaway. She was delighted, but this whole incident has been such an awkward and painful recollection that there was no celebratory sense around the news. It is a hurtful memory for Niamh.

I was completely out of order. I made a huge mistake. It was almost unforgiveable, but now that I've been given a second chance, I don't intend to betray that trust or love again.

I rang Mickey Harte shortly after I spoke to Niamh. He was as delighted as I was. Harte has always stuck by me. He has consistently shown massive trust and faith in me, both as a person and as a footballer. And the timing couldn't be better now in trying to pay Mickey back.

I was sitting in the stand with our substitutes the day Donegal beat Tyrone in 2011. We should have wiped them out in the first half. The stats at half-time showed how we had created thirteen more scoring chances than Donegal, yet we were still only ahead by two points. We completely threw away that game. We created the Donegal monster; and it's been killing us ever since.

Back in 2011, Tyrone were aiming to win three Ulster titles in a row. We still had our sights set on another All-Ireland until the Jim McGuinness machine rolled into Clones and changed everything.

The Armagh–Tyrone domination of Ulster football which had stretched over thirteen years was over. A new team was about to bring another fierce and distinct aura to the soul of Ulster football. Sunday is Donegal's sixth successive Ulster final appearance. It's our first since 2010. They have beaten us now in four championship matches in the last five years. Our failure to overcome Donegal in that time has been one of the defining realities of the modern Harte era.

Our championship match in Ballybofey in May 2015 encapsulated everything about our rivalry. The match was played in an atmosphere of naked hostility and hatred.

Fourteen assorted cards, including two reds, were dished out. A brawl erupted at half-time. We thought we could take them in the second half but, ultimately, we couldn't.

Serial defeat to Donegal has been a black stain on Harte's modern legacy and it's one we are all desperate to remove now. We feel ready. We are confident. We're unbeaten in eighteen games. Some of those wins may have been in Mickey Mouse matches, but the only team to have beaten us in over twelve months is Kerry.

We know we are as good as Donegal, but we have to go out and prove it. We dedicate our lives to this cause, but the cause has never been more serious.

As a team, we feel that our time has come. It's time to slay the monster.

I'm just fed up of Donegal, full stop. Defeat heaped on top of defeat. Bad memory stacked up on top of more bad memories.

I sat on the bench in 2011 and 2012, not even getting a minute's game-time in any of those Donegal matches. I did play against them in 2013, but Donegal beat us by six points. Colm McFadden took me for a goal. We were shite. The weather was worse. Incessant rain never relented all day. We returned to Omagh afterwards and tried to numb the pain with a flood of drink.

I had parked my car beforehand in the private car park of the workplace of a friend. After coming out of a night-club around 2am, the rain was still pelting down hard. I was trying to ring Andrea to lift us, but I couldn't because my phone was dead. I had a phone charger in the car, so myself and Tiernan McCann went back there, for shelter as much as anything else.

I turned on the ignition to spark up the charger. I had no intention of driving. I wouldn't have been able to anyway, even if I wanted to. I turned on the heat in the car to clear the condensation from the window, but as Tierney and I were chatting, I was pressing my foot on the brake, which was intermittently causing the brake lights to flash.

About a few minutes later, there was a bang on the side window. I rolled the window down. Two policemen were standing outside in the torrential rain, the raindrops dripping off their hats like a fountain.

'What are you doing here?' one of them asked.

'What does it look like?' I replied. 'I'm sitting here out of the rain.'

'Do you own this vehicle?'

'I do yeah, but I'm not driving it. I'm waiting for my girl-friend to lift me.'

'Have you got your keys on you?'

'I do, yeah.'

'Well, then I'm going to have to breathalyse you.'

'For what? I'm not driving the car.'

I got pure thick with the two of them. 'For fuck's sake, I haven't been out for a drink in six months. I've just come back here to shelter from the rain. If I was driving the car, why would I be hanging around here? I'd have been gone twenty minutes ago.'

The cop was completely arrogant, but I was drunk and he knew what he was doing. He told me to get out of the car. I did the breathalyser test, which I obviously failed. I was told

I was being arrested for being in possession of car keys while drink-driving.

I went nuts. I refused to step into the police car. They tried to put me into the back seat, but they couldn't physically get me in the door. A couple more officers arrived, they handcuffed me and the four of them forced me into the back seat.

I was dicing with jail big time. As well as the drink-driving offence, I was also charged with resisting arrest and assaulting an officer. The case was thrown out, because I was on private property and the police had no right to be there.

I got lucky. I could have been locked up while Tyrone were making their way to an All-Ireland semi-final that season. In my own head, I was blaming Donegal for my actions, reasoning that the defeat earlier that day had triggered the reaction. Of course it hadn't.

But on weeks like this, you'll pull motivation from anywhere to take these boys down.

Sunday 17 July 2016

We all met in the car park off the Ballygawley roundabout at 9.30am. At 9.45, the bus departed for our base before the game, the Westenra Arms Hotel in the heart of Monaghan town.

With an early start of 2pm, the pre-match meal was a choice of a late breakfast or lunch. Our normal menu of pasta and bolognaise had been changed to pasta and chicken, which caused some unease for the guys who like to stringently adhere to routine. I don't know whether it was a mix-up with the hotel or what, but the food was still top class.

After everyone had eaten, we all went to a private room and said the rosary. We had already been to Mass together in Garvaghey the previous evening, but saying Our Lady's prayer has become a special ritual for the squad before all games this summer.

Mickey Harte told us a personal story before we played Derry. A woman came to visit him. She told him about a dream she had of the players saying the rosary. A few days later, a priest arrived at Mickey's door with thirty-six rosary beads, the exact same number as on our panel. Harte, who is an intensely holy and spiritual man, took it as a sign. After telling us about the sequence of events, he handed out the thirty-six rosary beads to every one of us. I keep them in my gear bag.

We've been saying the rosary since before the Derry match. We alternate the decades. Mickey leads the first, third and fifth. The players and backroom staff say the second and fourth, with just Mickey himself responding.

The atmosphere in that moment is always powerful. I usually sit up the front and belt out the verses. I'm almost a contradiction; like a priest one minute before turning into a headhunter two hours later. It isn't a show though, because the rosary has always been special to me since my time in Cuan Mhuire in Galway. I had to go to Mass every day. We said the rosary every evening at 6pm. Prayer did provide some solace during that darkness, but Our Lady has always been the one I have often turned to in my time of greatest need.

Despite the perception of Tyrone as a team with a black soul, most of our boys are religious. All of us go to Mass. Anyone who doesn't, we take our lead from Mickey anyway. If he thinks saying the rosary can win us an Ulster title, we will do it in a heartbeat.

We would all do anything for that man. Harte has had his critics in the last few years, but nobody in this group doubts his greatness for a second. He has driven on to try and build another All-Ireland winning team and that relentless pursuit has been even more inspirational to us, considering the trauma and heartbreak the man has endured in that time.

His beloved daughter Michaela was murdered on her honeymoon in Mauritius in 2011. Mickey's heart is still broken but, on a higher level, he still feels a special connection to his daughter. He believes that that's the work of God and the work of Michaela, because her faith was so strong that Michaela believed it was her purpose in life to work her way towards God.

Alongside her father, Michaela was as much a part of the great and modern Tyrone footballing odyssey as anybody else. She loved Tyrone as much as any other person from the county. We can only imagine how much her loss still pains Mickey. But we know how close Mickey feels to his daughter through his unwavering faith. We can almost feel that power of connection during the rosary.

After we had finished our prayers, Mickey gathered us around him. He began to speak, slowly but with great conviction. He told us it was our time now. The moment had come for us to turn the tide on Donegal. It wasn't so much what he said, it was more the emotion and feeling he put into it, that resonated so loudly with everyone. The room was charged with fervour, and loaded with raw emotion. It was the best speech I ever heard in my life. I was fighting back the tears.

In that moment, it felt like Mickey Harte had just won us the Ulster title. But now we had to go out and win it for him. And for the people of Tyrone.

In the fifty-seventh minute of the match, I had joined an attack on the Donegal 65-metre line. Odhrán Mac Niallais came in hard to tackle me, but I got by him and was suddenly in open territory. I gave the ball to Ronan McNabb, who played it in to Tiernan McCann. All the while, I had kept going up that outside channel. Tierney still had possession, but he roared at me to go and I went around the back of his man. As soon as I took the return pass, I fired Paddy McGrath out of my way. Suddenly, I was seven metres from goal.

I could hear this wild roar of anticipation from the Tyrone crowd. I knew the chance was on, but I still expected the Donegal swarm defence to arrive and gobble me up. I let fly with my left foot but I only snatched at the shot. The ball skewed off my left boot and went wide of the goal.

I collapsed to my knees. I put my hands over my head. 'Why the hell didn't I just fist it over the bar?'

I should have scored. I score goals the whole time in training. I backed myself, but I shot with the outside of my left foot. What was I thinking? It was the wrong decision, but you only have a millisecond to make up your mind. I wasn't used to being in that position in such a big match, but it was hard to stay focused. The heat was brutal. A claustrophobic game was getting tighter and tenser by the second.

By that stage, scores were like gold dust. I scored a point – my first in the championship – in the first half. Scoring my first goal now would have broken this game apart.

I normally don't find myself in those scoring positions, but I was so high up the field because of the role I was playing. I normally never stray too far from the D, primarily because I'm often detailed to man-mark the opposition's best scoring forward. The week before the game though, Mickey came to me with a different job brief, and Michael Murphy's name attached to it.

I was to follow Murphy wherever he went. I knew that would mean chasing him all over the field, but Harte felt that I could punish Murphy whenever we had the ball.

Anytime Monaghan have played Donegal in recent years, Vinny Corey has always been given that job of tagging Murphy. He has done well on him on occasions, but if you watched both games this year, the drawn and replayed Ulster semi-finals, it looked like Corey was so preoccupied with stopping Murphy that he just wasn't able to get involved in the play.

I felt I could stop Murphy and also get him on the back foot. Most of the time I went forward, he was nowhere near me. When he wasn't, I was still fit enough to get down the field and back into his orbit before the Donegal counter-attack got that far.

Myself and Murphy were at it from the start, the usual

stuff of belting and thumping and jawing away at each other. I was slagging him off about his weight. He was giving it to me back just as hard. When I scored the point, we were running back out the field together. 'Where were you, lad?' I asked him. 'You were nowhere to be seen.'

Murphy never opened his mouth to me again after that. In fairness to him, anything he said to me was the sort of harmless stuff that always goes on in matches.

Neil McGee and myself had a running commentary going between us throughout the match, but it was some craic. We were laughing away at each other through most of the dialogue.

I was running up the field at one stage. 'Aboy McCarron, I have you, now that you're in my territory,' said McGee.

'You have not got me, McGee,' I replied. 'And you won't either.'

'Have you got the job of picking up the big man [Murphy] today?'

'I have, aye.'

'You're a much better player than Justin McMahon anyway.'

Half the time I was within McGee's range, he was showering me with compliments. 'Aboy McCarron, you're flying it.'

At one stage, I said to myself, 'This boy is fucking nuts.'

I didn't know whether he was being serious, or if he was trying to fuck with my head, or if he was just nuts.

The McGees, Neil and Eamon, have this reputation for being wild trash-talkers. Maybe they are, but they have always been sound to me. When we played Donegal in Ballybofey in 2015, Eamon was spotted shouting at me at one stage on camera. Oisín McConville was in the BBC studio and he wondered if Eamon was sledging me, which, if he was, Oisín said was totally wrong, especially after what I had been through.

Eamon never said a bad word to me. He was actually asking me what stage of recovery I was on at that moment. He was being totally genuine too. Eamon even rang me afterwards to clarify the matter, in case other people had said that he was slobbering to me about my past.

The Donegal fellas are hardy boyos, which you'd always expect them to be, but they have never verbally abused me, or brought up my past in huge games against them in the last two years – with the exception of one of their forwards, which I fully expected to hear.

'Are you going to make any more porn movies?' he roared at me once.

I just laughed at him. The same player is a brilliant talent, a super player, but I think he needs to concentrate more on playing football than mouthing off. If he does, he can be one of the best players in the country.

I marked him last year. At the start of the match, I broke a ball away from him. 'Not today,' I said to him.

Maybe I shouldn't have said anything, especially when opposition players have enough ammunition to blow me to smithereens, and particularly when it was my first big, high-profile game since the porn incident. Still, it was just a reflex statement about my intentions for the day, but he placed the cartridges in his gun and unloaded both barrels.

'Go away and ride, Fergus,' he said to me.

I thought it might have been something just said to

me in the heat of the moment. I know now that it clearly wasn't.

I expect to hear that kind of stuff. To be honest, I've expected to hear far more than what has been said to me. I'd often have it levelled at me on a pitch that I'm gay, but that isn't even worth thinking about. I'm not gay and I know it.

There is no point explaining yourself to fellas on a football field. It's pointless. When my team-mates hear it, they always stand up for me, but it honestly doesn't bother me because I have steeled my mind to deal with whatever taunts come my way.

Before every game, I visualize the most destructive and vitriolic verbal abuse that could be aimed in my direction. It's so bad that nobody would even contemplate saying it but, if they do, I'm ready for it. If someone does taunt or sledge me, I just use it as motivation. Boys don't realize that it does them more harm than it does to me. It just fires me up even more.

When you do hear those unpleasant comments, at first it does jolt your senses, even though you thought you had shock-absorbed your mind from that intended destruction. Once you have dealt with that initial stream of invective though, it's never as distressing when the next wave arrives.

The worst verbal abuse I ever got was against Monaghan in the 2015 All-Ireland quarter-final. It was so sustained throughout the match that I must have been targeted.

'Keep away from me, McCarron. Go away and ride someone else.'

'If you need money, go off and do more porn.'

'You're only a gambling cunt, McCarron.'

'Get off the field, you gay fucker.'

They were Ulster champions, but it was our second time in three years beating them in an All-Ireland quarter-final in Croke Park. I took great satisfaction in reminding them. I just didn't get personal.

'I might have done what I did, but look at the scoreboard, boys. You're getting beat here. You're gone out of the All-Ireland.'

I lost all respect for some of the Monaghan players that day, but the most hurtful moment of all arrived when someone, who I thought was my friend, seemed to sink to that same level.

To me, Ryan Porter was a god. He was almost family. He had been with us in Dromore from the start of our journey. Ryan was a central figure in us becoming the force we were, and still are, in Tyrone. He coached the team to three senior championships and six senior leagues. Massive.

We knew very little about Ryan before he was brought into Dromore by Kevin 'Herbie' O'Brien. Herbie knew Ryan from playing football with Omagh. He was a decent player who was forced to give up the game at a young age after doing his cruciate knee ligament. Ryan was always into weights training. He went off and got his qualifications. Ryan was just like Peter Donnelly, our trainer with Tyrone now; young, hungry and ambitious. He always wanted to know more. He always wanted to be better.

Porter was an excellent trainer. The word was soon out about him everywhere around Tyrone. Ryan was clearly a central component in us winning all we did. Malachy O'Rourke, who lives in Tyrone, was well aware of Ryan's capabilities. When he took over Monaghan in the autumn of 2012, he recruited Ryan. Two Ulster titles in three years are testament to Ryan Porter's coaching.

I always had time for Ryan. We used to have some great chats. He was with us for so long, and had been through so much with our group that he was like one of us. Even his father became a staunch Dromore supporter and he still goes to Dromore games.

At one stage of that 2015 All-Ireland quarter-final, Ryan was on the field. I can't remember what he was doing there. I didn't think he had any business to be on the field and I challenged him:

'Ryan, get off the fucking field,' I said to him. 'What the hell are you doing out here anyway?'

His reply cut me in two. 'What's it to you, Fergus?'

I know I don't have the respect of a lot of people but, after all we had been through together, I thought I at least had the respect of Ryan Porter. Championship football is dog-eat-dog stuff but, even in the middle of a right battle, I still expected some form of loyalty from a friend. Obviously, I didn't get any.

I lost the head with Porter. 'I thought you were above that,' I said to him. 'You mean nothing to me any more. Go and fuck off out of my sight.'

It was obvious that there was serious agitation between us. I was really animated. Spittle was splattering from my lips. The crowd picked up on it. The Tyrone supporters would have been fully aware of the connection between me and Ryan.

It appeared as if he regretted the incident straightaway.

Five minutes later, Ryan was on the field when – as far as I knew – he had no reason to be near me. 'I crossed the line there,' he said.

I didn't entertain him for a second. I didn't accept his apology. Ryan knew exactly what he was doing. He tried to hurt me. He would have known more than any other member of that Monaghan set-up what I had been through, of how sick I had been to put myself in the position I did. Looking back, maybe I misread the situation, but I was hurt to the core.

Trying to come to terms with such a massive trauma in my life was a difficult process. I know it will always be used as a machete to cut me with, but that laceration goes far deeper, and the pain is much more acute, when someone you thought was your friend slashes you with a handful of words.

All the visualization I had done, to prepare for the worst, was tested to the limit that day. Porter didn't say a great deal, but he knew how much that comment would hurt me. It was like a member of my family delivering those words. I would have died for that man.

I know how this works. Boys will do absolutely anything to win. They'll look for an edge everywhere. I see it myself first-hand with Dromore and Tyrone, but I've always been more comfortable emptying a boy with a shoulder than with malicious words.

I talk on the pitch, of course I do. I mouth a fair bit, but I have never got personal. A lot of players, though, have no problem crossing that line. They have the same attitude towards verbal abuse that the modern Australian cricket team – who were definitely associated to sledging – had to the practice. The Australians merely saw sledging as a craft. They always disparaged the sledging debate too, reasoning that those who were unsettled lacked the necessary fortitude to succeed anyway. That's how many GAA players, and coaches and managers, view verbal abuse now; as a means to an end.

Tyrone are no angels, but the practice appears to be rampant in Ulster. I'm sure it is down south too, but the only really bad verbal abuse I got was from Ulster sides. I honestly thought I would have had to listen to far more, but I think part of the reason I haven't is because boys saw how low I was, and accepted that I must have been at my wits' end to do what I did.

I'm very appreciative that the vast majority of GAA players never said anything hurtful to me. Even when I got stuck into them during matches and they didn't shy away in responding, they kept the personal stuff out of the exchanges.

Of course there will always be people somewhere more than keen to bring it up, even within my own county. Once when we played Carrickmore, a couple of their subs were roaring abuse at me. I know there was another incident at a club game where a row almost broke out in the stand over something that was said about me. It is a sensitive subject, but that doesn't deter some people from having a go.

No matter what I do for the rest of my life, I will always be the GAA player who did male gay porn for cash to feed his gambling habit. Even saying it feels like an ordeal, never mind doing it. That crazy moment will always be part of my life. You can't just erase something that big with time. But I'm trying my best to ensure that it doesn't define me, or perpetuate the perception most people have of me.

On the bus journey into Clones before the match, as we made our way through the throngs climbing the big hill towards the ground, we passed the Hibernian Hotel in Fitzpatrick Square. For a few seconds, my mind wandered back to those glorious days in the early part of the last decade when Tyrone and Armagh ruled Ulster like high kings.

The Dromore crew always arranged to meet outside that hotel. Ulster final day in particular was like a communal gathering of Dromore people, everyone high on excitement and stoked by pride that one of our own – Ricey – was flying our flag on that hallowed turf. Now, Ronan McNabb, Niall Sludden and I had taken up that charge.

When we were young, those epic matches at St Tiernach's Park were burned into our consciousness. You wanted, and hoped so badly, that some day you might be out there. Those tight, taut, absorbing games, when the tension was so high it was almost asphyxiating, only seemed to heighten that desire to be there in the middle of it all.

Now, I was.

We looked in trouble when Donegal forged ahead by four points just after half-time. Donegal normally don't get beaten from that position, especially in Ulster finals, but we always believed we could win.

I thought about Dromore again. When we won our second championship in 2009, we were winning the game handy enough at half-time against Ardboe. Whatever happened to us in the second half, who knows, but we folded. Ardboe got on a roll and we couldn't stop their momentum. They led by two points in injury time. The game looked over, but we never believed it was. We had possession. I drove forward. Ricey and Seán O'Neill pushed up the field. O'Neill gave the ball into Kevin Donnelly, who was pulled down by the goalkeeper for a penalty. Collie McCullagh buried it in the bottom left corner and we won by one point.

By the fifty-third minute of this Ulster final we'd levelled the match at 0–8 each. As the sun beat down mercilessly, the tension was stifling. Neither team was backing down. Two incredibly proud sides kept coming at each other, blow for blow, point for point.

The endgame was on a knife-edge. Donegal went ahead with time almost up. Then Seán Cavanagh replied with a score for the ages, a ball kicked so high that it seemed headed for the heavens. The end result was like a gift from the gods.

We had momentum now, just when we needed it most. Peter Harte took responsibility and boomed the lead point from distance, the ball slicing through the dead heat like an arrow. Kieran McGeary then pushed us two ahead. There was no way back for Donegal.

At the final whistle, I headed for Mickey Harte. I hugged him. Among the din and chaos and explosion of Tyrone emotion, I whispered in his ear. 'That was for you, Mickey,' I said. 'Thank you so much for all you have done for me.'

We did do it for Mickey. The man has been through hell since Tyrone last won anything. When I spoke to Seán Cavanagh afterwards, he said that as soon as the ball left his boot for his last point, he was sure it was going nowhere. Seán thought he had ballooned it. The ball was hanging in the clouds for an age. I was thinking afterwards that maybe Michaela was pulling it over the crossbar with her outstretched arms from heaven.

Maybe she really was.

CHAPTER 19

EXPERIENCE

Friday 22 July 2016

I got a call from an inter-county footballer two weeks ago. He wanted to meet, as soon as I possibly could. I asked him if he could come to Dublin. We weren't training this evening so, at 5.15pm, just after I left work, I met him in a café in Santry.

The boy was struggling, big time. Gambling had taken over his life. He had lost a lot of money, but the manner of his gambling habits – betting thousands in a short period of time – was having a highly destructive impact on his life. He had lost his girlfriend. His job was on the line. God only knows where it was all going to end, if he didn't get help.

I regularly get those calls, either from people struggling with addiction, or family members affected by that strain. Lately, more and more people are contacting me with those concerns through Facebook. A few more have even emailed me, having got my address through Linkedin.

I try and make myself available to as many of those people as I can, but the volume of calls has rapidly increased in recent months. In March, a mother rang me about her fifteen-year-old son. She was in an awful state with worry. He was gambling so heavily that he cleaned out her credit card balance.

I can't help everybody, but I often wonder does society realize how big this problem is? Or how big it could become? Only recently, former All-Ireland winning Derry footballer Johnny McGurk was handed a thirty-month prison sentence for stealing to feed his gambling habit.

Before Antrim Crown Court, Johnny pleaded guilty to the theft of £572,206 from the firm he worked for, and 34 other charges involving fraud by abuse of his position of trust over a five-year period. McGurk admitted to placing single bets of up to £3,000 a time. He even emptied £38,000 from his joint account with his wife to spend on gambling. Judge Marrinan said the case had devastated Johnny's life and he accepted that he was shamed and remorseful. The judge said Johnny, without any other blot on his character, deserved credit for a guilty plea and his assistance to police. Passing sentence, the judge said McGurk admitted that the thrill of the wins was 'like playing football again'.

That is often at the heart of this problem. It was something Oisín McConville first spoke about in 2007. There was a time when winning big games with Armagh and Crossmaglen was never enough for Oisín. He always wanted more; another adrenaline rush, another experience where he could win or lose it all.

'You play out your footballing career on a stage, in front of 80,000 people at times,' wrote McConville in his book *The Gambler*. 'You can't stop to think for a second, but then the final whistle goes and everyone goes home. I, on the other hand, always wanted more excitement and more adrenaline.'

This addiction can grab a hold of anyone, but sports-people often seem more vulnerable than anyone else. In 2011, Offaly footballer Niall McNamee also went public about the gambling addiction that cost him an estimated €200,000 and left him with outstanding debts of around €80,000. Oisín and Niall were brave enough to highlight how dark this secret is. That pathway has been followed by a new stream of young GAA players also prepared to tell their stories and create greater awareness around an insidious disease that is devastating a section of society.

In May 2016, Galway hurler Davy Glennon spoke of how gambling took everything from him. He lost thousands of euros, but gambling ravaged him of far more than just money. Glennon lost his friends. He lost all respect for himself. 'Addiction takes over your life and I don't think it was me,' said Glennon. 'It ate me. It had me a totally different person. I was living two lives: the life that everybody wanted to see, and my own life. Addiction brings you down and changes you. I didn't care about anyone. I didn't care about myself.'

Glennon's own addiction forced his parents to seek counselling themselves. They attempted to stage an intervention when they organized a meeting with Oisín in Dublin, but

Glennon only agreed to see him as a token gesture. Glennon kept reconciling with himself that he could deal with the addiction. He couldn't.

It came to a head on the day of the Leinster hurling final against Kilkenny in July 2015. Glennon was substituted after twenty-seven minutes. He was in turmoil. Penniless, devoid of direction and hope, Glennon thought he had reached the point of no return. His parents had stayed in Dublin that evening to attend a concert. Home alone, he contemplated taking his own life.

A text from his younger teenage brother Ronan inadvertently stopped him. He was getting a lift home from Dublin from one of his cousins. Glennon didn't anticipate his brother's arrival. He hopped into his car and went looking for the quickest and easiest way out.

'I didn't know where I was driving to, but I was saying to myself that it was all over and I had to do something,' said Glennon. 'It was 11 o'clock at night when I got a text from him [his brother] to leave the door open because he would be home. It triggered with me then: "What are you doing?" So I turned on the road and went home. It took my head away from what I was doing. I couldn't do it. It got me around, but I was at breaking point all that week. How was I going to do it? What's the easiest way? I didn't want to hurt myself but just get out of town. I wasn't trying to kill myself, but I wanted to kill the life I was living.'

Davy broke down to his mother the following Thursday morning. He checked in to Cuan Mhuire that evening. Glennon got through it. Like Mickey Harte, Galway manager Micheál Donoghue called Glennon over the winter to invite him to return to the Galway panel. Step by step, Davy has built his life back together.

Other young GAA players have faced that same battle. Recently, Stevie O'Donnell from Tipperary Mid-West Radio broadcast an insightful but harrowing programme entitled 'Gambling Report' which aired on *Morning Call with Joe Pryce*.

Three young Tipperary men relayed their stories to O'Donnell: 2006 All-Ireland minor hurling winner Timmy Dalton, former county minor footballer Brian Glasheen and Tadhg Lonergan of Kilsheelan-Kilcash, gave distressing accounts of their addictions.

The sadness and sense of hopelessness in each of their stories was like listening to myself. At one stage, Glasheen feigned sickness so he could explain why he wasn't eating. He didn't have any money to buy food, so he would pick the mould off bread and live on toast and water for days. Glasheen admitted to stealing from his former employers to feed his habit, acquiring €97,000 worth of credit cards over a five-year spell. He knew he needed help when he wasn't able to purchase small treats for his infant daughter.

Dalton became heavily involved in gambling after he finished at minor level. Lonergan though, was laying bets in the hundreds of euros as early as thirteen at Tramore and Leopardstown racecourses. His situation escalated to the stage where he also considered taking his own life. 'I could go to bed and I could cry myself to sleep,' said Lonergan. 'I had the thoughts of suicide and "What good am I here? I'm no good to anyone." I had a letter written and I was on the way out.'

Every week I go to GA meetings, I hear the same recurring and harrowing stories from gambling addicts. You get the odd person who has identified that they are stumbling and are close to breaking point, but they are extremely rare. Most are only present because addiction has already broken them, and their world has fallen apart.

Something has to be done to try and deal with this disease that's spreading like wildfire. And I hope, in some small way, that I can assist in that firefight.

I knew if I was to come home to play with Tyrone and Dromore again that I had to get work. I wasn't making a cent in Athy, but I had a routine which was good for me. I had a purpose in life. If I went home and sat around on my arse, I knew that I could be back gambling again within six weeks.

The difficulty was, where was I going to get work? Who was going to employ me? Tyrone supporters were delighted to have me back as a footballer, but were they fully ready to associate with me in a daily environment? The vast majority of Tyrone people didn't want to touch me, or be seen to have anything to do with me.

My reputation as an employee had also been trashed long before I did gay porn, so my options were extremely limited. I didn't have any qualifications, which further curtailed the possibility of getting work. I needed somebody to help me out. Martin Sludden was the one person who stepped up.

Martin is a big Dromore man. He is a great friend of mine, but I think Martin's kindness was in some way connected to being able to relate to that feeling of public opprobrium, and the isolation often attached to it.

Martin refereed the 2010 Leinster football final when he allowed a hugely controversial Joe Sheridan goal in the dying seconds of injury time for Meath to stand. The decision denied Louth a first provincial title in fifty-three years and some of their supporters wanted retribution. He was attacked on the pitch afterwards, and two supporters were fined €1,000 for the assault.

Martin knew he had made a mistake and he admitted it afterwards, but he had to deal with the very difficult fallout. He was threatened. Hate mail regularly arrived at his door. His reputation as an inter-county referee never recovered. The whole saga had a huge effect on Martin's life. I think that's why he reached out to me.

He was a subcontractor for Sandvik in Ballygawley, one of the world's leading manufacturing facilities for mobile crushers and screens. I'll always be very grateful to Martin for giving me a chance. I started in January 2015, but it was the worst job I ever had in my life.

I would never shy away from work but there was very little real work to be done. The jobs, which mostly entailed lifting heavy parts onto pallets, arrived in sporadic bursts, so I was just hanging around for most of the day. I wanted to work. I didn't want to be idle, or look like being idle, so I actually spent more time hiding than working.

I was employed with seven foreigners, Lithuanian guys. I didn't bother with them. They didn't bother with me. They spoke their own language, I suspected that they were talking about me most of the time, and it used to drive me demented.

I knew I had to start somewhere again, but that job was

soul-destroying. I simply had to suck it up. I had to get people to trust me again, especially the Tyrone people. It was a tough time, but I just kept my head down. I was driving a wee shitty car. My career prospects were nil. I despised everything about the job, but I accepted that hardship as part of the process I had to endure on the path back to wider respectability.

Mentally, the job was breaking me. It was a dangerous environment for me to be in. I thought about jacking it in, which could have left me exposed and vulnerable to gambling again. There was no way I was returning to that life, so staying in the job may have suppressed that compulsion.

I wasn't in a good place. Old traits were coming back, especially anger. Eventually, I snapped.

One day in August 2015, an older man was moving pallets around on a forklift. We were waiting to unload the material, but it was a three-wheel forklift and the man was having difficulty manoeuvring it. He was slow and the Lithuanians started complaining about him.

The guy was in his late fifties and only on a three-month contract. He wasn't likely to get work again if he lost the job, but this Lithuanian boy mouthed off to his boss about having him fired.

I went nuts. I approached the boy with venom. 'Why did you do that? You're a cheeky bastard. You're in this country making a living. You're lucky to have work and you're trying to get a man from this country out of a job. I'd love to drive your teeth down your throat.'

'Is that a threat?' he asked.

'You're damn fucking right, it's a threat.'

I was hoping he'd make a move, because I was ready to smash him up. I knew if I did that I'd have a gang of Lithuanians all over me, but I was ready to take them all on.

The boy marched straight up to the HR manager and made a complaint against me. I was called up before her half an hour later. I didn't think I had any case to answer. I felt I was standing up for one of my co-workers, who was being treated poorly by another co-worker. Race or background had nothing to do with anything. 'If I had to do it again, I would,' I said. 'I've no regrets.'

What I learned in recovery is that if you do something and have no regrets about it, that's fine. I knew my reaction was probably going to cost me my job, but I didn't mind. I was looking for a way out. I had just taken it. I walked out the door and never went back.

I was really appreciative of what Martin had done for me, but, for my own sake, I needed to travel a different journey. I also needed to be closer to Niamh. I had been living at home in Tummery since January, but Niamh was still in Athy. She would come up, or I would go down, but there was no future in that arrangement.

I was debating about returning to Athy, to live there with Niamh. I told Mickey Harte of my plans. He was adamant that he would find me work, but I didn't want to be beholden to anybody. I didn't want someone to give me a job just because I was a Tyrone footballer. I wanted to earn it myself.

I started looking at job applications in Dublin. I had good sales experience. I always felt I was good at dealing with people, especially in business. I didn't have qualifications, but I had that worldliness that no amount of letters can give you. I sent around my CV, which was a big next step on the journey. Then, it was a matter of whether somebody would take a chance on me.

I got two interviews within the space of a week. One was for a sales job with a company who outsourced business for Vodafone. The second was for a business development position with Temple Recruitment.

The guy at the head of that first company was a big football man from Kerry. I know that he rang Oisín McConville to check me out. He also rang my previous employers, *Gaelic Life* and *The Dealer* for a reference. He told me that, despite all the harm I had caused in those jobs, they still spoke well of me. He offered me the job on the spot. I was thrilled.

I didn't need to go to the interview with Temple Recruitment two days later, but I decided to go along anyway. The owner-director, Geraldine Doherty, was an impressive woman. She wanted to bring in new business and she liked my attitude.

Geraldine is from Derry. I assume she knew about my background. I know her brother, Anthony, was definitely aware of my past, because he is a big football man. He spoke to me about it at our Christmas party last year.

I'm not sure if Geraldine even checked me out, or my history with my previous employers. She is a smart business woman. She wanted the best for her business. You are either cut out for sales or you're not. And I am.

Ten people applied for three positions and I was offered one of them. I knew recruitment was a growing industry. I felt it was the right fit for me. I accepted the offer. I started in September 2015 and I've been there ever since.

I love the job. It suits me. My brief is to try and bring in new business by winning new contracts. We cover a broad range but the company regularly goes after work from the big boys: Google, AIG, PayPal, PricewaterhouseCoopers, that kind of market.

There were times when I thought I would never work again in a proper job, that nobody in their right mind would ever hire me over what I had done. I wondered if moving abroad was the only possible way I would be employable again. During those dark days, I never expected to be operating in the business circles I am now.

I filled a position for a transport planner recently. He was a massive Dublin fan and he copped who I was. He was delighted, but most people don't have a clue who I am. Those who might know me, or who may be aware of my past, respect you for what you do now, not the crazy stuff you did in the past. They have a vastly different perception to the keyboard assassins who continually want to fire off rounds. Business people would almost respect you more for having overcome adversity, rather than focusing on the adversity which continually fascinates others.

Good salespeople are hard to come by. I know, because I'm always looking to recruit them.

When I was in Athy, Liam McLoughlin asked me if I ever thought about becoming a counsellor, if I had any interest in pursuing a qualification in that field. I had but I didn't think I had the capabilities to make that happen. I didn't even finish school, never mind go to college. I hadn't the confidence even to believe I could follow that path.

Liam never saw that as an issue. From my work in Athy, he knew what I was capable of. He felt I had huge potential as a counsellor, especially after what I had been through. Adversity had shaped me as a person. Overcoming it was now beginning to define me.

Liam told me about this PCI College course in Kilkenny in counselling and psychotherapy. The course is designed to be the first step to a career in counselling, as well as providing the opportunity to apply for a BSc Honours Degree in Counselling and Psychotherapy.

I approached the Gaelic Players Association, who have a funding facility in place through their Education Programme, and they fully supported me. The course ran for eight months and I loved every minute of it. For the first time in my life, I suddenly had a clear career goal.

When I started the course in October 2014, I was still living in Athy, which was no distance from Kilkenny. When I moved home to Dromore to play with Tyrone again, I took one day a week off work with Sandvik to drive to Kilkenny. Football and college kept me going during that time when the rest of my working week was basically just eating me alive.

Learning more about counselling helped me learn more about myself. The certificate course was still only scratching the surface on how much you could really learn, but I wanted to take my education as far as I could. In September 2015, I started the four-year degree course in Dublin.

It's not your normal college life of lectures and the good life. It's full-on, heavy stuff, real-life shit. Everybody works hard. A lot of our work is done in triads and dyads, between a counsellor, client and an observer, with each member of the group sharing simultaneous interaction.

Having somebody observe how you deal with a client is pressure in itself. Having so many groups working in one room increases the distractions. In one way, it's a totally unrealistic setting. In another, it's a real test of you as a counsellor, and an ideal way to train and prepare yourself for the difficulties of this job.

It's raw and edgy, but I've always felt really advanced in that field through my experiences from Cuan Mhuire, and the self-management work I continually did on myself before I stepped inside a college door.

There have been times when I've felt a wee bit bored, and wanted to kick on more, but I try and take the positives from everything now. I have never been a patient person, but having to sometimes sit through stuff, that I know inside out, is good for me just to learn some patience. As a counsellor, you're always looking at a weakness you might have, and to work on those little frailties. Lack of patience was an automatic weakness that I have been able, or tried, to improve on through a basic desire to see the potential in everything.

I'm finished first year now, but there is always more to be done. I still have twenty-five hours of counselling work to have completed before September 2016, to enable me to start meeting clients in second year. That is probably the toughest of the four years. Along with work, and college, and football, I will also have 100 clients to see over 100 hours. That will be a challenge in itself.

Most of those clients will come from addiction or treatment

centres, people with little or no money, who are referred onto trainee counsellors like us. It's a cheaper service, but the little money we receive is used to pay a supervisor for every five clients we see. Every counsellor has a supervisor, no matter how good they are.

I have accumulated a world of life's lessons, but I'm still only twenty-eight. I still have another world of learning to do. If I am going to take somebody on a journey, or help that person overcome a difficult journey, I have to live through it too. I have to be fit to take that person to the destination they need, or hope to arrive at. Already, I feel excited about that challenge. I feel confident about meeting that challenge too, from having been there myself.

When I worked in the drug unit in Athy, I wasn't qualified to speak to people on a one-on-one basis, because I wasn't a counsellor. Yet I spent so much of my day in their company that I was able to mentor them through that interaction.

I heard all sorts of stuff. Cuan Mhuire in Athy took in a lot of patients from Cloverhill Prison in Dublin. Some of those boys had murdered people; others were facing a long stretch behind bars for other desperate crimes. More were just trying to get clean, or get their sentences reduced.

When I was sick, the person I harmed most was myself. Some of those fellas I mentored were so high on drugs that they had to harm other people to make themselves feel better, to try and keep that high going, even to stay alive.

Their lives were blighted by a different form of gambling addiction to mine. Some of them owed drug dealers thousands of euros from drug debts. When they couldn't pay up, the drug dealers often extracted that money in a far more sinister manner. They were effectively hired thugs, sent to maim or disfigure fellas who the drug dealers wanted to sort out. If they didn't carry out that job, they'd be maimed themselves, or possibly killed.

The cycle of addiction, especially drug addiction, is often perpetuated through manipulation of people who are vulnerable. The general perception of drug addicts is one of disgust and abhorrence. They're labelled junkies and scumbags but, honestly, some of those people are the most genuine you could ever meet. You don't see that on the streets, because their minds are just distorted and warped from addiction.

I grew up in Dromore, a big football town. All we knew was football. I looked up to Ryan McMenamin: I wanted to be like him, to live the dream like he did. A lot of drug addicts in addiction centres were raised in parks in Cork, Limerick, Dublin, Belfast, or somewhere else. Their parents may have been heroin addicts. All they see are drugs. Everywhere. The drug dealers are driving around in big fancy cars, wearing nice clothes, living in big houses. Those guys are who the drug addicts aspire to be. It's the reason so many are doomed to a life of poverty and misery.

I've honestly been blessed to work with some great people in the drug rehab centre in Athy. I helped them, but they were helping me too. Out of everything I have done, working with those people has been the most rewarding experience of my life.

When I was gambling and wrecking my life at eighteen, everybody around Dromore knew I had a problem. Most thought it was a craze that I would grow out of. It wasn't. I didn't. I needed help. People always need help.

We accept now that gambling is a huge problem. If the issue isn't addressed properly now, it will become a pandemic in five to ten years' time. Comparing the rate of distress calls the GPA receive, gambling has overtaken depression. We can't keep kidding ourselves. We know the people in our own towns. We know what is going on. We can't ignore this problem any longer.

An elite footballer or hurler, or any sportsperson, can't really do damage to their body because they, or at least they should, treat it like a temple. Outside of a few drinks after the odd game, the only way many sportspeople can often get a buzz is through gambling. You can gamble anywhere, and young people now are at it everywhere.

I know of kids as young as thirteen and fourteen gambling on their phones during classes in school. What are those kids going to be like in five years' time if this issue isn't addressed now? Despite what they say, or what the PR people they hire get them to say, some betting companies don't give a fuck.

There is a clear contradiction in current Irish legislation relating to minors and betting, particularly when it comes to gambling on juvenile sports events. Under existing gambling laws, under-18s are prohibited from entering a bookmaker's, and yet adults are able to bet on a variety of matches involving minor players. As a result, despite not being able to place bets themselves, young players are nevertheless exposed to the influences of gambling at a young age, opening them up to pressures that could lead to problem gambling in the future.

At the end of 2015, the GAA's community and health

section, on behalf of the GAA, requested that the new Gambling Control Bill prohibit any bookmaker from opening a book on a sporting event involving juveniles. They also made the same submission to the Department for Communities in Northern Ireland, their social policy team.

Paddy Power and BoyleSports did recently make the decision to stop taking bets on any Under-18 or schools matches in Ireland. The response from bookmakers everywhere else, though, was totally predictable: if there is a demand for betting on under-age games, it is in the interests of the business to offer the product.

Anyone can become addicted to gambling, just like they can become addicted to alcohol, but studies show how young elite athletes are three times more likely to become addicted to gambling. Up to July 2016, over 100 players have contacted the GPA about a severe gambling addiction. Hundreds more players have accessed their critical counselling support. Through the GPA's player and rep network, it's clear that gambling and social gambling is now a cultural norm among GAA squads.

Over the last year, the GPA has been working on a project to try to advocate for change in how we prevent, address and treat this huge societal issue. Separately, the GPA are also seeking support to formalize a more robust lobby group to tackle the wider issues at play with government, gambling companies and the GAA. But addiction is an emotional-health issue anyway and needs to be approached as such.

It is easy to become addicted, especially by such saturation marketing. Believe me when I say this, people are targeted. When I was gambling thousands and thousands of pounds online, I'm sure people in that company were monitoring my gambling habits and behaviour. Gambling companies have some of the best analytics teams in the world. Why didn't somebody stop me then? They stopped me afterwards when I didn't have a red cent. They probably knew by then that I had nothing left.

The companies have some methods in place to deal with these issues, but they are only tokenistic. They are not really serious about controlling this problem, because it's not in their business interests to really address it. A contribution was made to the National Gambling Helpline but it was only peanuts. They'd make it back in one decent bet.

I don't think there is nearly enough money put back into recovery, and helping people to recover after the addiction has destroyed their lives. Nobody was there to help me. That's fair enough. I didn't want help. I only wanted to bet, and to make money. The betting companies are there to exploit that market, but they should have trained people on site to read the signs of a compulsive gambler. If those signs are obvious, that person should be refused a bet. If you put me in a bookie's office for one day, I guarantee you I could draw up a list of compulsive gamblers from just observing. With trends and patterns online, are you telling me that they can't tell when someone is a compulsive gambler?

Most of these guys who run these places are ruthless bastards. They treat the big gamblers like royalty, wining and dining them and keeping them sweet so they can try and win all that money back. As for the guys like me at the other end of the scale, they just swallow you up and spit you right back out.

I'm not saying this out of hatred for bookies. I can walk past a betting office now and it doesn't bother me. But I have seen what they can do, and what they continue to do. It was my addiction. It was my choice, but they will take everything from you, allow your addiction to destroy you, and then fuck you on the side of the road like a dead dog.

I'm not going to take on the whole world, but I have sat down with the GPA and thought of the best ways of trying to get our message across. Most of my ideas can be distilled into two forms: a public advertising campaign, with real-life traumatic stories, for maximum effect; and heavily targeting the schools, as far down as kids just about to leave primary schools. We cannot take a chance by assuming those kids have not already been impacted by the blanket marketing coverage attached to gambling.

Oisín McConville and Niall McNamee have led the charge on this issue. They have done, and continue to do, great work in schools. But how much can those crusaders really do? How far can their message really stretch? They need support to get help to the young people who may already be on the road to suffering like we did.

There is always someone who wants to talk, who needs to talk. In March, I spoke with an inter-county player just out of recovery. He told me that when he saw me spiral out of control in 2014, he swore to himself that gambling wouldn't take him down like it chopped me down. Well it did.

A gambler will always think differently. Until the shit really hits the fan, you won't admit you have a problem. By then, it's often too late.

Creating greater awareness around this problem should

also create awareness about mental health, about seeking help. There is a sad mentality in this country towards that resource. The natural inclination is to think, and believe, there has to be something wrong with you to have to see a counsellor. If someone thinks they could be heading down a dark road, or if they are already on that path, talking to someone with experience of dealing with those matters is the realistic next step. It should be the natural next step.

If you're sick, you go to a doctor. If you think your mind is not well, why would you not treat the most important part of your body?

A counsellor doesn't cure you. You cure yourself. A counsellor just guides you through that process. A psychotherapist may delve deeper by excavating into your childhood, but you are still the person who does all the work to get yourself better.

In time, I hope to have my own counselling practice. To help those affected by addiction, alcoholism, depression, or whatever troubles stalk their daily lives. I think I can, primarily because I have been there myself.

When I was getting counselling, I often turned on my counsellor. 'What the fuck would you know about my problems? You've never gone through what I have. How can you tell me what to do?'

Even if you are in a bad space, and are not willing to help yourself, you're still more likely to talk to someone who has been through that ordeal.

You may respect that person more.

CHAPTER 20

AGONY

'GAY PORN STAR ON PUBLIC ORDER RAP'
Irish Daily Star, *26 July 2016*

As soon as I arrived on the steps of Dublin District Court, there were two photographers waiting for me. Their presence wasn't a shock. In all honesty, I was expecting them to be there. At least I looked sharp. I had come from work, so I was wearing a grey suit and a white shirt which I had ironed that morning. I didn't bother with a tie.

I was up for the incident which occurred back in May. It was my second court hearing on the charge, having already appeared in early June, the week before the drawn Cavan match.

The allegation was of engaging in threatening and abusive behaviour at Anglesea Street ten weeks ago. When the case was called, the court Garda sergeant told the judge she was instructed that it was possible there would be another charge, in addition to public order, which would have to be clarified. Judge Walsh said the matter could be dealt with at my next court hearing.

I thought I'd be out the door and in the clear, but now I've been remanded on continuing bail to appear before the judge again sometime in October. More photographers will probably be waiting for me again on that day. Here I am again, court proceddings hanging over me like a black cloud.

Diary of a week of a big championship game
Tuesday 2 August 2016

Finish work at 5pm and turn the car north. The routine and the route is familiar by now; onto the M50, up the M1 towards Drogheda, through the toll bridge, turn off at junction 14 for Ardee and Derry, up through Carrickmacross, Castleblayney, into Monaghan, through the border and past Aughnacloy, into Ballygawley and onto Garvaghey.

The journey normally takes just over two hours. I always stop for coffee and a sandwich in the Applegreen Service Station just off the M1. The odd time, just to break up the monotony, I'll refuel my body and stretch my legs at a shop and petrol station outside Monaghan town.

The road is long, especially after a day's work, but the time on my own gives me my own space. It allows me time to think. Once training begins, everything is hectic again.

I'm back on the road to Dublin, where I moved in 2015, just before ten. I ring Niamh. I stop for diesel and more coffee. I won't be home until midnight. I'm tired, but the buzz from the training session is still coursing through my body. The boys were fizzing tonight.

We are primed for Saturday.

Wednesday 3 August 2016

Jim Breen is the founder and CEO of PulseLearning, one of the world's leading e-learning companies. After taking part in *The Secret Millionaire* television programme on RTÉ in 2012, Jim realized he had been battling with depression for most of his life.

The huge reaction to his public admission inspired Jim to set up 'Cycle Against Suicide', an initiative aimed at raising awareness of the considerable help and support that are available for anyone battling depression, self-harm, at risk of suicide, or those bereaved by suicide.

I met Jim last year at a talk in Crossmaglen. I cycled 50 km of the 250-km route before stopping off in the south Armagh town, where I was one of a number of speakers. Jim had asked me to speak but he conducted a Q&A session with me. I just shared my experiences, of how close I was to not being on this earth any more.

I have kept in touch with Jim ever since. He asked me recently to be an ambassador for the 'Cycle Against Suicide' campaign. I was delighted to put my name to such a worthy and important project.

Over 10,000 people have already taken part in the event over the last three years. This year's cycle is taking place next month and Jim asked me to travel across to RTÉ this morning to help launch the event. I was just one of a number of ambassadors more than keen to lend their support.

Back to work afterwards. And then up the road again to Garvaghey for training this evening.

Thursday 4 August 2016

After work, I went shopping. I needed a couple of new suits so I went down to Best Menswear in the Dundrum shopping centre. When I got home, Niamh had dinner on the table.

I felt wrecked today, probably from training sessions on successive days, and all the mileage clocked with it, both on the field and on the road. I was in bed with Niamh by 8.45pm. We flicked on the laptop and watched a movie.

We normally take turns in selecting what to watch. It was Niamh's turn tonight, so she wanted to see this chick flick called *The Choice*. Based on Nicholas Sparks' 2007 novel of the same name about two neighbours who fall in love at their first meeting, I was expecting it to be a load of shite. It actually wasn't that bad.

Friday 5 August 2016

The beauty about Dublin is that you can just silently melt into the blur and haze of city life. I often go for lunch here in this little coffee shop in the Northwood Business Campus. Nobody knows me. Nobody ever comes near me. Nobody ever wants to talk football, that's for sure.

If they did, I'd have no problem discussing it, even the day before an All-Ireland quarter-final. I'm fully ready. I'm not even nervous. I've barely even thought about the match in the last twenty-four hours. I know what I have to do. And I'll do it when the time comes.

I'm ready. The team are ready. Mayo struggled to beat Westmeath last weekend. Westmeath had two sweepers in the first half, but their defence still allowed Jason Doherty to walk the ball into the net.

Our defence will be vastly different to anything Mayo have faced yet this year. We don't play in straight lines. We are set up in diamonds. Every single man knows exactly what he is doing, what he is supposed to be doing. We spend countless hours on this stuff, on getting our defensive structure right. I see some of these other teams putting men behind the ball and they haven't a clue what they are doing.

Mayo are a good side. They have huge experience. They will be up for it, but I just believe that we are a better team, that we have better players. If you compare the teams man-for-man, I think we are better equipped to win the match.

We have been dying to get into Croke Park, and its vast prairies of space, all summer. If we get our running game going, we'll be hard to stop. Especially if Mattie Donnelly, Peter Harte and Tiernan McCann take off.

We owe Mayo too for the 2013 All-Ireland semi-final defeat. Peter Harte was buried that day by a perfectly timed shoulder from Tom Cunniffe after only eight minutes. It ended his match but Peter was only a cub back then. The distance Peter and the team have travelled in the meantime reflects how much stronger he and we now are.

I can't wait for it. I feel great. Super-confident. No disrespect to Tipperary, but this is effectively an All-Ireland
semi-final too. The stakes are huge. The prize is massive
tomorrow, but we are primed to grab it.

The boys will be leaving Tyrone shortly because we are
staying in Carton House this evening. Once I finish work,
I'll get my hair cut and head out to meet them.

It's warm today. It's promised warmer tomorrow. I'm
heading over to the pharmacy now to get some Dioralyte
sachets. To be well hydrated, I need to load myself up
with rehydration salts, sugar, glucose and electrolytes.
Especially with the amount of running we plan on doing
tomorrow.

Saturday 6 August 2016
All-Ireland Quarter-Final
Croke Park

Half-time
Tyrone 0–7
Mayo 0–7

I was raging. I took the floor and vented my anger.

'Boys, what the fuck is going on here? Lads are playing
with fear. There's something not right when me and Colm
Cavanagh are going up the field trying to get attacks going.
Are boys hiding here or what? Are you scared? What the fuck
is going on?'

Colm Cavanagh expanded on my core point. 'He's

right, boys,' he said. 'It's a sad state of affairs when me and McCarron are the guys initiating attacks.'

I was spending nearly as much time in the Mayo half of the field as I was in our own. I have no problem getting forward, but that's not my job. I was looking for lads to run off my shoulder, for players to give me better options. Nobody was making those runs. Apart from Niall Sludden, and Mattie Donnelly in the second quarter, nobody was taking the game to Mayo.

Mickey Harte approached me. I knew he would. I was on a yellow card. 'Look Cathal,' he said, 'we can't risk you getting another yellow card here. So we're taking you out of the full-back line.'

I was told to push out into our pack, where I wasn't tied to any one player. Bar our full-back line, nobody else really marks anyone, unless they have been detailed for a specific man-marking role. That suits me fine, but I was annoyed with myself because I felt I could be more effective if I was still tagging Cillian O'Connor. But the yellow card fucked all that up.

I was even more pissed off with the manner of how I picked up the card. Aidan O'Shea was trying to buy himself that second of separation, to steal a yard on me before the ball was kicked in, so he pushed me in the back. I felt it should have been a free out. I lost the head with the umpire.

'Did you see that, umpire? Did you not see him pushing me in the back there?'

The umpire told the referee what I said and David Gough doled out the yellow card.

He was probably right, but I really wonder about referees sometimes. I always thought Gough was a decent referee, but I got my fill of him during the match. I was trying to speak to him. I was trying to speak to him politely.

Myself and big Aidan were at it the whole time we were marking each other: belting, thumping, mouthing away at each other, harmless chat. O'Shea didn't score off me. We had a right battle but I felt I was wronged – genuinely – on a couple of occasions.

'David, all I'm looking for here is a bit of fair play,' I said to him at one stage late in the first half.

'Cathal, you're on a yellow card now,' he said back. 'I don't want to hear any more of it.'

The Mayo boys never said anything nasty to me. I shouldn't have said anything to the umpire. I hold my hands up, but getting a yellow card for that offence is a joke when compared with some of the shit that's routinely said on a football pitch. Some players can lacerate you with vile, personal abuse – within earshot of the referee – and nothing is ever done about it.

What's the difference between using aggressive language towards an umpire, and directing vitriolic verbal abuse at a player? To me, there is a significant difference. Yet from my experience, there appears to be little or no distinction in the eyes of a referee.

According to the rulebook, verbal abuse to an opponent or team-mate is a black card. Why is nobody ever sent to the line for that offence? Unlike some sports, it's more difficult for GAA referees to police verbal abuse, because they roam all over the field while players are left alone with their men, free to engage in nasty and hurtful exchanges if they so wish. But are you telling me that referees don't hear some of the stuff that is said? Of course they do.

When we played an Ulster side in the league in March, there was some desperate personal shit said to me, about my past. Really nasty, personal and hurtful abuse. The referee heard it. For God's sake, some people in the crowd even heard it.

I know someone who was talking to the referee in the car park after the game. He was getting into his car when they struck up a conversation.

'Jeez, that Cathal McCarron has to listen to some terrible stuff on the pitch,' the referee said.

'Well, why don't you do something about it?' the person asked.

'Nah, I wouldn't interfere in something like that.'

What the f . . .? Are there are any rules for referees? Are they not supposed to carry out their duties as set out in the rulebook? Are they not supposed to protect the players?

When we played Derry in the championship in May, I was verbally abused right in front of the referee at one stage.

'G'way McCarron and ride a man. Fuck off this pitch and do more porn.'

The referee may say he didn't hear it, but referees should know exactly what's going on. Especially when it comes to my situation. When has a player even been cautioned for saying something vicious to me? Never. Referees have heard what was said, but they have never taken any action. They haven't the balls.

I'm not looking for protection. I'm well able to look after myself. So are most footballers, but I'm hoping some day that a referee will send off a player in a big championship match – in any match – for verbal abuse. Everyone will wonder what he was doing. If the referee is going by the rulebook, he should just be doing his job.

All that might sound rich coming from a Tyrone player. We're portrayed as the masters of the dark arts, the ultimate team of sledgers. A crowd of thugs.

I can honestly say I have never said anything nasty or personal to a player on the pitch. I have never heard any of my Tyrone team-mates sink that low either. The boys on the team of the last decade were big into the verbals, goading and taunting. Some of those boys would have said anything, and done anything. This team wouldn't; it's not in our nature.

Most of these boys just want to play football. Nobody will walk over the top of us, but we laugh at how we are often portrayed. Against Mayo, we got in the faces of some of their players. Our actions were deemed unsportsmanlike and sinister. That is just our passion. If anyone doubts me, or thinks I'm lying, ask any of the Mayo players if anything nasty was said to any of them. I can guarantee you there wasn't.

People think we are continuously sledging. Is telling a boy to fuck off sledging? Sure, you could say that to your brother ten times a day and he wouldn't even think anything of it. He might even say it back to you ten times as often, if you were having a running argument.

I won't deny it's a part of Tyrone's footballing culture. But it is not in the DNA of most of these current Tyrone players to act in the manner in which we are collectively portrayed.

These boys come from good families. They've been brought up well. You'd be surprised how holy and religious some of them are. Of course we get up to stuff, but every team needs a few boys who will lay down the law. We are no different to Donegal, Kerry, Dublin, Mayo. None of those boys will allow another team to walk all over them. We won't either. We won't allow anyone to bully us.

We are no angels. I just think we are more smart than mean. If a boy is coming straight through on goal late on and we are two points ahead, of course I'm going to pull him down. I will do anything I can do to win a game. What's the point in playing Kerry and getting beaten in the greatest game of all time? That's what's wrong with a lot of southern teams. They're happy to play in great games of football and get beaten. We want to win. And we will do whatever it takes to win.

The reflex response is that there is no honour or respect or dignity in that attitude. That winning ugly and dirty is not really winning. That doesn't make any sense to me. For most teams that have won championships across all sports, right around the world, they understand that history only deals with the bottom line, and not detail or specifics. History only records who won, not how they won. The purists and connoisseurs might have a different perception of those champions, but those winners have the fulfilment that many other teams spend a lifetime silently longing for.

I won't deny that Tyrone have a bad name. When our Under-21s played Tipperary in the 2015 All-Ireland final, the Tipp management refused the Under-21s Tyrone manager access to their dressing room afterwards. Tipperary said they were deeply unhappy with Tyrone's 'cynical' tactics.

The word afterwards from Tipp was that Tyrone had allegedly sunk to new depths in terms of sledging; that they had researched the names of the girlfriends of some of the

Tipp players from their Facebook pages; that the Tipp players were shocked by how 'personal' Tyrone actually got.

The perception around Tyrone got even more poisonous a few weeks later after an Ulster minor championship match when a Tyrone player was accused of taunting his Donegal opponent over the death of his father. I can't confirm or deny that story.

I swear to God, I never heard that story about the Tipperary Under-21s until somebody from another county told it to me. Maybe it's true. But whatever the minors or Under-21s did, we didn't do it as a group of senior players. Whatever our predecessors did, whatever way they might have influenced the culture in Tyrone, you should be able to make up your own mind as a player about how you go about your business.

What's the worst thing I have ever said to an opponent? If someone starts on me, I'll give it back with interest, but never in a personal sense. If I'm getting the better of a guy, I might tell him that he is finished in that particular game, that they are already preparing a substitute.

'You're going off now, the board is about to go up with your number on it.' The boy would look over himself, because he would know it was probably about to happen.

What's the worst thing I ever heard any of our boys say? We played Mayo in the league in 2015. Big Justy McMahon won a ball and ripped through three Mayo boys. One of them hit him a slap. 'G'way, you're fouling now,' said Justy. 'Why didn't you foul last year against Kerry when you let them walk through you? You shit yourselves again. You always shit yourselves in big games.'

The Mayo boys may have thought of us as a crowd of filthy-mouthed thugs, but a lot worse is repeatedly said to us, especially in Ulster. The Ulster championship hones and informs that impulse to survive its guerrilla warfare. You become as cold and cynical as the opposition seeking to take you down. Being concerned by what people think of you, as you go about your task, isn't even an afterthought.

In football, you have to play with anger. We are hard. We are in your face. We play on the edge. We often take it to the edge, but we don't go around slobbering with runny mouths.

In all my time playing under Mickey Harte, he never once targeted a player in any way, never mind telling us to verbally abuse someone. Mickey is the holiest and most religious man I know. I don't think he would contradict himself by preaching practices that don't fit in with his faith. He wants us to play hard, clean football. If you get booked, he will invariably haul you off. If you're a liability in his eyes, you won't even get on the field.

Some of these ex-players turned TV pundits who keep hammering us must have collective amnesia. Have they forgotten some of the games they played in, and some of the stuff they got up to? Despite the perception, or how we appear on the pitch, we are no worse than any of the top teams. Do people honestly think Dublin, Kerry and Mayo don't practise the dark arts?

Anyway, with the way David Gough is refereeing this game, you can't look sideways because he is so strict.

*

I'm fucked with cramp. My calf muscles are tightening up like a vice, but I'm still running, still trying to make something happen in a game that we can't get control of. There are three minutes of normal time remaining in this match and we are still one point behind.

Our captain and leader Seán Cavanagh was sent off for a second yellow card in the fifty-eighth minute. We don't have him to try and bail us out like he did in the Ulster final. Being reduced to fourteen men is taking its toll too on a baking hot day, and against a team set up to take us on at our own game.

I was getting forward as often as I could. Peter Harte came across from the Hogan Stand side. A cordon of Mayo bodies was set up across the half-back line to block his path, so I made a run across Peter to try and pierce through the cover. His switch pass bought me some daylight and I had time and space to get off a shot.

I was about 40 metres from goal. I'd normally hit that shot with the outside of my boot, but I was moving and lined up on my right, and wrapping my foot around the ball was a safer option from that position. I got good contact, but as soon as the ball left my boot, I knew it was veering off-line. I watched it sail through the tense and dead air, just tailing off about a foot outside the post. I closed my eyes and raised my head towards the heavens. Fuck it. Would we get a better chance?

We did. Mayo were desperately trying to hold on. They weren't interested in pushing forward. They were guarding possession and trying to kill the clock like old hands should. In injury time, they strung a long sequence of passes together, but we eventually turned the ball over. We won a free, 55 metres from goal, but I was confident that our goalkeeper Niall Morgan, who had already missed two earlier frees, would nail it. I was standing right behind Niall when he struck the ball. I was tracking its trajectory and flight path all the way, but my heart began to sink as the ball veered off to the left.

We still didn't give it up. We turned the ball over again from the Mayo kickout. Darren McCurry swung his left boot from a difficult angle in front of the Cusack Stand, but the shot shaved the opposite post.

While the game is still alive, I always believe we will win; that we can win.

But I knew the endgame was approaching. We unleashed a barrage of shots on Mayo's chin, but we couldn't knock them over. They're still standing. We're stumbling. The final bell is looming. Seconds later, it rings.

Mayo 0–13
Tyrone 0–12

I lay down on the baking Croke Park sod. Rolling beads of salty sweat were dripping from my forehead and stinging my eyes. I put my hands over my head. I felt like crying.

One of the Mayo players came over and shook my hand. He said something encouraging. I didn't even see who it was. Shortly afterwards, Jonathan Monroe, one of our young subs, clasped my hand and hauled me up off the ground. I can't remember the words he spoke. I stood there motionless, my hands on my hips, staring into a vacant space. There were close to 82,000 people in the stadium by then. To me, the place felt empty.

Aidan O'Shea approached and wished me well. So did Andy Moran.

'Great to see you back, Cathal,' he said as he hugged me. 'Best of luck to you in the future.'

'Make sure you go and win it now,' I said to Andy. 'Make sure that you lift it this time.'

Mayo are a serious team. They deserve to win an All-Ireland. We knew they would be a huge challenge. I'm not sure if we were overconfident. At times, we played like we had that mindset, but I don't believe we were complacent. We played shite. And we still should have won.

As I trudged off the field, regrets were already coming at me in waves. How did we lose that game? What was wrong with us today? Why the fuck did I pick up that yellow card?

Cillian O'Connor did some serious damage to us. He kicked three points from play, a massive haul in a game this tight. I had no problem playing in the pack, but it was killing me that I couldn't tag O'Connor inside. Cillian got off one shot when I was marking him early in the game, but I got my fingertips to the ball and blocked it. O'Connor is a serious player, but I still felt I could have tied him up more, and reduced his influence, if I was left on him.

The walk in through the tunnel was torturous. The dressing room was horrendous; the worst I was ever in after a game. It is sinful to compare losing a football match with death, but it felt like death. Boys were in shock. Everyone had their heads down. Grown men were openly weeping. Fellas were in a bad, bad way. I've seen Seán Cavanagh after plenty of games, but I've never seen him as destroyed. It took a huge toll on the man.

The silence and sense of devastation was everywhere. We never once felt we were going to lose. Maybe that added to the sense of shock. It was our first defeat all year too. No disrespect to Tipperary, but it felt like losing two games, an All-Ireland quarter- and semi-final. A glorious chance to reach an All-Ireland final had slipped by. It's even more disappointing when you know how much more is in this team. It was a wasted opportunity. Wasted.

I got up and walked into the warm-up area. I sat up against the wall, my elbows resting on my thighs, my hands cupping my head. 'How did we lose that game?' I kept asking myself. 'How did we not win that game?'

Ronan McNabb was collapsed in a heap at the other side of the warm-up area; my clubmate, a lifelong friend and neighbour from the next field, the guy who I roomed with the previous night in Carton House. I got up. I walked over to Ronie. I caught him by the arm and pulled him up off the ground.

'Come on to fuck, lad,' I said to him. 'We will get back here again.'

Ronan and I learned in Dromore that hurt and pain makes you stronger. Better. More determined. More resolute. It drove us to another level in the club, because we used it like rocket fuel. Personally, I know full well how much gain can be accumulated from pain. If we can store this hurt we are feeling now, and unleash it the next time we're back in

Croke Park for an All-Ireland quarter-final, God help who-ever is lining up against us.

It's a long road back to this point, but I've no doubt we will get back here. And when we do, we won't fuck up like we just have.

CHAPTER 21

NIAMH

Wednesday 17 August 2016
Coombe Women & Infants University Hospital, Dublin

Niamh lay on the table. The doctor tucked some paper inside the top of her jeans before putting gel on Niamh's tummy and then moving this hand-held transducer device over her skin. After a couple of seconds, a black and white image appeared on the screen, a fluid picture forming through ultrasound waves. There it was, right in front of us – our little baby at twelve weeks.

The heartbeat was audible. The doctor was explaining to us in detail the anatomy of the baby from the haze and whirr on the screen: the skull, the heart, two arms, two legs, the baby's pelvis. Of how the baby's skeleton is currently made of cartilage before hardening into bone in the coming weeks. I was transfixed on the monitor, of the little life growing inside Niamh's tummy. A glorious projection of our future.

I was so happy. I couldn't stop smiling. The same excitement and happiness lit up Niamh's face too. I was holding her hand. I squeezed it a little tighter when I caught her eye. I winked at Niamh. The glint in her eye captured the beauty of the moment, the power of the experience.

I was sitting down watching TV at home a few weeks back when Niamh called me upstairs. She had just done a pregnancy test which turned out positive. She was pregnant. It's a big moment in anybody's life. I hugged my girlfriend tightly. I told Niamh that I loved her, that I would be there for her. We will do this right. We will give it our best shot.

I am so happy and excited about our future together. I can't say enough about Niamh, about how much she has supported me. We just hit it off from the first moment we met. She never judged me from what she had heard about my past. Niamh was strong enough to make up her own mind. We have had some difficult moments in our relationship, but I love her so much. I can't wait to start a family with her.

She is a beautiful girl. She has a beautiful heart and a beautiful soul. My family adore her too. We just fit. I've never really discussed this with her, but I think Niamh is proud of me. She understands the difficulties and setbacks I have faced and overcome in my life, of the person I have become, of the person I am still trying to become.

Niamh appreciates how addiction is a part of my being, of how it is hardwired into my DNA. She keeps me right. Niamh is my rock. It's hard for non-gamblers to understand a gambler's mindset, but Niamh gets it better than most people affected by that horrendous world of gambling addiction.

It's not just a disease. When you are in recovery, you are still rebuilding and reconstructing yourself as a person from the damage that gambling caused. Niamh is always watching me for my own good, monitoring my self-discipline. If I wasn't going to my GA meetings, she wouldn't be long letting me know about it.

Niamh appreciates how important it is for us that I remain well, that I can never get complacent towards this disease, and that I continue to treat my addiction with the seriousness it requires. She saw what gambling did to me in the past. Niamh appreciates the lethal damage it could potentially do to me, and us, in the future.

She has been deeply, deeply hurt in the past by the destructive side of my personality, but she has still believed enough in me, and in us, to know that we can have a wonderful future together, both as a couple, and now as a family.

She is so protective of me. If anyone says anything negative about me at a football game, Niamh won't take it lying down. You always hope that the girl you love will show you the loyalty and trust that forms the essence of that love, but Niamh has been very brave too. When so many people told her to ditch me, she didn't. She has always stood by me. I did really hurt her, but Niamh always knew I was a good person. She trusted her instincts and feelings when the easiest option would have been to run. She always believed in me even when I didn't believe enough in myself, when I didn't believe enough in us.

Niamh's family are delighted with the news. In a neat sense of symmetry, it is Niamh's birthday today. The news that the baby is healthy is the best present she could have wished for. We are going out with Niamh's family tomorrow night to celebrate.

It is a wonderful feeling to be planning the birth of your child. It feels so right. I am so happy. But if I'm being totally honest with myself right now, a part of my heart is also more broken than ever today.

When you study psychotherapy, it's not like a normal college course where you sit in a lecture hall and take down notes. It often feels like a GA meeting, where we gather around in a circle and talk stuff through. I may be wrong, but I think a lot of people who study psychotherapy are there for a reason: either something traumatic has happened to them or a family member, and they want to be better equipped to help people through that process in the future.

We share a lot in our group in college. In early May, I told the class of twenty that I had a daughter. A beautiful girl who I cannot see, who I have no access to. Out of respect for the privacy of my daughter and her mother, I won't refer to either of them by their names here, but when I told my group about my daughter I became very emotional. Tears welled up in my eyes. I think the group were shocked by how much the admission dismantled me, of how distressed I became.

My daughter will be eight in November 2016. I haven't seen her in four years. I cannot even remember the last time I saw her. I just can't. I have no recollection of that moment. The saddest thing of all is that she could walk past me in the street and I wouldn't recognize her.

She is the only grandchild in our family. It breaks Mummy's and Daddy's hearts that they can't see her. It is killing me too. But I accept that this predicament is largely of my own making.

I first started dating the mother of my child when I was eighteen. We went out for a year and a half. A few months after we broke up, she texted me one day to tell me that she was pregnant. We got back together, but it was a sham arrangement on my behalf. I panicked. I was scared. I wanted out.

She was a really good-looking girl, but I didn't love her. There wasn't enough of a spark there to keep the fire going. I wanted to be with other women. I just basically wanted to do what suited me.

She was keen for us to get a place together, but I refused. I didn't want commitment. We were a couple only in name. We weren't getting on together. Her town was an hour's distance from Dromore, so we would only see each other once or twice a week. I was gambling like hell. Tyrone were in the process of winning their third All-Ireland title so that was my only other focus along with gambling. I was just horrible to the girl. A complete fucking dickhead.

We broke up just before the 2008 All-Ireland final, a couple of months before my daughter was born. The break-up was inevitable, but the timing was down to pure selfishness. I didn't want a girlfriend with me at the All-Ireland final banquet. I knew there would be a team holiday later in the season. I wanted to be single for that trip too. This woman was carrying my child, but I was only thinking of myself.

Part of me didn't care. That is the truth. I was thinking like a child. 'It will be alright,' I would say to myself. 'I'll see my ex when I see her. I'll see the baby when it's born. I'll get it sorted then.'

It was a crazy rationale, but that's how my life was set up. That mindset governed everything, including big life decisions. I wasn't thinking like a normal person should. I didn't deal in consequences. I didn't understand the meaning of responsibility.

I was a complete coward. I couldn't face up to anything. I deflected everything. I ignored everything. I was making good money working at the time, but I wouldn't even dream of paying a bill. When those bills came through the door, I wouldn't even look at them. When a second letter came through the door, I'd fire it into the bin. I dismissed everything. I respected nothing. I had respect for no one. Especially the girl who was carrying my child.

'Everything will be alright,' was my mantra. Everything wasn't alright, everything wouldn't be okay, because I was a total fucking arsehole.

I wasn't there for my daughter's birth. I don't even know where I was, probably in some dark and drab corner of a betting office. My daughter's mother texted Eimheár later that day to relay the news to me and our family.

I was numb. Initially, the reality did hit me hard. My family were extremely disappointed in me, but I honestly can't say if the whole experience had any real impact because that's how I felt during most of those years – numb. I had feelings, but there was no substance to any of my emotions.

I didn't see my baby until about three weeks after she was born. Barry and I visited my new daughter in her mother's house. It was a special feeling to hold your own child for the first time. I wanted to be part of her life. Her mother and I worked out a plan for the future. I would pay child maintenance. I would have certain visiting rights. I had great intentions, but gambling wouldn't allow me to follow through on my promises or good intentions.

When my daughter was still only a baby, when her mother probably needed my assistance most, I wasn't there for her. Maintenance payments were only sporadic. Money I had set aside to help them was often spent on backing horses. Arrangements to visit my child were often cancelled at short notice to go gambling. There were times when I couldn't go to see my daughter because I didn't have enough money for diesel to get me out of Dromore. On other occasions, I deliberately didn't go because it was an excuse not to pay maintenance, and save that money for gambling.

I let my child down. I let her mother down. I didn't support her in the manly, or decent, way I should have. I was a selfish bastard, but none of those actions were borne out of conscious decisions. It's not an excuse, but gambling just fucks you up in the head; I could have £5,000 in my wallet and I'd starve myself. I wouldn't even pay £2 for a sandwich, because I'd be saving every penny for gambling. When addiction overpowers you to that extent, everything else – even your daughter's welfare – gets pushed away.

After I came out of recovery in Galway in 2010, I had a much bigger presence in my daughter's life, primarily because I was able to. I paid maintenance. I visited once a week, and at the weekend. After a while I was allowed to take my child to visit her grandparents in Dromore. I was never allowed to have her for a night, which was understandable. At least I had a consistent presence in my daughter's life.

The more I grew to love my girl though, the more I wanted to see her. I took her mother to court to try and gain greater access. The court date was a disaster. I was hanging around all day. I felt that no one was on my side. I didn't feel I was going to get anywhere. Maybe it was old paranoid traits kicking in, but I panicked again. I walked out the door before the case even came up.

My ex was a brilliant mother. She did a great job in raising our daughter on her own. Even when I was sober from gambling, there were times when I gave her reason to doubt me. There were weekends when I couldn't see my child because I was going away down the country for a league match with Tyrone. That often caused friction between me and her mother, but I think taking her to court – while it failed – also showed her how serious I was about being part of my daughter's life.

The door was opening a little. Before my child started Montessori school, I went with her mother to an initiation evening for parents.

My daughter always called me Cathal. It was how she knew me from how her mother and her grandparents talked to me. That used to sting me. I would have liked her to call me daddy. When her mother wasn't around, I used to tell my daughter to call me daddy.

She was too young to understand. I was more like a close friend who called to see her every so often, a nice person, who was even nicer again to her on her birthday. That wasn't enough for her to consider me her daddy. It was a name that meant nothing to her.

When I relapsed again, when gambling overpowered me again, my connection to my child became weaker. The visits became less frequent. So did the child-maintenance payments. As I descended into the depths of addiction, I became more powerless to maintain a relationship with my daughter. I was desperate, absolutely desperate to keep seeing her. And yet, the addiction wouldn't allow me to.

Promises were broken. Old scars reopened. I wouldn't turn up when I was supposed to. I wasn't mentally in the right place to be a father again. Even with the limited access I had to my daughter, I wasn't able to do what a father should in that position. That time I spent with my child was precious. And yet gambling wouldn't even grant me that much calm in an angry ocean of disorder – she just became part of the blur of chaos and anarchy that gambling dictated. I have tried so hard, so hard, to locate that last image, those last few precious minutes, which I spent with my daughter. And I can't. I just can't. I have zero recollection of those few months in 2013. That's how fucked up my mind was at that time.

I still have a precious picture of my child in my mind. Every father says that their daughter is a little princess, but she really was something special: a beautiful wee child, with lovely hair and a gorgeous smile.

I'd give anything to see her now: to see what she looks

like; to hear how she talks; to find out her interests, her hobbies. Just to talk to her would mean so much to me. It breaks my heart that I can't. But I hope I will.

Some day.

The last time I spoke to the mother of my child was when I was in London. I asked Daddy to make contact with her. I can't remember if she rang me, or if I rang her, but we spoke on the phone.

She told our daughter that I was working in London. I think she felt sorry for me at the time. She knew that I was on the run in London. She was civil and kind, and she was trying to ensure that I still maintained some contact with my child when she knew I couldn't possibly visit her because of the distance and circumstances. But once the porn story broke, it was as if I ceased to exist in her mind. She clearly didn't want to have anything to do with me any more.

I have tried so hard to contact her since then. I have called, texted, emailed, sent her a Facebook message, and never received a single reply. I tried to make contact again a few weeks back, with the same outcome. Daddy has spoken to her on occasions. She will take his call and chat away, but as soon as my name is mentioned, the conversation is effectively dead.

I can fully understand why the mother of my child would want to protect our daughter. After all the harm I did to myself, after all the shame and embarrassment I brought to my name, she wouldn't want her daughter near somebody capable of sinking into such an abyss of degradation.

She saw both sides of me: the gambling addict who caused

her so much pain and hurt; and the reformed addict who struggled but who still tried to do his best for his child. Yet I broke once before. Maybe I will break again. If I do crack, I could do something worse. Given that my daughter is at such an impressionable age now, her mother maybe doesn't want to take that chance.

I'm sure my ex-partner has seen me on the front pages of newspapers in the last six months for incidents that – taken at face value – would disturb the mother of any young girl. I can understand her concern. She was always a great mother. I'm sure she still is. Of course she wants to protect our daughter, but I just wish she would give me a chance to show how much I have changed, to see how much work I have done to make myself a better person.

When our baby was born, I wasn't fit to be a father. I hope when she gets older that she can somehow understand what gambling did to me, of how it impacted on my ability to be a stable presence in her life when she needed me most.

I was living in a fantasy world. I hadn't even made my name as a Tyrone footballer, but I was thinking that the game would set me up for life: a job, security, get me whatever I wanted. It's only looking back now that I realize how chaotic and destructive my life was. It was no place for a child.

When I am well, everybody around me is well. Even when I came out of recovery in Newry, I needed more time to get better. There was no point in me re-entering my daughter's life if I wasn't stable and consistent. I had to fully focus on myself to establish that base and that consistency. Now that I feel I have, I hope that the mother of my child will some-day appreciate how difficult that journey has been for me to try and make my way back into my daughter's life again.

If I wanted to see my daughter again, I could. I could just arrive unannounced at the door of her mother's house. But I would never do that. I wouldn't have the neck on me to do it. To be totally honest, I couldn't face it anyway.

It wouldn't be fair to my child. From a counselling perspective, I appreciate how traumatic something that big could be for a seven-year-old. I have no right to land back into her life on a whim. I have no right to demand to see her. If I am to see my daughter again, if I am to be a part of her life once more, I will do this in the correct way. I don't want to cause any trouble. I'm at the stage of my life that I just want peace.

I'm busier now than I have ever been before: work, football, college, doing my own counselling hours, going to GA meetings, helping people out as much as I can. A new baby is on the way. But having my child back in my life is as important as anything else.

My daughter will be making her First Holy Communion soon. I desperately want to be there for that moment. So do Mummy and Daddy. It's killing them as much as it is me, but they fully understand how delicate this subject is.

I'm not sure if the mother of my child has a boyfriend or partner now. If she does, maybe my daughter recognizes that person as her father. I have to accept that. I often wonder if she follows football. Does she shout for Tyrone? Does she shout for Cathal McCarron, not knowing that he is her real father?

My daughter deserves to know her father, but I appreciate how difficult it is for her mother to make her peace with me. I really hurt her. I treated her so badly. I can't take that back. I can't make up for lost time, but I'm doing so much to try and be that person that I wasn't capable of being when they both needed me the most. I hope she can find it in her heart to give me that chance.

Of all my regrets in life, losing my daughter is the biggest. I always said that if I had a child again, I would do everything in my power to be there for that child, to give that child the support that I couldn't provide to my firstborn.

I desperately want her back in my life. Niamh knows that too. She is always pushing me towards my daughter, to try and ensure that she becomes a huge part of my life again. And if that happens, Niamh will welcome her with open arms.

Our future is bright. It's a really exciting and happy time. On my journey, it's a massive step to be planning a new family. But my daughter will always be part of my family.

PEACE

'God grant me the serenity to accept the things I cannot change | Courage to change the things I can | And wisdom to know the difference.'

That first verse of Reinhold Niebuhr's 'Serenity Prayer' is inked into the bicep of my left arm; words set among the gallery of symbols of a Polynesian tattoo running from the top of my shoulder to ten inches above my wrist. Each image, each word, represents some of the struggles experienced throughout my life, but there are other reflections and images on my body which I also draw inspiration from.

Every drop of ink carries a deep and personal meaning. The twelve arrows represent the twelve weeks I spent in recovery; the fishes inside my forearm are a symbol of the peace of mind recovery has granted me; just below that circular detail is a line from the Bible: 'Let he without sin cast the first stone.' The Roman numerals at the bottom-front of my forearm translate to 1 April 2013, the second time I entered into recovery, and the first day of my new life away from gambling.

I had always wanted a tattoo. When I was in Athy, I found out about Lisa Mackey, a tattoo artist from the area. I contacted Lisa. I told her my reasons for wanting a tattoo, and the meaning I wanted it to have. Lisa made some suggestions and I set out my ideas around those concepts. She drew some patterns on my arm with a pen. Eventually we settled on a Polynesian tattoo design.

There are numerous titles and strands to a Polynesian tattoo, but we agreed on a spearhead design. In Polynesian culture, those arrowheads express courage and willpower; innate elements of my own character, and strengths which have helped me overcome the many difficult battles I have fought in my life.

The tattoo is so large, and so intricately designed, that it took five four-hour sittings to complete. It wasn't much fun. The needles move in an up-and-down motion, carefully puncturing the skin before pushing the ink just below its surface. Lisa was constantly wiping off traces of blood. Most people can take the pain for no more than two hours, but my pain threshold has always been high. Some parts of your inner arm, especially around your elbow, are extremely sensitive to pain, but I just sucked it up and got it done.

The ink that Lisa used has a high level of pigment, which makes it less susceptible to ageing and sun. But in time, the tattoo will have to be touched up with more ink, just to keep its design detail and appearance sharp and well defined.

That is a metaphor for my life now. I always have to keep working on myself; I can never hope that everything will stay the same as it is now; I can never get complacent. If I ever think that I have this addiction beaten, I probably will fall back into gambling again.

That's why I treat this disease with the utmost respect. It's why I have to be so much on my guard. It's similar to that feeling before a big football game: that fear, that nervousness, it keeps you on edge. It keeps me sharp.

Every compulsive gambler worries he will relapse. Of course it is a possibility, but I will do everything possible not to let that happen. I can't allow it to happen. I know if it does, it could be the end of me.

I have to be so vigilant. I have said it to Niamh so often: 'If you think there is anything wrong with me, even the slightest little chink, question me. If you think everything is not right, don't let me try and convince you that everything is.' More than likely, it won't be.

I'm sober from gambling for nearly three years now, but I honestly can't say I won't ever bet again. I still get urges to bet. That insatiable desire is so powerful it can consume you. Those cravings usually arrive when I'm doing nothing, when I'm bored, or if I'm sitting on my own watching sport on TV. Sport can be more exciting when you have a bet on. That impulse prods your subconscious, but before the craving can hit, I counteract the threat with a prayer to Our Lady. More often than not, I'll say the 'Memorare', to ask Our Lady for her intercession.

The compulsion will usually go again after about a minute, but that's how powerful this disease is. You can do everything possible to firewall your system, but the virus will still try everything to get past those defences. That is not just me. It's what every compulsive gambler has to fight every day of their lives.

Sometimes when I'm at GA meetings listening to what other people have been up to, those stories can flash like a red siren. 'If I relapse,' I think to myself, 'I could end up worse than that man.'

I would never go longer than one week without going to a GA meeting. If you go more than a week, you are pushing it. Sometimes, I might try and go to two GA meetings in seven days. You can't take any chances. I can never take any chances with anything. I don't do the Lotto. Even when boys come round to the house selling €1 club Lotto tickets, I don't buy them. I wouldn't even put a pound into one of those 'Lucky-Hook' machines you'd see at a fairground or an arcade. Something as simple as winning a teddy bear could be a trigger point to get me gambling again. There is no need for me to take that risk.

I'm confident that I won't crack, but it's never a certainty. The painful memory of where I went won't be enough to keep me away from gambling. What keeps me away is staying involved in recovery, remaining in that loop. The pain of the past will never keep you away. Even if you killed somebody, you would still return to gambling if you could.

My biggest fear in life is that I will relapse, that I will plunge back into the depths of gambling despair again. When I relapsed before, look what happened. If I relapse again, God only knows what I might do. I might do far worse than what I did in London. I could kill somebody. I could kill myself. It's not worth thinking about.

I don't think about what might happen in that future. I only think about now, of what I can control in this moment. And fighting this battle. Day after day after day.

God has granted me the serenity to accept that there are so many things in my life that I cannot change. Those dark moments will always be with me. That moment in London will always be a part of my life, but I think I have learned to accept that decision for what it was at that time. I won't say it was a mistake. It was a decision that gambling forced me into. Addiction drove me to those depths. Given the path I was on, who knows what I could have done?

If I can talk about that day in counselling now, I will. I have dealt with a lot of the traumatic issues associated with that moment with my counsellor. It's never a closed subject. It will always be there. Often, there are times when the gravity of what I did hits me in the face like a sledgehammer. When I think of hundreds of thousands of people watching me having sex with a man, I sometimes have to check myself: 'Did I really do that? Did I really sink to that level?' It's almost as if that whole incident happened in a parallel universe, involving some strange person.

I think that attitude and mindset frames the general perception everyone who doesn't know me seems to have of me. When I meet people, especially those aware of me through football, often I get the impression that they are expecting this dark and troubled soul, as if I must be some kind of mysterious and preternatural figure to do what I did.

My club manager Ciaran Meenagh mentioned that to me recently. He works in Derry and is continually bombarded with questions about me.

'What's that Cathal McCarron guy like to deal with?'

'Is he hard to handle?'

'What's his personality like?'

'Is he as crazy as he seems?'

From the outside, I can understand that perception, that fascination so many people seem to have with me. I realize why some may think, 'That man must be a fucking nutcase.' Others wouldn't be that kind. To debase myself in the manner that I did, I must be a sicko. Many others are still surprised that I'm playing inter-county football. I wouldn't be if Mickey Harte thought I was a nutjob. Yet for some football teams, it suits them to form that image of me, and to almost exploit it.

Because of the work I have done on myself, through my rehab and counselling, it honestly doesn't bother me how others perceive me now. I don't want to sound arrogant or cocky, but it really doesn't. There was a time when it did play on my mind. But not any more.

All I care about is what my family, Niamh, my friends, and those close to me think of me. I know I'm doing my best. I don't always get it right, but I'm trying. If some people want to continually associate me with the trouble, strife and mayhem of my past, that's fine. Most of them don't know the road I have travelled for a 28-year-old. Most men would never see it in a lifetime.

What I did will always be part of my life. You can't erase it that easily. But what I have done, and what I plan to do in the future, I hope will overshadow those mistakes, and dilute their negative legacy as time goes by. I hope that people will remember me for being a good footballer, a guy who had his troubles but who has come through them.

It's still a struggle. It will be a struggle for a while yet. In the time that I have been sober from gambling in the last two and a half years, I have made big mistakes. I have brought shame on myself, and my name, again and again.

Just because I'm not gambling, that doesn't mean I won't do something crazy again. I've no doubt I will make more stupid decisions, but I also feel that I'm still adjusting to a level of normality in my life. For a long time, my normality was a blur of chaos and dysfunction.

I have character defects. I always will. I think they have more or less been assimilated into my character now, ingrained in my mentality. It's like treating addiction. You can work on it, suppress it, but it will always be there.

Many of those explosive tendencies, those volatile idiosyncrasies, are connected to my personality. I'm fiery. I can get angry. I'm outspoken at times. I'm passionate. When I do go off the rails, everything becomes reconnected to my past, like the recurring porn headlines. I just have to keep working hard on controlling that part of my personality.

I'm an addict. I'm still in recovery. That's not an excuse for any of the errors or miscalculations I have made since I have been in recovery. But addiction comes at you in many ways; it attacks in so many insidious forms and guises. When I went on Tinder looking to meet women last year, I knew it was wrong. I knew it was being callous and disloyal to the girl I loved. But the gamble, the thrill of the risk, was the attraction. It took getting caught to jolt my senses again, to make me realize how crazy I was. Pressing that self-destruct button made me appreciate how lucky I was to have Niamh.

It also made me realize how much I have to keep working on myself, and those character defects, all of the time. Anything which I think is a weakness now, I try to strengthen, like a cracked beam on a roof that needs reinforcement. Because I can't afford, or allow, the roof to cave in.

'Am I sorry for what I did?

'Well ... are you? [Parole board officer]

'Not a day goes by I don't feel regret, and not because I'm in here or because you think I should. I look back on myself the way I was ... stupid kid who did that terrible crime ... wish I could talk sense to him. Tell him how things are. But I can't. That kid's long gone, this old man is all that's left, and I have to live with that.'

Ellis Boyd 'Red' Redding,
The Shawshank Redemption (1994)

I often think of the words Pat McGinn said to me the first time I met him in Newry. 'Cathal, did you kill anybody?' Pat asked.

'No.'

'Well, it's alright then. This can be fixed.'

I often use Pat's quote now. When I am talking to somebody who is in the depths of despair like I once was, I ask them that same question Pat once posed to me. And then I provide the answer. 'Well, this can be fixed so.'

At the time, it's easy to think that your world is about to end, that there is no future in this life for you. There is. If you are in trouble, the suffering can cease if you seek, and get, the proper help in recovery.

When I was in Cuan Mhuire in Galway, so many people there told me how lucky I was, how I was still only twenty-one, how I had my whole life ahead of me. Some of those people were in their fifties. A few had destroyed the best years of their lives from alcohol. They had ruined the lives of their families. Recovery set them on a new path. They still had plenty of good living to do, but decades of regrets can't be easy to shift.

I have lots of regrets, deep sorrowful regrets. I wish I could take back some of the hurt and distress I caused. There are times when I wish I could go back now and talk to myself as a young kid, talk some sense into him, just like Red wished he could.

Yet I didn't kill anyone, like Red did. I'm not an old man, like he was. And if I could go back in time, what would I say to myself? That young fella of ten or eleven, who was trying to stop his parents from fighting, who was confused and upset: what could I really tell that little boy?

I have caused a lot of harm to a lot of people, none more than myself. Being in recovery can't just wash those regrets away, but I think I can help a lot more people now from the road I have travelled. It would be nice to be able to make some positive impact on people's lives now from sharing those experiences. If doing some desperate damage to myself enables me to make a difference now, I can more than live with that pain and regret.

Those experiences have also granted me a different perspective on life. When I was younger, I was never a big family man. Maybe that stemmed from childhood and the hurt and pain I often associated with that time. Yet my family is my number one priority now. I don't take anything for granted any more.

I don't know what the future holds for me. I will play football for as long as I can. I need football in my life, both for recovery and normality. I had a solid season. I won an *Irish News* Ulster All-Star. I'll probably be nominated for a GAA All-Star. I will be trying my best to win another All-Ireland. Whether it happens or not, it won't define me. I don't want it to define me as a person.

I hope to have a good life. I want to have a good professional career, whether that is in recruitment, or having my own counselling practice some day. Pursuing that path is something I aspire to, but becoming so involved in counselling is as much to help me as anybody else. It keeps me right. It keeps me in the loop.

Most of all though, I just want to live a normal life.

Already, I'm enjoying that experience. I get a buzz now from something as regular as paying bills. That just feeds into my sense of responsibility as an adult. It feels so good to have a good credit rating, to be able to trust yourself to do the right thing with money. Especially when money meant so little to me for so much of my life, when it represented the very symbol of my self-destruction.

When you are an addict in recovery, it takes a lot to pull yourself together again, to become proud of yourself again. I want to be proud of myself. I want to make Niamh and my family proud of me, for far more than what I do on a football field.

The other day, I got a letter from the football player I spoke to in July, the guy I met in Santry. I sat in the car before I went to work and read his words. He was in Cuan Mhuire in Galway. It's a difficult time. He is struggling but he is getting there. He thanked me for my time, and for my advice. 'I'll never forget it,' he wrote.

To me, that is recovery. That is why I got well. And why I am trying so hard to stay well.

I was walking down Grafton Street in Dublin last week when I passed this homeless guy. He looked to be in a really bad way. He was wrapped up in a blanket. He was cradling a wee dog. I never carry money any more, purely to reduce the risk of having money to gamble, but I had some change in my pocket. There was no point giving it to him. He probably would have drunk it. So I went into a shop, bought a coffee and a Mars bar, and gave it to the homeless guy.

He couldn't thank me enough. It wasn't much, but at least the coffee and chocolate would give him energy for a few more hours anyway. The few minutes' chat we had together probably meant more to him. It showed the poor fella that, however fleeting it was, at least somebody cared.

The death rate from homelessness in Dublin is shocking. Who's to say that that boy isn't dead now? If he is, at least I tried to make some tiny positive impact on his life while he was in this world.

I could have been that homeless guy. To be honest, I'd have been even lucky to be that guy. I'd probably have been dead. If I kept going the way I was, I would have taken my own life.

All that stopped me that day in London was the knowledge that people were reaching out to me; that they were trying to help me. If I didn't have Mummy and Daddy and Barry, Paul Coggins, my sister, my friends, I would have killed myself.

I was so close to jumping in front of that train. I don't think I could have gone any closer to doing it. I remember moving my body forward, imagining the act in my head, motioning myself forward to get it over and done with. I wanted the pain to go away. I wanted to be free of this gambling disease, and all the agony it caused me. I just wanted to close my eyes. And never have to open them again.

I kept looking at my phone. I saw all the missed calls, the texts dropping into my inbox. I was thinking of my family, and how they would feel if I did what I was there to do. In the middle of that train of thought, Barry rang again. I turned around and walked out the door.

That call provided that little shard of light. It gave me some hope. Those people who can't even see a tiny pinprick of light in the distance are the unfortunate ones who take their own lives.

Through my counselling, I understand the circumstances and mindset around suicide even more. Addiction brought me to the edge of that cliff, to the edge of that platform. But at least I had that insight and rationality that people who suffer from depression cannot summon. They can see absolutely no way out of the darkness. They cannot understand why they are paralysed by such pervasive sadness. At least I could see the people who cared about me. People who are that depressed cannot see anything from the darkness.

I understand that mentality more than ever now. I want to try and help those people. I even pray for them when I can. I don't pray as much as I used to, but prayer is still an important part of my life. There was a time when I would get down on my two knees every day and thank God for guiding me on the right path. Not long after I met Niamh, I knelt at the end of the bed one night and started praying. I was almost oblivious to her presence. I almost forgot myself. She was looking at me in near exasperation, but I didn't care. It wasn't the image Niamh had of me in her mind, but I think that story reflects how I am perceived in this life.

I don't think I am how people think I am. People will judge me. People can think who I am. It makes no difference to me. I know who I am.

I don't ask God or Our Lady for much. When I'm saying the 'Memorare' before big games, my petitions don't include a good personal performance and a win. I'm just thanking Our Lady for the huge opportunity I have been given, and to give me strength to make the most of that opportunity.

Our Lady holds a special place in my heart. I say the 'Memorare' at least twice a week. I pray to her every single day. Sometimes I will get down on my knees, but I will petition Our Lady when I get up every morning. And thank her again before I go to bed at night.

'Please keep me away from a bet today.'

'Thank you for keeping me away from gambling today.'

Every day.

Every single day.

Christy O'Connor is a freelance journalist based in Ennis, Co. Clare. A former GAA McNamee Award winner for print journalism, his first book, *Last Man Standing*, was runner-up in the BoyleSports Irish Sports Book of the Year in 2005. His second book, *The Club*, was voted William Hill Irish Sports Book of the Year in 2010. In 2014, he co-wrote *Dalo: The Autobiography of Anthony Daly*, which was selected as *Sunday Times* Sports Book of the Year.